A matter of intelligence

MI5 and the surveillance of anti-Nazi refugees, 1933–50

Charmian Brinson and Richard Dove

Manchester University Press

Published by Manchester University Press
Altrincham Street, Manchester M1 7JA, UK
www.manchesteruniversitypress.co.uk

British Library Cataloguing-in-Publication Data is available

Library of Congress Cataloging-in-Publication Data is available

ISBN 978 0 7190 9980 9 *paperback*

First published by Manchester University Press in hardback 2014

This paperback edition first published 2015

Printed by Lightning Source

Contents

Acknowledgements

Firstly, the authors would like to thank the staff of the National Archives, Kew, where much of the research for this book has been carried out. We are also grateful to the following for access to unpublished archival material: Arbeiderbevegelsens Arkiv og Bibliotek, Oslo; Archiv der Sozialen Demokratie der Friedrich-Ebert-Stiftung, Bonn; Archiv für die Geschichte der Soziologie in Österreich, Graz; BBC Written Archives Centre, Caversham; Bibliotheek van het Vredespaleis, The Hague; Bodleian Library Oxford; Columbia University Rare Books and Manuscript Library, New York; Deutsche Nationalbibliothek, Frankfurt am Main; Deutsches Literaturarchiv, Marbach; Geheimes Staastsarchiv, Preussischer Kulturbesitz, Berlin; Home Office, London; Institut für Zeitgeschichte, Munich; Lambeth Palace Library, London; Politisches Archiv des Auswärtigen Amtes, Berlin; Schweizerisches Bundesarchiv, Berne; Staatsarchiv des Kantons Basel-Stadt; and Stiftung Archiv der Parteien und Massenorganisationen der DDR im Bundesarchiv Berlin-Lichterfelde.

In addition, we should like to acknowledge the help, cooperation and interest of Professor Rüdiger Görner, the late Joan Rodker, Ernest Rodker, Peter Lowe, Edna Sovin, the late Ellen Otten, Nicholas Jacobs, Merilyn Moos, Yvonne Wells and the late Yvonne Kapp.

Introduction

This is a book about the British Security Service (popularly known as MI5).[1] More specifically, it concerns one particular aspect of its past work – the surveillance of political refugees from Nazi Germany during the 1930s and 1940s. When Adolf Hitler became German Chancellor in January 1933, the Nazis began a reign of terror against their political and ideological opponents: Communists, Socialists, trade unionists, pacifists, liberals and intellectuals, many of whom were forced to flee, seeking sanctuary outside Germany.

A small but growing number of these 'political' refugees came to Britain, commanding the attention of MI5, which kept many of them under close surveillance. This study is based substantially on the personal and organisational files that MI5 kept on them during the 1930s and 1940s – or at least those that MI5 has chosen to release to the National Archives. Inevitably, this book is therefore also a study of the political refugees who were the object of MI5 scrutiny.

It is of course a commonplace that the vast majority of refugees from Nazi Germany and Austria were Jewish. Of almost 80,000 refugees present in Britain at the outbreak of the Second World War, some ninety per cent were Jewish, while only about eight to ten per cent were 'political refugees'. However, the distinction between 'racial' and 'political' refugees is often a pragmatic one, given that some of the most prominent 'political' refugees were also Jewish, though the term serves here to designate those who were persecuted by the Nazis primarily for their political beliefs, irrespective of their racial origins.

The predominance of Jews amongst the refugees prompts the question: how far was MI5's surveillance programme driven by anti-Semitism? Historians of the refugees from Nazi Germany have suggested in varying ways that the policies of the British government and its agencies towards the refugees – particularly on the question of internment – were driven by anti-alienism and anti-Semitism. Anyone reading the MI5 files in question will certainly find instances of casual anti-Semitism, reflecting very much the social prejudices of the day. We shall review such cases to see how far individual prejudice might have affected MI5's investigations.

MI5's surveillance of refugees and its strong advocacy of the internment of 'enemy aliens' in 1940 (and even before the outbreak of war) were not motivated by anti-Semitism, but by intense suspicion of Germany as a former and future enemy. The MI5 files thus illuminate a small but significant area of Anglo-German relations during the 1930s and 1940s. However, MI5's measures of surveillance were motivated even more by its fear and suspicion of the 'Red Menace', as international Communism was habitually called within the Security Service. Most of the 'personal files' compiled by MI5 on German and Austrian refugees were assigned to the category 'communists or suspected communists', a category sufficiently broad to embrace a range of differing and often conflicting left-wing – and anti-Nazi – opinion.

MI5's preoccupation with Communists may have distracted it after 1933 from monitoring the dangers of Nazi espionage in London, exemplified by the case of refugee turned spy Hans Wesemann, and the mysterious deaths of the left-wing activist Dora Fabian and her friend Mathilde Wurm. The Fabian–Wurm case remains unsolved, and we shall examine its implications for MI5, asking how far the Service was concerned to monitor Nazi activity in Britain and how far it was hindered in doing so by the refusal of the Home Office to sanction surveillance of the London office of the Auslandsorganisation (the foreign organisation of Nazi Party members) because of the government's reluctance to offend the Nazi regime.

MI5's surveillance of Communists, including German Communists, operated throughout the 1930s, continued seamlessly into the war years, persisted even when the Soviet Union became a war ally in June 1941 and flourished in the early post-war years of the burgeoning Cold War. The Security Service maintained extensive surveillance of the Communist Party of Great Britain (CPGB) and was particularly concerned to monitor its contacts with foreign Communists. They made relatively little progress in this respect because, in accordance with the strict instructions issued by the Communist International (Comintern), foreign Communist parties avoided all contact with the CPGB, although it will be shown that certain individuals who acted as agents of Soviet intelligence used the CPGB as a conduit for passing information to Moscow.

The MI5 files in question are mainly investigative in nature, gathering information in pursuit of a potential threat to national security. Our study too is investigative. It aims to trace the course of MI5 surveillance of anti-Nazi refugees from 1933 to 1950 (and even beyond, in many cases) investigating when – and why – this particular aspect of its operations began and what rationale, if any, it was based on. It will also attempt to evaluate how necessary or how successful it was, both in relation to the perceived threat to British security posed by the refugees and to the time and effort involved. Unsurprisingly, the answers to these questions may differ at different points in the history of the period, but they are rarely black and white.

In assessing the effectiveness of MI5's activities, it is necessary to take account of the constraints on its operations resulting from the lack of manpower and investigative resources available to it, particularly during the 1930s. We shall also refer to the difficulties arising from its relationship with government, particularly the Home Office, and indeed with other intelligence agencies like the Metropolitan Police Special Branch and the Secret Intelligence Service (SIS), popularly known as MI6.

The MI5 files in question contain an eclectic mix of police reports, internal memoranda, intercepted letters and phone calls, correspondence with SIS and the Home Office, reports by MI5 'watchers' and by informants. They make fascinating reading, though they are, by their very nature, tightly focused, conveying a one-dimensional picture of their subjects: as 'suspects'. They were, however, much more than mere 'suspects'. Many of them were figures of some cultural or scientific distinction, such as the writer Karl Otten, the composer and musicologist Ernst Hermann Meyer, the photographer Edith Tudor-Hart, the statistician Jürgen Kuczynski and the young scientists Karl Fuchs and Engelbert Broda. While all these 'suspects' were politically active, they also had lives outside politics. They had friendships and relationships, families and work, as well as political, social and moral concerns.

In our study, we have felt it important to present a more rounded picture of the individuals concerned, drawing on more personal sources such as letters and personal testimony, where available. Letters of course could be intercepted, and often were; most of the 'suspects' we examine in our study were the subject of a Home Office Warrant, authorising a postal intercept. However, we have also drawn on more retrospective sources, such as memoirs (their own and other people's) as well as on secondary sources, such as biographies. We acknowledge, of course, that we have the historian's benefit of relative hindsight, having been able to draw on sources that were not available to the security services.

MI5 kept watch not only on individual refugees, but on the organisations they founded, such as the Free German League of Culture (FGLC) and the Austrian Centre. The FGLC was the most important social and cultural organisation of German refugees during the years of the Second World War in London, offering its members and visitors a distinguished cultural programme of music, theatre, exhibitions and lectures. It was not however the largest organisation of German-speaking refugees in London, a distinction belonging to its Austrian counterpart, which at its height boasted some 3,000 members. Like the FGLC, the Austrian Centre had an astonishingly wide cultural programme – and like the FGLC, it also served as a surrogate for the political activities that the refugees were not formally permitted to pursue. In the eyes of MI5, both organisations amounted to little more than a 'Communist front' and it therefore monitored their activities assiduously, receiving regular reports from 'reliable' informants who were themselves refugees. Our study reveals the identity and evaluates the role and importance of these informants within the refugee community.

The MI5 file on the Austrian Centre was released as recently as 2010; the file on the FGLC is, at the time of writing, still retained. MI5 will say neither why nor when (or indeed if) it will be released, answering all inquiries with the routine response that 'this file does not meet our current release criteria'. What secrets this file holds must therefore be a matter for conjecture, though we have been able to reconstruct much of its contents by means of cross-reference.

Both individual refugees and refugee organisations enjoyed the backing of numerous British patrons, often leading figures in British cultural and political life, who offered financial, moral and political support, sometimes even interceding on their behalf with the British authorities. MI5's constant watch on these 'friends in need' also forms part of our narrative.

The MI5 of today is a much more open organisation than it was even twenty years ago, but it is still not fully transparent. Even today, it releases only carefully managed information about itself, remaining famously reticent about its activities. With regard to current operations, this is inevitable: as one prominent cheerleader for MI5 has put it, 'What's the point of a secret service, if it's not secret?'[2] However, there is still a lack of accessible and reliable primary material concerning its past activities which makes it difficult to ascertain what policies MI5 pursued, or what it did at any particular time, let alone to evaluate it in detail. This remains the case, despite a steady stream of books on the subject by outsiders claiming insider information, and more recently, the monumental official history of its activities.

Although the surveillance of German and Austrian refugees formed an important part of MI5's work during the period under review, it is a part which MI5 itself seems to have disowned or at any rate overlooked. The official history of the Security Service, published in 2009 and amounting to 1,000 pages, fails even to mention it;[3] nor is it mentioned in the 600 pages of the official history's 'unofficial' counterpart, *Spooks*.[4] The present study therefore seeks to close a significant gap in historical research. This would not have been possible before 1999, when MI5 started to release some of its historical files to the National Archives. At the time of writing, it has released over 5,000 files, though many more are still retained and a far greater number have simply been destroyed.

Notes

1 The terms 'MI5' and 'Security Service' are used throughout as mutually interchangeable.

2 Bernard Ingham, former chief press secretary to Margaret Thatcher, on the publication of Stella Rimington's memoir *Open Secret: The Autobiography of the Former Director-General of MI5*, London: Hutchinson 2001.

3 Christopher Andrew, *The Defence of the Realm: The Authorized History of MI5*, London: Allen Lane 2009.

4 Thomas Hennessey and Claire Thomas, *Spooks: The Unofficial History of MI5*, Stroud: Amberley 2009.

Part I

I spy 1933–39

1

Defending the realm: MI5 in the making

MI5's mission statement is displayed in its heraldic motto: 'To Defend the Realm'. The Service has been described by intelligence expert Nigel West as 'Britain's premier counter-intelligence agency'. However, it grew from modest beginnings. First established as the Secret Service Bureau in 1909 to coordinate intelligence against the perceived threat of German espionage, it was staffed by a thirty-six-year-old army captain, Vernon Kell, and a former naval Commander, fourteen years his senior, called Mansfield Cumming. At an early stage, it was agreed to divide the work of the Bureau into two parts: a Home Section, responsible for investigating and countering foreign (notably German) espionage in the United Kingdom, and a Foreign Section, responsible for gathering intelligence abroad on Britain's enemies. The former, under the direction of Kell, became MI5; the latter, under Cumming, evolved into the Secret Intelligence Service (SIS), better known as MI6.

The origins and early development of MI5 reveal much about the later organisation, illuminating its world view, ethos and modus operandi, particularly during the historical period spanned by this study. It was during the First World War that MI5 first became MI5. In 1914, the Home Section of the Secret Service Bureau became a part of the War Office. As a subsection of the War Office's Directorate of Military Operations, it was designated MO5 (Military Operations, Section 5), changing in 1916 to MI5 (Military Intelligence, Section 5). For much of its early life, MI5 was a part of the War Office; up to the reorganisation of intelligence services in 1931, Kell's immediate superior was the Secretary of State for War. Throughout these early years, the quasi-military ethos of MI5 was pervasive, most of its recruits coming, like Vernon Kell himself, from a military background. This ethos was echoed in the Service's structure, in which intelligence officers were assigned military rank, whether or not they were entitled to it on the basis of military service.

The military ethos of MI5 remained pervasive during the 1920s and 1930s. In the jargon of the Service, only those who worked in the 'Office' were referred to as 'officers' and enjoyed officer rank; those outside were referred to as 'agents'. No insider, the intelligence expert Nigel West assures us, ever used the word 'spy'[1] – though spying is of course what they were engaged in.

MI5 operated as a clandestine department of government. All officers signed an agreement not to reveal their employment or duties within MI5. The secrecy surrounding its operations gradually gave rise to a self-sustaining mystique that became virtually an end in itself. Officers were instructed to say that they 'worked for a rather dull department in the War Office'.[2] According to John le Carré, every secret service invents its own mythology. In the case of MI5, the mystery surrounding its operations has fostered its popular image as a glamorous and dashing organisation: a perception which the facts of its history scarcely justify.

The initial division of work between Kell and Cumming reflected their disagreement about their respective responsibilities; it also presaged a rivalry which persisted for many years, resulting in frequent territorial disputes between MI5 and MI6.

MI5 was established to combat the threat of *German* espionage. The focus on Germany as a potential and real enemy remained a major concern of the organisation until 1945, though during the inter-war period it was matched by concern about the 'red menace'. These twin preoccupations help to explain the surveillance of so many German 'political' refugees after 1933, most of whom were targeted as 'Communists and suspected Communists'. The Security Service only rather belatedly recognised the threat to British security represented by Nazi activity in Britain.

If the years of the First World War were years of exponential growth for MI5, staff numbers dwindled rapidly in peacetime, as other priorities appeared. At the Armistice in 1918, MI5 had boasted a complement of over 130 officers (of whom 84 were at London HQ), but a decade later (1929) this number had fallen to only 13.

In fact, the 1920s was a decade of decline and retrenchment for the Security Service. Kell even had to reassert its role as an independent agency, fighting off moves to merge it with other intelligence organisations or even to wind it up altogether. Kell's defence of MI5 was partly necessitated by the ongoing turf wars between MI5, MI6 and Special Branch, but was also a consequence of drastically reduced post-war levels of expenditure on intelligence.

MI5's prime responsibility lay in gathering information on subversive, and potentially subversive, organisations and individuals. It was only one of the agencies charged with preserving Britain's security: others included the Secret Intelligence Service (SIS), which came under the jurisdiction of the Foreign Office, and the Metropolitan Police Special Branch, responsible to the Home Office.[3]

The boundaries between these various organisations were a frequent source of friction and even rivalry. In its early days, MI5 had begun by collating and coordinating information gathered in the field by other security organisations. Despite its popular reputation, it had only limited power and influence and enjoyed only slender resources. Whatever the licence it enjoyed in certain activities, it was obliged to work within well-defined operational boundaries. It had, for example, no powers of arrest or prosecution, being obliged to work through Special Branch. Financial constraints also meant that it had only limited powers of investigation.

Christopher Andrew, the official chronicler of MI5, confirms that 'Between the wars more MI5 resources were devoted to the surveillance and investigation of the Communist Party than of any other target'.[4] MI6 had engaged in anti-Soviet operations since the 1917 Bolshevik revolution. Moreover, the Communist Party of Great Britain (CPGB) had been subject to Special Branch surveillance since its formation in 1920; cases had been brought against its members on charges such as sedition and breach of the peace. MI5 too began to address the perceived threat of communism which, for the next decade and a half, became its overriding concern.

During the 1920s, MI5 began to compile numerous 'personal files' on known and suspected Communists, as well as other 'political extremists'. It focused specifically on the CPGB, reflecting the world view that every party member was a foot soldier of the Communist International (Comintern) and therefore a potential spy for the Soviet Union. Its surveillance of Communists included both leading activists and rank and file Party members. MI5 paid considerable attention to the Soviet Trade Delegation, many of whose members were engaged in subversive activities. In March 1927, it launched its first anti-Soviet operation, directed against the Trade Delegation, the so-called 'Arcos operation'. Since MI5 had no powers of arrest, the operation was carried out together with Scotland Yard.[5]

The methods of surveillance available to MI5 were of course crude in comparison to those available today. It relied heavily on its Central Registry. Even before the First World War, MI5 had compiled (largely from police sources) a Register of Aliens, held in the form of a card index. By the spring of 1917, Central Registry had held 250,000 cards and 27,000 'personal files' covering its chief suspects.

The agency's main external weapon was the postal intercept. To intercept a suspect's post, it was necessary to have a Home Office Warrant (HOW), signed by a Secretary of State, in practice usually the Home Secretary. Many of the files released to the National Archives open with a warrant signed by 'one of His Majesty's Principal Secretaries of State' and contain numerous photographic copies of intercept letters. The widespread reliance on the

HOW was largely dictated by MI5's shortage of staff, which also made it reliant on other agencies to carry out some aspects of its investigations.

Both postal and telephone intercepts were carried out by the Investigation Branch of the GPO, the Postmaster-General receiving authorisation to 'detain, open and produce for my inspection all postal packets and telegrams addressed to [suspect].' As private use of the telephone increased, there was a growing requirement for telephone intercepts. This often proved problematic, however, since recording phone conversations was possible only by hand, a task made harder if suspects did not converse in English. Phone check records increasingly included the comment: 'Conversation in a foreign language – not understood.' The Dictaphone Company eventually came to the rescue, producing a device to record telephone conversations. Christopher Andrew notes that until 1937 it was not thought necessary to seek an HOW for a phone tap; he does not say why.[6]

During the 1920s, MI5 was a service of slender means, corresponding to its diminished responsibilities. While it had no powers of arrest, its powers of investigation were also severely limited by ongoing financial constraints. An ever-decreasing number of HOWs was recorded and there must also have been a drastic pruning of the number of 'personal files' (and therefore suspects). Moreover, 'B' Division, responsible for counter-espionage operations, lacked the capacity to run agents, being limited to the use of informants.

The year 1931 proved a turning point in the fortunes of MI5, enlarging the scope of its operations over the next decade and marking the recruitment of some of the key individuals involved in them. In that year, the government's Secret Service committee was re-convened in order to discuss serious differences which had arisen between the SIS and Scotland Yard. The committee decided that responsibility for investigating and combating 'Communist subversion' should be transferred from Special Branch to MI5. This meant that MI5 became responsible for all intelligence concerning the CPGB, and therefore also concerning the activities of the Comintern in Britain, a new responsibility which partly dictated MI5's later interest in anti-Nazi German refugees. At the same time, MI5 acquired the services of Scotland Yard's leading experts on counter-subversion, Hugh Miller and Guy Liddell. Miller was killed in an accident in 1934; Liddell became Deputy-Director of 'B' Division,[7] overseeing its counter-espionage operations.

A further proposal by the committee which had far-reaching consequences was that the SIS should confine its activities to countries outside the United Kingdom and the Empire. By the end of the 1920s, SIS had started to encroach on MI5's sphere of influence: it began running a string of agents on British soil, justifying its action by reference to MI5's inability to do so. SIS's agents were controlled by a young man called Maxwell

Knight. In the light of the committee's decision to limit SIS's field of operations, Knight – and his agents – also joined MI5 at this time.

At this point, MI5 was also divorced from the War Office[8] and was designated an inter-departmental service, supplying intelligence to (among others) the Home Office, the Foreign Office and the Committee of Imperial Defence. This reassignment of responsibility brought one considerable benefit for MI5. Under the re-organisation, SIS was to establish a new section – Section V (Counter-intelligence) under Valentine Vivian (later deputy Head of SIS) – which was to liaise with MI5. This measure introduced 'a period of close and fruitful collaboration' between the two agencies.[9]

Following the re-organisation of 1931, MI5 had just two divisions: A Division, covering administration, personnel and Registry, and B Division, responsible for counter-espionage and counter-subversion, whose Director throughout the 1930s was Brigadier A.W.A. Harker (known to his friends and associates as 'Jasper'). On joining MI5 in 1931, Guy Liddell became Harker's deputy, eventually succeeding him as Director in June 1940.

Liddell came from a classic MI5 background. He had served with distinction in the army in the First World War, having won the Military Cross, a background which fitted perfectly into the quasi-military ethos of MI5. Despite this dashing reputation, Liddell cut an unremarkable figure. A former colleague described him as 'avuncular' and 'rather dumpy'. Surviving photographs lend him the air of a benign bank manager. Few of those who passed him in the lift would have taken him for an experienced and dedicated intelligence officer. In the years after the First World War, Liddell had served with the Metropolitan Police Special Branch, dealing primarily with cases of Soviet espionage. It was there that he developed a preoccupation with the Communist threat – one he took with him to MI5. He also took his assistant Milicent Bagot, who was to become a formidable figure in MI5 in the 1940s and 1950s. Another crucial arrival, in January 1936, was Dick White, who later became the only man to head both MI5 and MI6.

Perhaps the most flamboyant addition to B Division was Maxwell Knight. Three times married, though also reputed to be homosexual, Knight has been described as 'colourful' and 'a gregarious eccentric'.[10] However, his political views were more than eccentric, chiming with those of the British Fascisti, the prototype British Fascist organisation he had joined in 1924. In mitigation, it should be added that 'Knight's early enthusiasm for Mussolini's victory over Italian Bolshevism was widely shared by mainstream conservatives.'[11] Knight became MI5's chief agent-handler, his 'M' section (so-styled because Knight, an inveterate conspirator, always signed himself 'M'[12]) eventually becoming section B5b in 1937, a section devoted to monitoring political subversion.

If Knight was the most colourful recruit to MI5 in the 1930s, the most significant was the young journalist Roger Hollis, who joined the Service in June 1938, becoming head of section B4a, dealing with Communist subversion. The son of an Anglican bishop, Hollis lacked the military background of so many MI5 recruits, but he rose steadily through the ranks to become Director-General of MI5 in 1956. He was nonetheless a controversial figure, his early experience as a journalist in Shanghai later fuelling persistent rumours that he was in fact a Soviet agent,[13] a remarkable claim to which we shall return.

The prime responsibility of the Security Service in peacetime was to gather information on subversive organisations and individuals. In practice, its operations centred on the surveillance of 'Communists and suspected Communists', a broad category which embraced many anti-Nazi refugees. Within 'B' Division, sections B4a and B4b were responsible for monitoring and investigating Communist activity, dealing with British and foreign Communists respectively. B4b was thus responsible for investigating German refugees, using Maxwell Knight's agents to penetrate refugee networks, largely in search of Communists or Communist sympathisers. MI5's overriding preoccupation with 'the Red Menace' is perhaps best documented by the extraordinary visit of Guy Liddell to Nazi Berlin in March 1933.

Notes

1 Nigel West, *MI5: British Security Service Operations 1909–1945*, London: Bodley Head 1981, pp. 21–2.

2 *Ibid.*, p. 18.

3 Special Branch is a term used to identify police units responsible for matters of national security. The first Special Branch unit (or Special Irish Branch as it was originally known) had been formed in 1883 as a unit within the Metropolitan Police to combat Irish Republican terrorism in mainland Britain. Thereafter, Special Branch had retained the main counter-terrorism role against the Irish Republican Army (IRA), leaving MI5 to act in a supporting role.

4 Christopher Andrew, *The Defence of the Realm: The Authorised History of MI5*, London: Allen Lane 2009, p. 142.

5 See Andrew, *Defence of the Realm*, pp. 153–8.

6 *Ibid.*, pp. 134–5.

7 MI5 usage alternated between 'branch' and 'division'. According to Andrew (p. 127), the term 'branch' was used in internal documents up to 1931, 'division' from 1931 to 1940 and then from 1943 to 1950. Since 'division' was used practically throughout the period of concern to this book, we shall refer throughout to 'divisions'.

8 John Court Curry, *The Security Service 1908–1945: The Official History*, London: Public Record Office 1999, p. 147. This publication reproduces the original report,

compiled by Curry in 1945–46 for internal distribution. Marked 'Top Secret', the report was intended 'for future guidance'. See 'The Security Service: Its Problems and Organisational Adjustments 1908–1945', The National Archives [TNA], KV4/1–3.

9 Curry, *The Security Service 1908–1945*, p. 103.

10 Andrew, *Defence of the Realm*, p. 123.

11 *Ibid.*, p. 124.

12 *Ibid.*, p. 134.

13 See Chapman Pincher, *Treachery: Betrayals, Blunders and Cover-ups: Six Decades of Espionage*, Edinburgh: Mainstream 2011.

2

Liddell in Wonderland: MI5 and the Prussian Secret Police

Adolf Hitler's rise to power in Germany made little apparent impression on the British security services. According to MI5's own in-house history, 'The Nazi threat attracted practically no attention in the Security Service between 1931 and 1933 and very little when Hitler and the Nazi Party came into power in Germany.'[1] This statement is somewhat disingenuous. In fact, MI5 was keen to cooperate with the new Nazi authorities, with whom it had a common interest in countering Communist subversion.

On 30 March 1933, Guy Liddell arrived in Berlin to meet his counterparts in the Prussian Secret Police (shortly to become the Gestapo). Liddell's mission to Berlin was not initiated by MI5, but undertaken in response to an offer of 'liaison' by the Nazi authorities. He was invited to inspect documents relating to the Comintern's attempts at subversion in the British Empire, a matter which was central to Liddell's responsibilities.

Liddell was aided during his visit by Captain Frank Foley, officially the Passport Control Officer at the British Embassy in Berlin. Foley was undoubtedly a man of courage and cunning. Educated by the Jesuits, he had initially felt a vocation for the priesthood but had subsequently left the seminary in France to pursue a more secular path, studying philosophy in Hamburg – and becoming fluent in German. Escaping from Germany in 1914, he served in the First World War and rose to the rank of acting captain before being wounded in action. His grounding in casuistry, his command of languages and his military experience all propelled him towards the Secret Service, which he joined even before the war ended. In view of his language skills, he was offered the post of Passport Control Officer in Berlin: in fact, a cover for his role as SIS head of station.

On this occasion, Foley was to act as Liddell's 'interpreter', though since Liddell, once a promising cellist, had actually studied music in Germany prior to August 1914, he had little apparent need for one. SIS, however, was actively involved in the operation. Liddell's visit was in fact treated as a 'joint operation' between MI5 and SIS, which 'kindly offered to pay half the cost, amounting in total to £106'.[2] It is opportune to remember at this point that Guy Liddell was a distant relation of Alice Liddell, the girl for whom Lewis Carroll had written *Alice in Wonderland.* Liddell's meeting with his Prussian counterparts in Berlin must have been a looking-glass moment, confronting him with a reverse image of his own organisation.

Liddell's report, entitled 'The Liquidation of Communism and Left-wing Socialism in Germany', established the framework within which MI5's 'liaison' with the Nazi authorities was to take place.[3] His counterparts in Berlin were two key men in the new Germany, each as dubious as the other. His host, acting as foreign-press liaison officer, was Ernst 'Putzi' Hanfstaengel who, as Liddell must have known, was a long-standing friend of Hitler's, and had lent him material and moral support in his days as a beer-hall orator in Munich. Hanfstaengel took Liddell to the Karl Liebknecht House, the former HQ of the German Communist Party, now occupied by the Nazi Secret Police and renamed the Horst Wessel House, after a Nazi 'martyr' murdered by Communists. There Liddell was introduced to Rudolf Diehls, Head of the Prussian Secret Police – which within a month was to become the Gestapo, with Diehls still as its Head.

Liddell was quite an astute judge of character – he accurately summed up Hanfstaengel as 'on the whole an extremely likeable person', even if 'quite unbalanced on the question of communism and the Jews'. He found Diehls less sympathetic, but equally accommodating: 'Although he had an unpleasant personality he was extremely polite [...] and later gave orders to all present that I was to be given every possible facility. At our first interview he said that it was his intention to exterminate Communism in its widest sense' (p. 5).

Liddell would probably have concurred with this end, though not with the means used to achieve it. He had come to Germany at a moment of political turmoil. Three weeks after the Reichstag Fire, the Nazis were still conducting an orgy of arbitrary arrest, detention and torture of political opponents – not only Communists, but Socialists, trade unionists and pacifists. Liddell was moved to comment that 'ruthless and often wholly unjustifiable acts are being committed' and confirmed that

> There is certainly a great deal of 'third degree' work going on. [...] A number of Jews, Communists and even Social Democrats have undoubtedly been submitted to every kind of outrage and this was still going on at the time of my departure. (pp. 8–9)

Furthermore, he remained sceptical of Nazi stories that they had frustrated a Communist coup attempt, dismissing them as 'childish arguments'. But he was a poor judge of political developments, apparently thinking that this reign of terror reflected merely the birth pangs of a new regime.

He could have been under no illusion about Nazi anti-Semitism, having witnessed at first hand the effects of the boycott of Jewish businesses which took place on 1 April, the second day of his stay in Berlin. Captain Foley had already testified to the widespread panic among Jews, even before the boycott. On 29 March, he had reported to London that 'This office is overwhelmed with applications from Jews to proceed to Palestine, to England, to anywhere in the British Empire'.[4]

Liddell's report on his visit also contains an appendix on 'The Anti-Jewish Movement.' While dismissing Nazi propaganda claims of a Jewish conspiracy, he nonetheless concluded that there was some truth in claims that corruption in government institutions in the Weimar Republic was due chiefly to the Jews:

> There have undoubtedly been some very serious cases of corruption in government institutions where the Jews had a firm foothold. For the last ten years it has been extremely noticeable that access to the chief of any department was only possible through the intermediary of a Jew. It was the Jew who did most of the talking and in whose hands the working out of any scheme was ultimately left.[5]

Liddell's casual anti-Semitism is unsurprising, being fairly typical of his class and generation. In fact, his social and political views were those of a patriotic conservative, to which – unencumbered by modern notions of political correctness – he gave frank expression. However, Liddell's visit to Berlin was not so much ideologically driven as opportunistic. His report concludes:

> There is no doubt that the moment chosen to establish contact with the present regime has been a good one. Those in authority are persuaded that they have saved Europe from the menace of Communism. [...] In their present mood, the German Police are extremely ready to help us in any way they can. (p. 17)

He and Foley were finally allowed access to the official files and were able to make 'liaison arrangements' for certain documents to be copied and forwarded to MI5 via Foley – a room had indeed been placed at the latter's disposal in the offices of the Political Police. There can be little doubt that this arrangement was implemented, if only for a limited period.

The file containing Liddell's report on his visit to Berlin has no sequel, as though the story began and ended there. There is no record of information received from Berlin, though it seems highly probable that the 'liaison' which had begun so promisingly must have continued. How long it continued can only be a matter for speculation. A year later, after Heinrich Himmler had taken control of the Gestapo, Rudolf Diehls lost his post – and very nearly his life – in the savage purge of the 'Night of the Long Knives'.[6] However, it seems highly likely that, for several months after Liddell's visit,

MI5 received information – via Foley – regarding Communist and other political opponents of Nazism and that this information was the basis for future surveillance of left-wing German refugees in London.

Notes

1 John Court Curry, *The Security Service 1908–1945: The Official History*, London: Public Record Office 1999, p. 109.

2 See letter MI5 (Eric Holt-Wilson) to Admiral Hugh Sinclair, MI 1C, The National Archives [TNA], KV4/111.

3 'The Liquidation of Communism and Left-wing Socialism in Germany', TNA, KV4/111.

4 Quoted in A.J. Sherman, *Island Refuge: Britain and Refugees from the Third Reich 1933–1939*, London: Frank Cass, 2nd edition 1994, p. 29.

5 'The Liquidation of Communism and Left-wing Socialism in Germany': Appendix 1, 'The Anti-Jewish Movement', TNA, KV4/111.

6 Diehls (1900–57) was a remarkable political survivor. As a protégé of Hermann Göring, he survived the Nazi period unscathed, becoming a member of the post-war government of Lower Saxony in 1950, a year in which he also published his memoirs, *Lucifer ante Portas*. His luck ran out in 1957, when he died following a hunting accident.

3

The undesirables: political refugees from Germany and Austria after January 1933

The commonplace view of the stream of refugees fleeing Germany (and later Austria and Czechoslovakia) after Hitler's rise to power has been of the flight of German-speaking Jews from Nazi racial persecution. The predominance of this historical narrative is perfectly understandable, given that some ninety per cent of the refugees from Greater Germany were Jewish. However, this narrative – retrospectively influenced by the enormity of Nazi genocide – disguises the fact that the first victims of Nazi persecution were their political and ideological opponents: Communists, Socialists, trade unionists, pacifists and liberals.

The majority of 'political' refugees who fled Nazi Germany did so – in contrast to the majority of their Jewish counterparts – before the end of 1933. On the night of 27 February 1933, the Reichstag was set on fire. While it has never been established beyond doubt whether the Nazis themselves were responsible, they certainly exploited the event to settle accounts with their political adversaries. Even before the flames had been extinguished, police and Nazi storm troopers, working from long-prepared lists, arrested over 4,000 opponents of Nazism, mainly Communist and other left-wing activists, including over a hundred cultural figures and intellectuals.

Those arrested were interrogated, beaten and often tortured. While some were released after a few days, others were detained for long periods and eventually thrown into concentration camps. Some, like the leader of the German Communist Party (KPD) and former presidential candidate Ernst Thälmann, were never to regain their freedom. The Nazis sought to justify their action by claiming that it had forestalled a planned Communist coup d'état, and despite the implausibility of such claims, the KPD was swiftly proscribed.

Many Communists and Socialists who had escaped arrest were forced to go underground or flee abroad, often departing in haste to escape arbitrary arrest and detention. Their flight into exile forced them to leave behind family and friends, and to abandon familiar surroundings and the social and political signposts which had guided their lives. They went initially to countries immediately bordering Germany and Austria, settling in France, the Netherlands and above all Czechoslovakia in expectation of an early return.

Their hopes proved illusory. By the summer of 1933, the Nazi regime had consolidated its power, using the process of *Gleichschaltung* (coordination) to bring all elements of society under the single control of the Nazi Party. In May, the Nazis moved to destroy the power of the trade unions, attacking and looting their offices and transferring their organisations to the control of the monolithic German Labour Front. Shortly after, the Nazis occupied all offices of the German Social Democratic Party (SPD), before banning the party as an enemy of people and state. Other parties were dissolved – or simply dissolved themselves. By July, the National Socialist Party was the only legal political party in Germany.

It was at this point that some refugees began to move on, leaving countries such as Switzerland, where they were made to feel unwelcome, for those where regulations were less stringent. However, many chose to stay where they were, joining political comrades in helping to rebuild the organisations and support networks destroyed by the Nazis. Many of the most militant political opponents of Nazism were concentrated in Prague, where both the KPD and the SPD (or SOPADE, as it called itself in exile) established their political headquarters outside Germany.

While the course of history in Austria followed a different trajectory, the consequences were very similar. In an attempt to outflank the Nazis in neighbouring Germany, the government of Engelbert Dollfuss embarked in March 1933 on its own path to Fascism. In a matter of days, it moved to abolish parliament, abandon the constitution and institute an authoritarian one-party state, the so-called 'Ständestaat'. Following the abolition of parliament, the Dollfuss government rapidly removed other restraints on its power, introducing press censorship and prohibiting strikes and demonstrations. The success of these measures depended of course on the elimination of its political rivals. The Austrian Communist Party (KPÖ) was formally banned on 26 May 1933, and its activists subjected to rapid and often brutal repression.[1]

However, most political refugees left Austria only after the brief civil war which erupted in February 1934, when the Dollfuss government used the army to crush a rash revolt by the 'Schutzbund', the militia of the Social Democratic Party (SPÖ). Among those who witnessed these brutal events was the young Kim Philby, who was to become the most prolific British traitor of his generation. The 'February events' were followed by the prohibition of the SPÖ. Many of the leading political cadres of KPÖ and SPÖ were arrested or forced underground, while others fled abroad, often to neighbouring Czechoslovakia. The Czechoslovak Republic, a parliamentary democracy now bounded on three sides by authoritarian one-party states, accepted refugees from both Germany and Austria and was prepared to tolerate their political activities – turning a blind eye when these sometimes seeped over the border.

During the early years of this emigration, Britain was not a favoured country of refuge. By the end of 1933, some 60,000 refugees had left Germany, of whom only about 2,000 had come to Britain, compared with ten times that number in France. Up to 1938, Britain remained a marginal destination for most refugees. At the end of 1937, when the number of refugees fleeing Nazi persecution had risen to some 155,000, only 5,500 had sought sanctuary in Britain.

This manifest reluctance to come to Britain was only partly the result of geographical distance. Britain was both economically and culturally remote from the European continent, absorbed with its role as the centre of a worldwide empire. When the refugee lawyer turned painter, Fred Uhlman, arrived in England from France in 1936, he found it 'a stranger country than any I had known, as far away from Europe as Peking', its people still apparently living in a golden Edwardian past.[2]

Uhlman was about to marry into the English aristocracy, but spoke little English. In fact, few German refugees could speak English and even fewer had social or political contacts in Britain. However, their failure to come to Britain was also a consequence of the unwelcoming immigration policies of the British government. British policy on refugees still largely derived from the Aliens Act of 1919, which had limited the liberal idea of asylum in favour of controls on the flow of immigration. The primary aim of this policy was to restrict immigrant numbers and exclude anyone who might become a charge on public funds. In 1933–34, Britain was only just beginning to emerge from economic depression: refugees were seen as potential rivals in the job market and with few exceptions were not allowed to work. To achieve entry into Britain, it was therefore necessary to show evidence of independent means or to have a guarantor, a function often fulfilled by Jewish organisations or, in the case of 'Aryan' refugees, by the Religious Society of Friends or other Christian organisations.

Superficially, foreign visitors to Britain were admitted with few formalities. Visas between Britain and both Germany and Austria had been abandoned in 1927 (although they were to be reintroduced in May 1938 in response to the fresh waves of refugees leaving Austria). Refugees arriving as visitors in Britain were admitted (or not) at the discretion of the

Immigration Officer at the port of entry, as the lawyer and journalist Rudolf Olden explained to a fellow-writer:

> Whether or not you get in here is a matter of luck. On the boat or after landing you will meet the Immigration Officer and your fate depends on him. Show him a confirmation from your English publisher that you have money here, or can at least expect some. That's the best way of preventing the Immigration Officer from getting the idea that you could be a burden on the public purse or are even looking for a job. Best of all [...] show him confirmation from an English bank that you have an account here.[3]

If allowed to land, refugees were admitted for a limited period, usually one month, and on the strict condition that they did no work, 'paid or unpaid'. They were required simply to register with the police at their eventual destination and to renew their permission to stay on a regular basis. Refugees staying in London, for example, had to report to the Aliens' Police at Bow Street police station, which acquired a daunting reputation in refugee folklore.

The essence of British policy on refugees was therefore that the United Kingdom was not a country of settlement, but of temporary refuge, that is, of transit. The only categories of refugee treated as an exception were those who already had considerable assets in Britain or who were able to transfer a business here, or who could show that they had a guaranteed income from elsewhere. All refugees were therefore considered undesirable; some, however, were more undesirable than others.

The political refugees

While the overall number of refugees leaving Germany, and of those who made their way to Britain, has always been the subject of keen debate, the proportion of *political* refugees in both cases has remained uncertain. There were, of course, no recorded statistics of the number of political refugees who left Germany and estimates of their number can only be made pragmatically.

Up to the end of 1933, some 60,000–65,000 refugees had left Germany, of whom over 50,000 were Jews who had been deprived of their livelihood, while the balance of some 10,000–12,000 were political refugees, representing roughly fifteen to twenty per cent of the total. Though it is clear that the proportion of political refugees to racial refugees declined sharply after 1935, their total number remains a matter for conjecture.

The distinction between 'political' and 'racial' refugees is a somewhat pragmatic one, blurred by the fact that some prominent 'political' refugees were also Jewish, though the term serves here to designate those who were persecuted by the Nazis primarily for their political beliefs, not their racial origins. However, there are some important ways in which political refugees differed from their Jewish counterparts. Firstly, the great majority of political refugees left Germany in 1933–34, whereas the peak of Jewish emigration from both Germany and Austria occurred in 1938–39 as the Nazi regime accelerated its discriminatory measures against Jews. Moreover, political refugees represented very much an elite: their number included many of the recognised leaders of the main left-wing parties and trade unions, as well as some of their most prominent members.

Perhaps the most crucial difference between political and racial refugees was one of attitude. Unlike many of their Jewish counterparts, who were prepared (however reluctantly) to regard their enforced emigration as permanent, the political refugees neither wanted nor expected to settle abroad. Their gaze was still directed firmly towards Germany in the belief that they could influence the political situation there. It was always their intention to return to a Germany freed from Nazism. And the majority of political refugees *did* eventually return home – if only to a devastated and divided country which bore little resemblance to the land they had left.

Even in the straitened conditions of exile, political refugees faced particular difficulties. Many had left Germany fleeing for their life and liberty, often crossing the border 'illegally'. Some had no passport and were forced to acquire temporary travel documents, often issued in their first country of refuge. More surprisingly, few of them had extensive political contacts in Britain.

According to figures compiled by the High Commission for Refugees for the three years from 1933 to the end of 1935, between 15,000 and (at most) 20,000 political opponents of the Nazi regime had found refuge abroad, including 5,000–6,000 Social Democrats, 6,000–8,000 Communists, 2,000 pacifists and Democrats, 1,000 Catholics and 2,000 other opponents of the Nazi regime.[4] What these figures inadvertently confirm is that the political emigration from Germany was not only diverse, but divided, united only in opposition to National Socialism. Despite the common ground of anti-Nazism and the painful experience of exile, they remained mutually mistrustful, pursuing the political differences which had disfigured the final years of the Weimar Republic.

In 1928, the Sixth World Congress of the Comintern had promulgated the policy of 'class against class', which identified the Social Democrats as the main political enemy, denouncing them as 'social fascists'. From 1929, the KPD adopted this divisive policy in Germany, making it impossible to form a broad anti-Nazi front with the SPD, thus smoothing the way for Hitler's assumption of power. Only in 1934 did the Comintern begin to change course, moving towards a policy of cooperation with other anti-fascist forces. The new policy of the Popular Front was finally declared at the Seventh Congress of the Comintern in August 1935, although it did not succeed in healing this split: over the next decade, the SPD continued to reject all offers of collaboration with the KPD.

The SOPADE lacked any real party organisation in Britain prior to 1939. Initially, it even lacked any idea of how many of its members had found their way to Britain. The SOPADE leader, Otto Wels, was forced to turn to William Gillies, the International Secretary of the Labour Party, asking him to draw up a list of SPD members who had managed to reach England. When the lawyer Franz Neumann, who had arrived in London in July 1933, assumed the task of creating an SPD party group in exile, he found it an uphill struggle. Neumann, who enjoyed useful contacts with the Labour Party and the Trades Union Congress (TUC), did succeed in organising a Socialist discussion group (the London Group of German Socialists) though he was obliged to admit, in a report to the SOPADE Executive, that this was a cross-party group which included ex-Communists like Karl Korsch and Franz Borkenau and various unaligned Socialists. Matters improved during 1934; by December, Neumann was able to report that, in parallel to the discussion group, he had succeeded in establishing a strictly SPD party group comprising about a dozen members. A year later, in December 1935, he informed the SOPADE Executive in Prague that the party group in London now boasted some forty-five members. However, in 1936 Neumann accepted the offer of a post in the United States, and SPD activity in London seems to have declined with his departure. When the party functionary Wilhelm Sander arrived in London in 1939, he wrote to the SOPADE Executive complaining that the party had not even a skeleton organisation there.

Communist exiles in Britain were no more numerous. When the Marxist economist and statistician Jürgen Kuczynski (whose name will recur in these pages) arrived in London in July 1936, the KPD group in Britain was still small, comprising roughly thirty to forty members, who were 'scattered throughout the whole country'.[5] They were, Kuczynski recalled, almost entirely comprised of bourgeois intellectuals, such as the economist Siegfried Moos and the composer and musicologist Ernst Herman Meyer, who was pursuing research into British chamber music. Kuczynski rapidly found himself the Head of the Party group in Britain. Under the watchful eye of the Security Service, the KPD group had to remain a clandestine organisation, limited in its capacity for independent action.

The remnants of the two major left-wing parties were joined in exile by the survivors of smaller parties and breakaway groups, including the Sozialistische Arbeiterpartei Deutschlands (SAPD, usually known as SAP), the Internationale Sozialistische Kampfbund (ISK) and the Neubeginnen Group.[6] Their capacity for political action was severely circumscribed by the restrictions on political activities imposed by the British authorities – as the surveillance files of MI5 eloquently document.

In addition, there were a handful of politically unaligned intellectuals in London, such as the lawyer Rudolf Olden, the playwright Ernst Toller and the aristocrat, Hubertus, Prince zu Lowenstein. The refugee population was not static. Both Toller and Löwenstein, for example, moved on to the United States in 1936. The Marxist academic Karl Korsch was forced to leave Britain in July 1935, when he was refused permission to extend his stay. He left London for Denmark and later the United States. Although the number of political refugees in Britain in the five years to 1938 therefore fluctuated, the number present at any one time could scarcely have exceeded 200–300, representing no more than five to six per cent of the small overall total of those who had found their way to Britain.

The 'personal' files so far released by MI5 confirm that virtually all 'suspects' were kept under surveillance as 'Communists or suspected Communists', a blanket designation covering individuals of very different – and often rival – political allegiances. Among those on whom MI5 kept 'personal' files were the Catholic Karl Otten, the pacifist Otto Lehmann-Russbueldt and the Socialist Dora Fabian as well as orthodox Communist cadres like the actor Gerhard Hinze, the composer and musicologist Ernst Hermann Meyer and his Austrian counterpart Georg Knepler. These were politically uneasy bedfellows who shared little – except the broad bed of MI5's central registry.

MI5's interest in the political refugees from Germany was out of all proportion to their numbers and influence, prompting the question why MI5 deemed such surveillance necessary. The answer is rooted in MI5's own history and the way it continued to dictate the security agenda in the 1930s. MI5 had originally been established to tackle the threat of German espionage and remained alert to the danger of German spies. However, during the 1920s its principal focus had shifted to combating Communist subversion, for which it had assumed principal responsibility in 1931. In Guy Liddell, who had spent a decade in this role in Scotland Yard, it had acquired the foremost expert in this field. While Liddell's attention was concentrated on the CPGB, he recognised that Communism was an international movement and had therefore also established a franchise for Soviet espionage in Britain and for the activities of the German Communist Party, which before 1933 had been the largest and most powerful outside the Soviet Union. The question remains: how was MI5 able to identify so many 'suspects' amongst German refugees?

Liddell's visit to Berlin in March 1933 had not been his first: his 'liaison' with the Prussian Secret Police had actually begun much earlier, while he was still with Scotland Yard. Even before 1930, there had been routine 'liaison' between Metropolitan Police Special Branch and the Prussian Secret Police concerning Communism.[7] These links, conducted through Frank Foley, the Passport Control Officer in Berlin, covered exchanges of information on visits by British Communists to their German counterparts, including 'Communist front organisations' like the League against Imperialism and the Friends of Soviet Russia – and reciprocal visits to Britain. There had, for example, been discussion of whether the Communist press impresario, Willi Münzenberg, and other Communists should be allowed to enter Britain.[8] At a further meeting between Scotland Yard and an official of the German Embassy in August 1930, it was established that 'closer collaboration [...] in respect of Bolshevik propaganda and intrigue would be helpful'.[9] Liddell subsequently visited Berlin on 10 October 1930 to meet his opposite numbers, though no record of the meeting has survived – perhaps because it had been agreed that such liaison 'was a thing to be kept within the knowledge of a very few individuals'.[10]

It is known that the wave of arrests of political opponents of the Nazis after the Reichstag Fire was carried out on the basis of lists of 'suspects' prepared well in advance by the Prussian Secret Police. It seems almost certain that the facilities granted to Foley would have included access to some or all of these names. Certainly, the limited number of personal files of German refugees so far released confirm that SIS (and therefore MI5) had details of the refugees' political activities in Germany before 1933 – information which must have come from a German source and been forwarded to London by Foley, SIS's man in Berlin. Foley certainly continued to be the fulcrum of British intelligence in Berlin, remaining in his post as Passport Control Officer until recalled to London in August 1939.

The mechanics of surveillance were fairly simple. If activists were not identified at the port of entry, they were soon picked up on registering at Bow Street. In other words, the surveillance of some political refugees began with their entry into the country, being initiated by Special Branch; many of the earliest reports in MI5 files were submitted by Special Branch. The file on Otto Lehmann-Russbueldt, for example, was opened immediately after his landing at Harwich, when he stated that the purpose of his visit was 'to discuss questions of disarmament with Lord Cecil and others', a response which immediately drew the attention of the security services.

Other 'suspects' were identified through their contacts. Edith Tudor-Hart, for example, came to the notice of MI5 after a Special Branch officer had observed her talking with several known Communists at a demonstration in Trafalgar Square.[11] In some cases, 'suspects' were identified by one of the handful of MI5 agents controlled by Maxwell Knight, who penetrated refugee circles by 'befriending' individual members. One notable example was, as we shall see, MI5's surveillance of the so-called 'Primrose League'.

Once opened, most files remained open for some years, often without yielding any apparently useful information. A few were opened and closed more quickly. One, in particular, came to an abrupt end: the case of the journalist and Socialist activist, Dora Fabian, whose sudden death in 1935 remains an unsolved mystery.

Notes

1 See Martin Kitchen, *The Coming of Austrian Fascism*, London: Croom Helm 1980.

2 Fred Uhlman, *The Making of an Englishman*, London: Gollancz 1960, p. 201.

3 Olden to Oskar Maria Graf, 1 April 1938, Deutsche Bibliothek, Deutsches Exilarchiv, Exil PEN, 75–175, 462.

4 Quoted in Werner Röder, *Die deutschen sozialistischen Exilgruppen in Großbritannien 1940–1945*, Bonn-Bad Godesberg: Neue Gesellschaft, 2nd edition 1973, p. 17.

5 Cf. Jürgen Kuczynski, *Memoiren: Die Erziehung des J.K. zum Kommunisten und Wissenschaftler*, Berlin/Weimar: Aufbau, 2nd edition, 1975. Heinz Schmidt, on the other hand, claims that the party group at this time 'rarely exceeded 10–15 comrades'. Cf. Heinz Schmidt, 'Erinnerungen', unpublished manuscript, Bundesarchiv Berlin-Lichterfelde [SAPMO-BArch], SgY30/1909/1. (p. 230)

6 The activities of these small splinter groups in Britain are described by Werner Roeder – albeit from the perspective of the SPD. See Röder, *Die deutschen sozialistischen Exilgruppen*, pp. 39–47 Roeder's study, based largely on sources in the Friedrich Ebert Stiftung, Bonn, concentrates almost entirely on the war years, coinciding with the period spent by SPD leaders in London and therefore has little to say on the years 1933–39.

7 Letter to SIS (Valentine Vivian), 7 March 1930, The National Archives [TNA], KV4/110/ 6a.

8 TNA, KV4/110/12a.

9 *Ibid.*, item 13a.

10 *Ibid.*

11 TNA, KV2/1012.

4

The mysterious case of Dora Fabian

On Thursday 4 April 1935, the bodies of two German refugees were found dead in a flat they shared in Bloomsbury, London WC1.[1] One was an older woman, the former Social Democratic (SDP) member of the Reichstag Mathilde Wurm, 60, who had been leading a relatively quiet life in British exile. The other was the much younger Dora Fabian, 33, a journalist, political activist and a former member of a breakaway German Socialist group, the Sozialistische Arbeiterpartei (SAP). Since the door of the bedroom in which they lay was locked from the inside, anxious friends had to call the police to force it open. Fabian and Wurm, who had in fact been dead for some days, were found lying in bed, facing one another, with a cup containing a brown liquid on a bedside table beside them. The flat was neat and tidy although the cleaner, who in the interim had unsuspectingly cleaned the rest of the flat, reported having previously found and cleared away the remains of a meal laid for three on the kitchen table.

Dora Fabian had been known to MI5 as a political activist for nearly two years. In fact, it had opened a 'personal file' on her in September 1933. This file (PF 42716) has not been released, though the reason for this, like the case it concerns, is shrouded in mystery. Fortunately, it is possible to reconstruct much of the file's contents by reference to the Metropolitan Police file on the Fabian–Wurm case (which undoubtedly would have been passed to MI5) and to two MI5 files which *have* been released, those on Hans Wesemann and Heinz-Alex Nathan, who in different ways were both involved in the Fabian–Wurm affair.

The mystery surrounding Dora Fabian begins with the circumstances of her escape from Germany. She was a friend and collaborator of the celebrated dramatist Ernst Toller, for whom she had done secretarial work in 1930–31. In the introduction to his *Letters from Prison*, published in 1936, Toller recorded that the letters which formed the nucleus of the book were rescued by Dora Fabian, who went to his flat shortly after it had been raided by the SA and removed two suitcases full of papers. When the police discovered what she had done, she was arrested and imprisoned, but resolutely maintained that she had destroyed the papers. Immediately after her release, she fled abroad, 'managing in some inexplicable way' to smuggle the papers out of Germany.[2]

Fabian did not come directly to Britain, staying briefly in Prague before travelling on to Zurich and Paris. She arrived in London on 8 September 1933, armed with an invitation from John Paton, the British ILP activist and sometime editor of the Party's paper *New Leader*. She was also in possession of ample funds and was granted permission to stay in Britain for one month, subject to the condition she did not seek employment. However, her real purpose in visiting London (though hardly one she would have admitted) was to attend the Legal Commission of Inquiry into the Burning of the Reichstag (also known as the Reichstag Fire Counter Trial), due to open in London a few days later. This event would not have escaped the attention of MI5. The brainchild of the Communist publicist Willi Münzenberg, the Commission was conceived as a counterpart to the official Reichstag Fire Trial, which was to begin in Leipzig later in the month. Münzenberg himself was unable to visit London, since he would have been refused entry to Britain. As early as March 1930, MI5 and Special Branch had discussed how to exclude Münzenberg, whom the MI6 head of station in Berlin Frank Foley (officially the Passport Control Officer) had called 'probably the most dangerous German in existence as regards British Imperial and internal interests'.[3]

The Counter Trial was very much a media event, intended to discredit the official Nazi trial in Leipzig: the *Daily Worker* called it 'the trial of a trial'.[4] Although organised by the Communist Party, it received wide support among political exiles. Among those who would testify to the Commission of Inquiry were Albert Grzesinski (the former Berlin Police President until his removal by the Nazis at the time of the 'Prussian coup' in 1932), the SPD Reichstag deputy Rudolf Breitscheid, Kurt Rosenfeld of the SAP and Ernst Toller. Fabian herself was involved in the trial as an official translator[5] – once again, a role which MI5 would scarcely have overlooked.

While Fabian would therefore have been a figure of some interest to British counter-intelligence, neither MI5 nor Special Branch seems to have opposed her remaining in Britain, which suggests that they were content to monitor her and her contacts. At the end of her first month, an application for extension of her permission to stay in Britain made on her behalf by the Jewish Refugees Committee was duly granted as were later requests, her final extension being approved up until 31 May 1935.[6] Following the Counter Trial, Fabian remained in London, using it as a base for intensive political work. She certainly did some work for the veteran pacifist Otto Lehmann-Russbueldt, notably editing and typing a fair copy of his book *Wer rettet Europa? Die Aufgaben der kleinen Staaten* (*Who Will Save Europe? The*

Task of the Smaller States).[7] She also renewed contact with Ernst Toller who had taken up residence in London after the Counter Trial.

When the bodies of Dora Fabian and Mathilde Wurm were discovered, the police found 'a large quantity of correspondence dealing with the activities of various international associations for German refugees'.[8] This was presumably addressed to both women, although Fabian in particular had been greatly involved in exile politics (despite the fact that such involvement was officially frowned upon by the British authorities and could even lead to expulsion from Britain).[9] Although having officially parted company with the SAP on ideological grounds early in 1933, Fabian was in correspondence with the SAP leader, Jacob Walcher, who with his wife Hertha was in exile in Paris, as well as in regular contact with members of the small London-based SAP group. In particular, she was concerned with raising money for the defence of SAP prisoners being tried in the Reich: for example, with the help of her close friend Fenner Brockway and the British Independent Labour Party (which was aligned with the exiled SAP), she managed to arrange for a British lawyer to attend the trial of Max Köhler and others, a group of twenty-five SAP members who in November 1934 were tried for treason in Berlin. In addition, Fabian was anxiously corresponding with the Walchers and others concerning the welfare and safety of her ex-husband Walter Fabian who, having remained in the SAP, was still living and working underground in Berlin.[10]

It is likely that Dora Fabian's correspondence with SAP members and others would have been among that found by the British police. It is equally likely that MI5 would already have seen it: as with many other 'suspects', she would have been subject to an HOW, authorising the interception of all mail sent to her address. The local police constable who was first called to the scene was soon joined by Detective Inspectors Campion and Hawkyard from Scotland Yard; and Campion, with a view to a possible political dimension, informed Chief Inspector Foster of Special Branch, 'as it seemed a matter that would interest that Branch ... At that moment there was nothing to suggest that the deaths were caused by anything other than by suicide, but in an early edition of the evening papers, veiled suggestions of a political crime were made, and I therefore had further enquiries made'.[11] Consequently, Inspector Jempson and Sergeant East from Special Branch also arrived to make their enquiries.

The inquest into the deaths was heard a few days later, on 10 April, at the Paddington Coroner's Court.[12] The courtroom was packed with both British and German observers, the former including well-known political figures such as Fenner Brockway and James Maxton MP, representing the Independent Labour Party; Ben Riley, who was a long-standing Labour Party colleague of Mathilde Wurm's; William Gillies, the Labour Party's

International Secretary; and the pacifist peer, Lord Noel-Buxton, who was frequently a source of support to the refugees from Nazism. German observers included Ernst Toller, who had travelled especially from Paris to attend the inquest and funeral of the two women; Rudolf Olden, the well-known lawyer, writer and journalist, whose wife Ika had been a close friend of Dora's; and, representing the exiled SPD (or SOPADE), the lawyer and political scientist Franz L. Neumann. The verdict reached was one of suicide while of unsound mind; but there were many in the refugee community as well as among the British friends and supporters of the refugees who found such an explanation totally unconvincing. At the inquest itself, witness after witness had reiterated that neither of the two women had seemed at all suicidal in the weeks and days leading up to their death. Disbelief at the official version of events was also expressed to representatives of the press by various Englishmen and women in public life such as Fenner Brockway[13] or the Labour politician Ellen Wilkinson,[14] who had known both women well, as well as by another prominent friend of Dora Fabian's, the Chief Opposition Whip and ex-Under-Secretary for War Lord Marley,[15] who had frequently called on Fabian for assistance with German refugee matters.

Indeed the case quickly grew into something of a *cause célèbre*, with public interest fanned by accompanying revelations of an unhappy love affair of Dora Fabian's with the exiled German writer and politician Karl Korsch. The inquest had revealed the existence of a supposed suicide note from Fabian to Korsch, written in shorthand, about which Korsch had chosen not to alert the police (and had thus possibly failed to save the women's lives), as well as a longhand letter from Korsch to Fabian breaking off their relationship, the two documents raising more questions than answers.[16] In addition, the case had given rise to rumours of German espionage on British soil. It was even suggested in heated press reports that the Gestapo, operating abroad, could have been implicated in the deaths.[17]

At the time the two women died, there had already been a number of cases pointing to Nazi activity beyond the German borders that had been widely reported in the international press. The engineer Dr Georg Bell, who had been accused of passing on information for publication in the antifascist Catholic journal, *Der gerade Weg*, had in March 1933 been pursued by the SA over the German border into Austria and killed there. A few months later, in August 1933, the philosopher Theodor Lessing, a long-standing opponent of the Nazis, had been murdered in Marienbad, Czechoslovakia, by local Nazis. The most notorious case of all up until that point was probably the abduction of the anti-Nazi journalist Berthold Jacob over the Swiss border into Germany (and from there to a Nazi prison) in March 1935, only a matter of weeks before the deaths of Fabian and Wurm. Implicated in the abduction had been a man by the name of Hans Wesemann (see also chapter 5) who for the best part of two years had been passing himself off in Britain as a Socialist exile, but who had recently been unmasked as a Gestapo agent.[18] After Wesemann's arrest in Switzerland on 20 March, a number of other political exiles, like Ernst Toller, came forward with accounts of how Wesemann had attempted to prey on them, and of how they had succeeded, by luck or by judgement, in evading him.[19] All these cases had been perceived as worrying in Britain; but the deaths of Dora Fabian and Mathilde Wurm, occurring as they did in the very heart of London, were seen as positively alarming by the general British public and, more particularly, by the beleaguered refugee population in Britain.

The case was rendered still more disturbing by the fact that, in the days leading up to her death, Dora Fabian had been assisting the Investigator of the Swiss Police Authorities, Dr (Anton) Roy Ganz, who had been sent to Britain to look into the British-based activities of Hans Wesemann. Fabian had invited Ganz to use her flat as a base for his enquiries and had arranged a series of interviews for him there (indeed Fabian's passionate involvement in investigating the case, literally up until the day she died, was widely cited as another strong counterargument to the suicide verdict). The suspicion that the Gestapo could have had a hand in the women's deaths therefore seemed all the more plausible, particularly since it was also reported in the press and elsewhere that Fabian and Wurm had twice before during their period of exile had their flat broken into, it was thought by German agents. The first occasion had allegedly been in February 1934, when valuable items had been left untouched while papers had been disturbed; the second occurrence was a few months later when the flat had been ransacked, following which the two women had fitted Yale locks to their doors to prevent a further intrusion.[20]

While the public at large became increasingly exercised by the reports of these events, British official bodies were equally anxious to dampen down the agitation. A memorandum dispatched from Scotland Yard to the Home Office, contained in the Metropolitan Police file on the case, indicates the importance that both organisations were placing on dispelling public disquiet. For example, although Special Branch had been very involved in investigating the women's deaths, it was thought advisable that this should not become apparent at the inquest: 'Having regard to the political excitement over this suicide, it is unnecessary and undesirable to complicate the inquest by calling in a Special Branch officer.'[21] Certain aspects of the case could be explored at the inquest but others – the women's possible anxiety regarding their British residence permits, for instance (which might have indicated Home Office culpability) – were not. A minute on the inside cover of the Metropolitan Police file makes it clear that the

Scotland Yard memorandum was compiled prior to a meeting with the Coroner, these notes being intended for his prior information and guidance. And indeed, the Coroner went out of his way to depoliticise the inquest: in fact, 'at intervals', when political motives were suggested, he observed that he could not have politics introduced into his court.[22] This repeated instruction was perceived by those who viewed the case as a fundamentally political one as totally inappropriate; and indeed the whole inquest was seen as disturbingly unsatisfactory by the dead women's supporters in failing to unearth the real facts of the matter.

The identity of the women's last supper guest was never established, for instance, and nor was that of a man, a German speaker on intimate terms with Fabian (but not Karl Korsch), whom the cleaner had seen in the flat shortly before their deaths. Korsch's evidence was felt to be contradictory and evasive but he was not pressed for clarification by the Coroner; on the contrary, the Coroner explicitly permitted him, as a married man, to gloss over his relationship with Dora Fabian. The shorthand note, presented to the court as Fabian's suicide note, had been transcribed by the German Embassy, it emerged; this fact hardly served as a recommendation of the accuracy of the transcription, nor as a testament to the political *nous* of the British police. Moreover, even if the note was interpreted as going some way towards explaining Dora Fabian's suicide, no explanation was forthcoming concerning that of Mathilde Wurm. Yet the deep disquiet at the conduct of the inquest and its verdict felt by the dead women's friends and supporters was in no way shared by the British authorities: Norman Kendal, for instance, at Scotland Yard, who was in charge of the Criminal Investigation Division and Special Branch, wrote of the inquest to Norman Brook at the Home Office: 'I think it went very well.'[23]

And just as the direction and result of the inquest appear to have been predetermined by the authorities, so too those questions on the case that were raised in the House of Commons – on 5, 8 and 11 April 1935 – failed to elicit anything approaching a satisfactory answer from the Home Secretary. Captain Charles Waterhouse, for example, attempted on three occasions to ask for a Home Office statement on the subject, 'in view of the fact that *The Times* and other responsible newspapers are putting a sinister connection on the deaths of these ladies', but was told that the local Coroner would investigate the case 'in the ordinary course'.[24] Sir Charles Cayzer, who was much concerned with the related Jacob–Wesemann affair (and raised it in the House on no fewer than six occasions), took the opportunity to enquire about 'the presence in this country of any counter-refugee organisation engaged in undesirable activities';[25] he was informed that since enquiries into the Fabian–Wurm deaths were still proceeding, a Home

Office statement would not be desirable. A third MP, Major Abraham Lyons, worrying along similar lines, enquired about the numbers of 'foreign political organisations or organisations supporting foreign political systems' in Britain and requested that these be shut down immediately. In reply, Lyons was merely told by the Home Secretary, Sir John Gilmour, that 'appropriate action would be taken should occasion arise'.[26]

Yet, despite the soothing answers, it is clear from those files that are available on the Fabian–Wurm case that the British authorities were seriously concerned at this time about the presence of Nazi agents in Britain. This is very evident, for example, from the MI5 file on Hans Wesemann as well as from his Home Office file (there is, as one would expect, a considerable overlap between the two files).[27] It is also apparent from the comparable files kept on the journalist and sportsman Heinz-Alex Nathan (later to make his name as the Germanist Alec Natan) who was a friend of Dora Fabian's in exile.[28] The equivalent files held on Dora Fabian either no longer exist (in the case of her Home Office file) or, as already mentioned, have not been released (in the case of her MI5 file).[29] Many Security Service files which would be of the greatest interest to the present study remain unavailable, Fabian's among them, though the Wesemann and Nathan files make for fascinating related reading. In addition, the British official view of the Fabian–Wurm deaths is frequently revealed in the Metropolitan Police file on the case which fortunately was released on request.

From these sources it emerges that, quite apart from their suspicions of Wesemann, the British authorities suspected Dora Fabian's lover, Karl Korsch, of being a Nazi agent (and although their suspicion was never officially substantiated, Korsch was indeed expelled from Britain in the summer of 1935). This may be attributed at least in part to Inspector Jempson's Special Branch report of 26 April 1935, 'Re Hans Wesemann and others', held in Wesemann's MI5 file, informing the Home Office of its belief that Korsch 'played a sinister role in the suicides of Dr Dora Fabian and Frau Wurm at 12, Great Ormond Street on 1.4.1935'. The report, which was also informed by the confessions that Wesemann had made to the Swiss police about his relations with the German Embassy in London, noted that, through the Embassy, Wesemann 'was working for a secret department of the German police which is exclusively concerned in watching German political refugees abroad, luring the most dangerous back to Germany or taking other steps to render them innocuous'.[30] It noted further that, after the Fabian–Wurm deaths, Roy Ganz had returned to London to investigate the role of some of Wesemann's associates there and, as the fifth point in a list of five: 'To see Karl Korsch.'[31] Ganz had interviewed Korsch in Jempson's presence (without Korsch having initially been aware of the latter's identity) and Jempson had gone on to record the following in 'Re Hans Wesemann and others':

> The theory held by the German refugees in this country and abroad is that Korsch knew Dora Fabian had given information to Dr Ganz concerning the Jakob [*sic*] case, and reproached her for having done so. She discovered that Korsch was a Nazi agent, and the shock of this, coupled with the fact that she had betrayed to him many things concerning German refugees in London, caused her to commit suicide.[32]

As mentioned above, Heinz-Alex Nathan was another refugee to fall foul of the British authorities in this same connection. When Nathan had heard of the two women's deaths, he had reported to the police on how Fabian had shortly beforehand asked him for a loan of some money (a request with which he had not complied). Despite the fact that Nathan had made his statement to the police voluntarily, he was still perceived as being implicated in the Fabian–Wurm affair, with Jempson reporting further:

> This man is also suspected by the German political refugees in London of being a Nazi agent, because they know nothing of his antecedents, and is a frequent visitor to the German Embassy in London.[33]

There was, Jempson reiterated towards the end of his report, 'no evidence in the possession of the police to confirm the theory that the last two men named [Korsch and Nathan] are Nazi agents'.[34] Three days later, Norman Kendal wrote to Norman Brook, enclosing a copy of 'Re Hans Wesemann and Others' for Home Office consumption and sending another off to MI5.[35] MI5, so it emerges from Kendal's letter, was particularly interested in investigating Wesemann's Anglo-German contacts, the Hitzemeyer brothers, and what Kendal termed 'the military side of the case', that is, the Hitzemeyers' apparently shady business deals in British military bases where they sold suits and other goods.[36] Kendal then went on to express his views on Korsch and Nathan rather more forcefully than he had done previously, as well as on Elisabeth Günther, a German national working in Britain (though not a refugee), who was thought to have acted as an intermediary between Wesemann and the Gestapo.

> In the meantime, the suspicion that Korsch, Nathan and Günther are secret German Police Agents is fairly strong [...] You may consider whether, when their permission to stay runs out, it is necessary or advisable to allow them to stay any longer.[37]

Although the evidence on this is not entirely clear, Elisabeth Günther does indeed appear to have left Britain later in 1935.[38] Karl Korsch, as already noted, was required to leave in the summer of 1935, despite representations being made on his behalf by Walter Adams of the Academic

Assistance Council.[39] Moreover, the rumours about him continued to spread. When Korsch left Britain, he attempted to make a career for himself in the United States but things did not go particularly well for him there either, a fact he attributed, some four years on, to 'my reputation among the German emigrés'.[40]

As for Heinz-Alex Nathan, while he was not compelled to leave Britain, he remained linked with the Fabian–Wurm deaths, and therefore suspect in the eyes of British officialdom for some time to come. On the outbreak of war, Nathan was one of the few refugees to be interned as a category 'A' enemy alien, that is, as an alien constituting a high security risk. He appealed against this decision to the Central Advisory Committee under Norman Birkett QC, his appeal being heard on 13 December 1939.[41] The day before, MI5 had sent the Home Office some pointers, 'Observations of MI5 on the Case of Heinz Alexander Nathan', reminding the Advisory Committee of Nathan's former links with Dora Fabian and, through Fabian, with 'an extremely unpleasant Nazi agent called Hans Wesemann'.[42] Nathan found his hearing a gruelling experience, not least because, to his surprise, he was interrogated on the Fabian–Wurm deaths – which he had almost forgotten – and on his part in them. He became flustered and, failing to recall perfectly the sequence of events of some five years previously, contradicted a statement he had made in 1935 about Dora Fabian's financial position. As Nathan himself later wrote:

> My confusion must have left a bad impression, for the next questions of Mr Birkett indicated clearly that he thought me an accessory to the affair which had always been shrouded in mystery for me and in the eyes of public opinion, which presumed at the time that the suicide was a disguised political murder.[43]

Predictably, Nathan's appeal was turned down and he was interned for four years in all, an unusually long period of time. He himself, who had more than enough time in internment to consider such matters, placed the blame variously on Rudolf and Ika Olden for having supposedly spread rumours about him,[44] or on the German spy Ivan Petkov who had reportedly included his name in a list of alleged German agents in Britain in return for his freedom.[45] Neither of these theories is borne out, however, by the Advisory Committee's report on Nathan's hearing which instead stressed its dissatisfaction at the answers Nathan had given to questions on both the Jacob–Wesemann and Fabian–Wurm affairs and noted further: 'The information before the Committee suggested that the ground for Dr Fabian's suicide was that somebody had informed the German authorities of Wesemann's action of luring Jakob [*sic*] into Germany'.[46] Although the logic here is questionable (since the German authorities would in any case have been well aware of Wesemann's activities), the inference is clear: the British authorities, while concluding that the two women had indeed committed suicide, were of the opinion that these deaths were to be explained in political rather than personal terms.

Hans Wesemann, for his part, had been arrested in Switzerland a couple of weeks before the Fabian–Wurm deaths for his part in the abduction of Berthold Jacob over the Swiss–German border. At his trial just over a year later, it was reported that in Britain Dora Fabian had consistently warned fellow exiles against him[47] and indeed a statement of hers on Wesemann was read out posthumously. Her suspicions of him had been based, *inter alia*, on a tip-off she had received from someone at the German Embassy in London that Wesemann was viewed there as a spy;[48] on the fact that Wesemann, despite being a refugee, had always had plenty of money; and on his habit of pocketing fees paid for newspaper articles by other refugees which he was supposedly helping to place.[49] The refugee newspaper the *Pariser Tageblatt*, reporting on the Wesemann trial, noted that at the time in question 'no-one apart from the clever Dr Dora Fabian' had recognised Wesemann for what he really was.[50]

While the presence of Hans Wesemann in custody had a generally calming effect on those alarmed by the Gestapo presence abroad, in particular the international refugee community, the role of the German Embassy in Wesemann's activities that emerged from the trial caused huge disquiet. The British press made much of it, with the *Daily Herald*, for instance, reporting the case under the startling headline: 'German Embassy as Spy HQ'.[51] Indeed the matter was raised in the House of Commons on five occasions, on 11, 17, 20, 25 and 28 May 1936. Just as had happened after the Fabian–Wurm deaths, however, the government managed to sidestep the request for a statement by means of a variety of avoidance tactics: on 11 May, for instance, the Prime Minister, Stanley Baldwin, announced in the House that the Foreign Secretary was awaiting a report from the British Minister in Berne[52] while on 28 May, the Home Secretary had this to say:

> Such activities are, of course, closely watched by the responsible authorities. Appropriate action would be taken in any case where it was considered expedient. It would not, however, be in the public interest to detail the measures which are taken by the authorities to deal with activities of this kind.[53]

British sources are less than helpful as to what communications may have passed between the British government and the German Embassy at this time since the relevant Foreign Office file on, *inter alia*, 'evidence implicating German Embassy in London' has not been preserved.[54] German official sources are more fruitful, however: it emerges from Auswärtiges Amt [German Foreign Office] documents, held in Berlin, that on 15 May 1936 an unnamed member of the German Embassy staff visited Ralph Wigram at the London Foreign Office with a statement designed to clear the German Embassy of the charge of involvement in spying on the German exile community. If the German report of the interview, marked 'top secret', is to be relied upon, Mr Wigram more or less dismissed out of hand the recent anti-Nazi enquiries in the British press and Parliament while doing his best to be agreeable to the German authorities:

> Mr Wigram immediately declared that the Foreign Office did not attribute the slightest significance to the English press reports nor to the questions in the House of Commons. For this reason the parliamentary question on 11 May had been deflected by the reply that it was necessary to await a report from the British Legation in Berne. In fact a report had not even been requested from the Legation. Mr Wigram considered the matter as closed, unless – as he put it – another foolish question should be asked in the Commons or some trashy newspaper ['Schundblatt'] or other should pick the story up again.[55]

The plight of the refugees from Nazi Germany, spied upon in exile, was clearly not the British authorities' prime consideration here.

So how did Dora Fabian and Mathilde Wurm die? Even if the British authorities were keen to bury the affair, the dead women's friends and supporters, both German and British, continued for quite some time to pore over every scrap of evidence in order to arrive at an explanation. Roy Ganz, of course, returned to London, officially on Swiss Police business, though his investigations evidently had something of a personal quest to them too.[56] It was reported that members of the London-based German exile community were keen to set up an enquiry of their own, though this apparently came to nothing. Other investigations took more of a party-political turn: thus the exiled SAP, formerly Fabian's party, joined forces with the affiliated Independent Labour Party in which Fenner Brockway played a leading role. At the same time the exiled SPD, as Mathilde Wurm's party, turned for help to the British Labour Party, while the Labour Party also instigated a separate line of enquiry through the Socialdemokratisk Forbund i Danmark, based in Copenhagen, and the Sozialistische Arbeiter-Internationale under Friedrich Adler. Finally, as late as 1937 and 1938, an American journalist, Clara Leiser, undertook quite extensive research into the affair with the help of two of Fabian's closest friends in England, the British Margaret Goldsmith and the political refugee from Berlin, originally from Austria, Margaret Mynatt, who will reoccur later in our narrative. While each of these lines of enquiry succeeded in opening up fresh facts for consideration, both personal and political, none of them offered a totally convincing explanation; and nor indeed did the Metropolitan Police file on the case when it was finally released in the 1990s.

A fictional account of the Fabian–Wurm case has recently been published in which the mystery surrounding the case has been 'satisfactorily' resolved.[57] However, reality is more intractable than that. The case itself remains unsolved, resisting the easy resolutions of fiction; indeed there are numerous questions that have remained unanswered to the present day. Why, for example, were two packed bags found in the flat after the women's death containing night clothes, washing utensils and the Sunday newspapers? Who was the mysterious third person who had shared the women's last supper with them and who was the German-speaking stranger observed in the flat shortly before that? If the two women did not commit suicide, as their friends insisted, why was the bedroom door locked on the inside? What, exactly, was the role of Fabian's former lover Karl Korsch, why was he not pressed to give a proper account of his actions by the Coroner and why was he then summarily deported from Britain? Why, even if Dora Fabian did commit suicide because of an unhappy love affair, would the much older ex-parliamentarian Mathilde Wurm have followed suit? Why was the Coroner evidently so intent on reaching a 'safe', that is, non-political verdict? And why, even though the Special Branch report on the case has survived, has MI5's personal file on Dora Fabian been 'retained' or perhaps destroyed?

What makes this case rather different, as far as the British authorities were concerned, from some of those considered elsewhere in this book is the relatively early stage in the years of German emigration to Britain at which it took place. In addition, and unusually, the official concern here is primarily with supposed Nazi agents rather than their Communist counterparts. Even the ex-Communist Karl Korsch, to take just one example, was seen as a putative Nazi agent. It is also worth noting that, even though British appeasement policies towards Germany cannot strictly be said to have started by 1935 or 1936, the preservation of good diplomatic relations between Britain and Nazi Germany was already of paramount importance. The Wigram statement, as given above, demonstrates clearly how it was considered expedient for the Foreign Office to play down the revelations at the Wesemann trial in order to avoid a diplomatic incident. Roy Ganz, on his first visit to London in March 1935, had already complained of the 'restrained conduct' [zurückhaltende Gebärde] on the part of the British police in the course of his highly political Wesemann investigations.[58] And similar police 'restraint' was apparent from the beginning of the Fabian–Wurm enquiries the following month, with the inquest proceedings, far from airing all the issues (as had been requested in the House of Commons), serving to obfuscate the admittedly complex facts of the matter still further. In short, the British authorities showed themselves determined to render the case harmless by downplaying and depoliticising it, no matter how or why Dora Fabian and Mathilde Wurm actually died.

Notes

1 On this, see Charmian Brinson, *The Strange Case of Dora Fabian and Mathilde Wurm: A Study of German Political Exiles in London during the 1930s*, Berne: Peter Lang 1997.

2 Introduction to Ernst Toller, *Letters from Prison*, translated by R. Ellis Roberts, London: John Lane1936.

3 Report from MI 1c to Special Branch, 14 March 1930, The National Archives [TNA], KV4/110/12a: 'Liaison between Metropolitan Police Special Branch and Prussian Ministry of Interior concerning Communism 1930'.

4 *Daily Worker*, 14 September 1933.

5 According to the Labour MP Ben Riley in 'Was It Suicide? Mystery of the Two German Exiles', *Forward*, 13 April 1935, p. 7.

6 See Metropolitan Police file on the case, TNA, MEPOL3/871/3A, p.1.

7 Otto Lehmann-Russbueldt to J.B. Hugenholtz, 27 December 1933, Bibliotheek van het Vredespaleis, The Hague, Corr. Hugenholtz.

8 See TNA, MEPOL3/871/2B.

9 For instance, Helmut Goldschmidt, the first leader of the exiled SAP group in London, had been deported from Britain in February 1934 after he had been overheard speaking at a political meeting.

10 On Fabian and the SAP, see Brinson, *The Strange Case*, pp. 142ff. SAP correspondence in exile is held at the Arbeiderbevegelsens Arkiv og Bibliotek, Oslo.

11 TNA, MEPOL3/871/3A, pp. 1–2.

12 This account of the inquest is based on TNA, MEPOL3/871/3a, pp. 8–10, and contemporary press reports.

13 Brockway 'could not find any explanation of the supposed suicide pact', while adding that Fabian had been concerned about her British residence permit coming to an end (*News Chronicle*, 'Two German Women Dead in Flat', 5 April 1935, pp. 1, 13).

14 According to Wilkinson, 'there was no apparent reason why either of them should decide to end their lives' (*The Star*, 'Refugees Dead in London Flat', 4 April 1935, p. 1).

15 Marley was of the view that, even if Fabian had committed suicide, then this would have been motivated by political rather than personal factors (see for example, *Manchester Guardian*, 'London Link with the Jakob [*sic*] Kidnapping', 5 April 1935, p. 11).

16 For example, re the identification of the writer of the shorthand note; re its meaning and the accuracy of its transcription; re when or whether the letters had been posted or delivered by hand; re the fact that, while it was reported that the couple customarily corresponded in shorthand, Korsch had chosen to write his letter to Dora in longhand, etc.

17 See for example, *Daily Herald*, 'German Refugees Poisoned: Women Worried After Flat was Raided', 5 April 1935, pp. 1, 2.

18 On Wesemann, see James J. Barnes and Patience P. Barnes, *Nazi Refugee Turned Gestapo Spy: The Life of Hans Wesemann, 1895–1971*, Westport/London: Praeger 2001; Charmian Brinson, 'The Gestapo and the German Political Exiles in Britain during the 1930s: The Case of Hans Wesemann – and Others', *German Life and Letters*, 51, 1 (January 1998), 43–64.

19 On Wesemann's written approaches to Toller, see for example Ernst Toller to Marie Meloney, 27 April 1935, Columbia University, Rare Book and Manuscript Library, New York, Spec. Ms. Coll. Meloney.

20 On the burglaries, see for example Otto Lehmann-Russbueldt, *Germany's Air Force: With an Introduction by Wickham Steed and an Appendix*, London: Allen and Unwin 1935, p. 24; *Everybody's Weekly*, 'Nazi Terrorism in London!', 20 April 1935, p. 12.

21 TNA, MEPOL3/871/4B.

22 See, for example, *Daily Worker*, 'Poisoned Women', 11 April 1935, pp. 1, 4.

23 Dated April 1935, TNA, MEPOL3/871/4A.

24 *Hansard*, 5th Series, *Parliamentary Debates*, House of Commons (HC), vol. 300, cols. 678, 679.

25 *Ibid.*, col. 803.

26 *Ibid.*, col. 1317.

27 These are TNA, KV2/2834 and Home Office (HO), Aliens Department, W2024.

28 TNA, KV2/1743 and HO, Aliens Department, N183.

29 It is not in fact known whether Fabian's MI5 file, originally numbered PF 42716, has been retained by the Security Service.

30 TNA, KV2/2834/78a, p. 1.

31 *Ibid.*, p. 4.

32 *Ibid.*, p. 6.

33 *Ibid.*

34 *Ibid.*, p. 7.

35 N. Kendal to N. Brook, 29 April 1935, HO, Aliens Department, W2024.

36 On Charles, Walter, Willi and Werner Hitzemeyer, see Brinson, *The Strange Case*, pp. 358–60.

37 Kendal to Brook, 29 April 1935, HO, Aliens Department, W2024.

38 See HO, Aliens Department, G1368.

39 See Adams to E. N. Cooper, HO, 25 May 1935, Bodleian Library Oxford, SPSL, 435, 1.

40 Korsch to Paul Partos, 12 June 1939, in Michael Buckmiller and Götz Langkau, eds, 'Karl Korsch: Briefe an Paul Partos, Paul Mattick und Bert Brecht, 1934–1939', in Claudio Pozzoli, ed., *Arbeiterbewegung: Theorie und Geschichte* (Jahrbuch I: *Über Karl Korsch*), Frankfurt a. M.: Fischer, 1973, p. 218.

41 For a transcript of Nathan's interrogation on 13 December 1939, see Nathan's MI5 file TNA, KV2/1743/42a.

42 TNA, KV2/1743/41a.

43 See Nathan's 'Erlebnisbericht aus der Internierung September 1939–August 1943, Institut für Zeitgeschichte, Munich [IfZ], Alex Natan Papers, F 203', pp. 129f.

44 *Ibid.*, pp. 131–2.

45 According to a note by Dr Werner Röder, dated 1 December 1969, entitled 'Mitteilung von Dr Alex Natan ... bei einem Gespräch im Institut für Zeitgeschichte am 22. Oktober 1969', IfZ, Natan Papers, F 203, p. 186a.

46 Report, dated 12 January 1940, from Advisory Committee to Under-Secretary of State, Home Office (Aliens Department), in HO, Aliens Department, N183.

47 See, for example, statement by Dr Anton Roy Ganz, Staatsarchiv des Kantons Basel-Stadt, Gerichtsarchiv KK2, 1936, vol. 15–16, no. 80, l.c., 863.

48 *Ibid.*, p. 254f. Fabian had reportedly been told this by an unnamed acquaintance (probably Nathan) who had previously been warned against Wesemann by a non-Nazi German diplomat in London, himself under surveillance (whom she had taken to be Baron zu Putlitz).

49 *Ibid.*

50 *Pariser Tageblatt*, 'Die Gestapo auf der Anklagebank', 6 May 1936, p. 2.

51 On 5 May 1936, p. 1.

52 *Hansard*, 5th Series, *Parliamentary Debates*, HC, vol. 312, col. 18.

53 *Ibid.*, col. 2169.

54 See TNA, Index to Foreign Office Papers for 1936.

55 German Embassy London to Foreign Office Berlin, 15 May 1936, Politisches Archiv des Auswärtigen Amts, Berlin, Rechtsabteilung, Schweiz, Streitfall Jakob, R42532.

56 On these and the other investigations, see Brinson, *The Strange Case*, pp. 291ff.

57 Anna Funder, *All That I Am*, London: Penguin 2011.

58 'Notiz', Schweizerische Gesandtschaft, London, to Abteilung für Auswärtiges, Berne, 29 March 1935, Schweizerisches Bundesarchiv, Berne, E 2200, London, 50.

5

Nazi spies and the 'Auslandsorganisation'

Given MI5's somewhat ambiguous attitude towards Nazism, it is pertinent to ask: at what point after 1933 did policy begin to change and when did Nazi Germany and its agents become a prime focus of counter-intelligence? An internal MI5 memorandum records a meeting taking place at the Home Office on 23 November 1933, at which it was decided:

> that MI5 should undertake to look after Fascism in the same way as they look after communism, and that the Commissioner of Police and the Chief Officers of Police should collaborate with MI5 in exactly the same way as they did at present as regards communism.[1]

MI5 stipulated, however, that it would be unable to assume the new duties until April 1934 and then only if additional funds were made available to pay for the necessary staff. The intelligence historian Christopher Andrew also suggests that the policy change occurred in around 1934[2] – but MI5's in-house history, written much closer to the events, claims that it was at least a year later: 'Until 1935 the staff of this branch [i.e. 'B' Division] was primarily concerned with matters relating to Communism and the USSR.'[3] Certainly Communism remained a most pressing concern for MI5 from the mid-1930s, but the Security Service also began to take seriously the threat of Fascism, both of the domestic variety and that being directed against Britain from Nazi Germany.

MI5's official version of these years is a sober story of action and occasional frustration in which the Security Service was more alert to the threat of Fascism than the government of the day. The report's author, John ('Jack') Curry, a former officer in the Indian Police, had joined 'B' Division in 1934 and made the investigation of the British Union of Fascists (BUF) his main priority.[4] It is therefore hardly surprising that his retrospective report (written in 1945–46) pays great attention to MI5's surveillance of Fascism.

The BUF was founded in 1932 by the charismatic and politically agile Sir Oswald Mosley. Inspired by Benito Mussolini, Mosley modelled his 'Blackshirts' on the Italian Fascist movement. The growth of the BUF had caused concern in the Home Office and when the *Daily Mail*, owned by the right-wing press baron Lord Rothermere, declared its support for Mosley with the historic headline 'Hurrah for the Blackshirts' early in 1934, MI5 was asked to monitor the new party, prompting Vernon Kell to write a series of reports for the Home Office and other government departments.

Kell was initially somewhat myopic about Fascism, which he thought was, to a great extent, 'a natural reaction from Communism'.[5] In his first report he stated that, whereas Communism was an international movement, preaching class warfare, 'fascism insists on the common interests of all classes in an intensified economic nationalism inspired by patriotic sentiment'.[6] Under the influence of his BUF 'expert', Maxwell Knight, Kell concluded that the BUF was a patriotic – and even democratic – party. However, the BUF's Olympia Rally in London in June 1934, at which there were violent brawls between Communist hecklers and BUF 'stewards', recalling similar violence between Communists and Nazis in Germany, made him reconsider. The violent incidents also cost Mosley the support of the *Daily Mail* and briefly moved the BUF to the centre of the political stage.

By March 1935, Kell noted somewhat complacently that the political threat of the BUF was beginning to decline.[7] Up to then Kell – trusting the advice of Maxwell Knight – had refused to believe that Mosley was receiving money from foreign sources. However, he was forced to change his mind following conclusive evidence that the BUF was indeed being funded from fascist Italy. He also warned that Mosley would be ready to accept similar funds from Germany, 'but it is very doubtful whether he is receiving any and almost certain that Hitler would regard it as an unsuitable investment'.[8] Kell remained confident of this, despite Mosley's declared admiration for Hitler and the renaming of the Party as the 'British Union of Fascists and National Socialists', though he did note the growing political convergence between the BUF and the Nazis, particularly evident in Mosley's growing attacks on the Jews.[9]

MI5 was certainly hindered in its investigation of the BUF by the refusal of the Home Secretary, Sir John Gilmour, to grant an intercept warrant on Mosley's mail in 1934. In fact, the Home Office consistently refused to authorise an HOW on Mosley, even after the news that the BUF leader had married Diana Mitford in a supposedly secret ceremony, attended by Adolf Hitler, at the house of the Nazi Propaganda Minister Josef Goebbels in July 1936.[10]

The long arm of the 'Auslandsorganisation'

Despite (or perhaps because of) its initial 'liaison' with the Nazi authorities, MI5 was alert to the threat of German espionage in Britain, represented particularly by the 'Auslandsorganisation' (or Foreign Organisation of Nazi party members). A British Foreign Office memorandum concerning the 'Auslandsorganisation' (AO) defined the latter's original aim as 'the permeation with the Nazi spirit of German residents abroad and the combatting of foreign propaganda and the Jewish boycott'.[11] MI5's B Division had already reported in 1934 'that the activities of the Nazi party organisation in this country deserved special attention'.[12] By 1936, it was recorded that there were 288 Nazi party members in Britain while the AO's London Headquarters was said to be 'in touch with some 1,500 people, some being British subjects of German extraction'.[13] The organisation in Britain was run by Otto Bene, a personal acquaintance of Rudolf Hess, who had come to Britain in 1927 as a hair tonic salesman; Bene ran his group on the strictest lines, expecting compulsory attendance from his membership at AO events. Interestingly, he consistently warned his group against participating in British politics or associating with British Fascists.[14]

Scotland Yard did take cognisance of this fact,[15] but MI5 remained concerned about contacts between members of the 'Auslandsorganisation' and some of the leading personalities in the BUF. There was, however, official reluctance to allow MI5 to investigate further: in January 1934, the Home Office had refused MI5's request for a postal intercept on the AO's London office.[16] Even Kell himself was initially reluctant to investigate the AO, though was persuaded to do so by MI5's 'B' Branch and by Sir Robert Vansittart at the Foreign Office.[17] By 1935, the year of the abduction of Berthold Jacob and the deaths of Dora Fabian and Mathilde Wurm (see chapter 4), MI5 had prepared a report on the ramifications of the AO, also noting the number of German journalists in Britain and their probable links with the Nazi Party. More than that, 'among the press correspondents in London are two of some prominence who are definitely known to be connected with espionage work'.[18] The climax to the growing British official nervousness in 1935 at the thought of National Socialists in their midst was probably the expulsion from Britain at the end of that year of Hans Thost, the London correspondent of the Nazi newspapers *Völkischer Beobachter* and *Der Angriff*, for suspected espionage.[19]

By 1936, Ralph Wigram at the Foreign Office was minuting MI5's belief that the AO 'is a grave potential danger to this country and that the longer it is left to develop here without interference, the graver will be the potential danger which it constitutes'.[20] Indeed, during 1936 serious consideration was being given by both the Foreign and Home Offices to the question of suppressing Nazi and Fascist organisations in Britain. On 29 July 1936, the matter had been discussed at cabinet level but no action was taken to curtail the activities of the AO on British soil; at a time when the government was attempting to promote contacts with the German and Italian governments, the moment was thought to be 'inopportune for taking the action proposed'.[21] A year later, a further memorandum was reviewed by the Joint Intelligence sub-committee which concluded that MI5 'should continue to study these problems', but recommended 'no important increase in the staff of the service for dealing with these matters'.[22]

In 1937, B Division prepared an additional analysis of the 'Auslands-organisation' which was submitted to the Home Office, the Foreign Office and the Directors of Intelligence of the three services. The submission emphasised concerns of sovereignty, pointing out that the AO was 'an extension on British territory of the machinery of the Nazi state', and that 'its branches functioned as subsidiary organs of the German police system'.[23] However, once again no action ensued – and indeed more rigorous surveillance would have run counter to the policies of government, particularly after Neville Chamberlain became Prime Minister in 1937, pursuing a policy of 'appeasement' of the Axis powers.

The case of Hans Wesemann

In fact, the 'Auslandsorganisation' and visiting journalists did not represent the only possible channels for German espionage on British soil; this could be achieved through refugee circles as well. The confusion prevailing in the ranks of the German political exiles, particularly in the early years of emigration, made it a relatively simple matter for one of their number to disguise or to shift political allegiance and spy on fellow exiles. This is exemplified by the case of the formerly Social Democratic journalist Hans Wesemann who in London presented himself in German refugee circles and in British progressive ones as a genuine Socialist refugee.[24]

The details of Wesemann's initiation into espionage on behalf of the German Embassy in London, and ultimately the Gestapo, come from records of the German Diplomatic Service, which was well aware of his activities, rather than from files of the British Security Service, which remained unaware of them until well after the event. It is recorded that about a year after his arrival in Britain, on 27 April 1934, Wesemann arrived unannounced at the German Embassy, in a state of utmost agitation, and requested an interview with one of the diplomats. He proceeded to explain that while he had initially been drawn to his Socialist comrades in exile, he had since undergone something of a 'conversion' and wished now to inform the German authorities of their anti-Nazi activities and contacts.[25] From then on, and at substantial financial benefit to himself, Wesemann reported on the publication and propaganda plans of some of the most prominent members of the German political émigré community in Britain: on the elderly pacifist Otto Lehmann-Russbueldt, for example, from whose desk he removed some incriminating anti-Nazi correspondence,[26] or on the celebrated exiled writers Rudolf Olden and Ernst Toller.[27] He made repeated reports on the activities of the Socialist politician Gerhart Seger who, having escaped from Oranienburg concentration camp, was currently taking refuge in Britain while gathering support for the release of his wife and child who were still detained in Germany.[28] Others on whom Wesemann reported included Hans Preiss who ran an anti-fascist bookshop near the British Museum that served as a meeting place for the political exiles[29] and the very active Prince Hubertus zu Löwenstein who, during the three months he had been in London, had been engaged in various types of anti-Nazi propaganda.[30]

Wesemann also reported on the comings and goings of non-resident German exiles who were visiting Britain for political purposes. The legendary Otto Katz, emissary of the Communist impresario Willi Münzenberg, for one, often came to Britain bringing with him anti-Nazi materials for the benefit of British sympathisers and the British press.[31] The leading Social Democratic politician Max Braun had arrived in Britain to give a lecture,[32] so Wesemann informed the German Embassy, while the journalist Victor Schiff was involved in discussions with the British Labour Party.[33]

In addition, Wesemann reported on the activities of some of the refugees' most influential British sympathisers, such as George Bell, Bishop of Chichester, who was said to be intending to approach German church leaders,[34] or members of the House of Lords like the Liberal Lord Lothian who was reportedly attempting to intervene with the German government for the release of the SPD politician Ernst Heilmann from a concentration camp.[35] The Jewish Lord Reading, the trade unionist Walter Citrine and the Religious Society of Friends who were involved in relief work with the German refugee community all featured in Wesemann's regular reports to the German Embassy.

One of the strategies that Wesemann used repeatedly in order to obtain information was to offer to assist fellow exiles in placing material for publication. Lehmann-Russbueldt, for one, would later complain of how Wesemann had passed on an article of his to an English newspaper whilst retaining the fee for himself.[36] Using an assumed name, Wesemann wrote to the celebrated statistician and pacifist E.J. Gumbel, in exile in Lyons, to ask after the progress of his work and to offer to assist him in finding a British publisher.[37] Another intelligence-gathering strategy was to attempt to arrange meetings with persons he targeted as 'useful'. In June 1934, for instance, he wrote to Kurt Caro, a well-known journalist in exile in Paris, to suggest that he should attend the forthcoming National Peace Congress with him in Birmingham – and that he should bring with him the eminent Georg Bernhard, editor of the best-known émigré newspaper, the *Pariser Tageblatt*.[38] Interestingly, a later Special Branch report describes how, at the Trades Union Congress in

Weymouth in September 1934, Wesemann was observed to be 'anxious to avoid some of the delegates' but 'equally anxious to make the acquaintance of others, principally those known to be refugees from Germany'.[39]

All the information gathered by Hans Wesemann was passed on by the German Embassy in London to the Gestapo in Berlin, where it was recompiled into reports entitled 'Information about émigré circles in London active against Germany'. If, when viewed dispassionately today, much of the information he provided seems fragmentary or indeed inaccurate, Wesemann himself appears to have had no doubts as to its significance,[40] and the German Embassy was evidently of the same opinion.[41] At the same time, however, the Embassy was becoming uneasy as to its role in the matter.[42] As a result, in August 1934, bearing a guarantee of safe conduct from the Embassy, Wesemann returned to Germany to engage in direct talks with a representative of the Gestapo.

From then on, Wesemann's activities became decidedly more dangerous. In the autumn of 1934, he visited the Saar to inform on the anti-Nazi separatists like Max Braun who were campaigning there prior to the 1935 referendum. Braun would later describe Wesemann's suspiciously predatory behaviour towards him as part of a possible abduction attempt.[43] In January 1935, Wesemann brought about the arrest of Werner Kohlberg, the German representative of the English firm Liberty's, by first encouraging him to make defamatory remarks about the National Socialists and then denouncing him to the Gestapo.[44] That same month he was directed to Copenhagen from where, on an unknown pretext, he lured an exiled German trade unionist, Carl Balleng, and his wife back to Germany where they were arrested. Since Wesemann's name was not immediately associated with the Ballengs' disappearance, he could be issued with his next assignment, which was to abduct the anti-Nazi journalist Berthold Jacob, living in exile in Strasbourg, whose exposures of covert German rearmament and other military matters were an intense irritation to the Nazis.

Wesemann, who was well acquainted with Jacob from pre-emigration days, had early on made contact with him in exile by offering to find a British publisher and British subscribers for his anti-Nazi news-sheet, the *Unabhängiger Zeitungsdienst* or *UZD*.[45] In the autumn of 1934, Wesemann had received the instruction to keep a close eye on Jacob's movements and there had been an episode in Saarbrücken in November 1934 which, like the Max Braun case, may well have been a preliminary abduction attempt, when Wesemann had led Jacob into a deserted area close to the German border.[46] In March 1935, following on from the Balleng abduction, Wesemann succeeded in luring Jacob from Strasbourg to Basle by promising him a new passport, talked him into getting into a car and had him driven over the German border where Jacob was arrested.[47]

Up to this point, British security had not paid a great deal of attention to Wesemann. It is true that in October 1934 MI5 had requisitioned copies of papers from Wesemann's Home Office file and had intercepted a letter between Wesemann and Otto Katz,[48] but that was about the extent of it. However, after the Jacob abduction, MI5's now keen interest in Wesemann was illustrated by the appearance in his MI5 file of lengthy Special Branch reports with titles like 'Re Berthold Jacob and Others' (27 March 1935) and 'Re Berthold Jacob' (4 April 1935). Then, on 5 April 1935, Dora Fabian and Mathilde Wurm were found dead in their London flat; since the deaths were widely thought to be linked with the Jacob abduction and therefore with Wesemann, these too received detailed comment in Wesemann's MI5 file.[49]

In the meantime, Hans Wesemann had been arrested in Ascona, Switzerland, in March 1935 for his role in the Jacob abduction; the case came to trial in Basle in May 1936. After a hearing lasting three days, Wesemann received a three-year prison sentence, being finally released in March 1938. Thereafter, with help from the Gestapo, he emigrated to South America.

It is evident from Wesemann's MI5 file that the British Security Service was concerned firstly at the prospect of Nazi espionage being directed against the German refugee population in Britain but secondly at Communist influences discernible within that population. The third aspect of the Wesemann affair to worry them was the possibility of the ideological contamination of the native British population by the Germans in their midst. As mentioned in chapter 4, while in Britain Hans Wesemann had had a great deal to do with five brothers by the name of Hitzemeyer who possessed dual Anglo-German nationality (though being 'essentially German in character and sentiment' as Special Branch noted ominously).[50] Of great concern here was the fact that the Hitzemeyers were engaged in trading in British military camps. MI5 summarised its suspicions on the subject as follows:

> It has not been definitely proved that the Hitzemeyers were carrying on espionage, but owing to their relations with certain soldiers in these camps, they were in an excellent position to do so, and it seems likely that they reported once a week to Wesemann, who handed on the information to the correct quarters.[51]

These elements, that is, Nazi espionage and Communist subversion within the refugee community and the possible infiltration of the native British population, continued to tax MI5 throughout the pre-war and wartime periods.

An inside job

MI5's frustration at Nazi espionage was certainly tempered by the fact that, early in 1936, it began to receive significant intelligence from inside the German Embassy. Its source was Wolfgang Gans zu Putlitz (code-named P.), a diplomat who had been posted to the London Embassy in June 1934, becoming the head of its Consular Department. Indeed, according to Dora Fabian, within a short time of Putlitz's arrival in London, a non-Nazi German diplomat in London – almost certainly Putlitz, she contended – had sent a message to the exile community that Wesemann was a Gestapo spy.[52] In addition, as he describes in his autobiography, Putlitz had cultivated a relationship with the Home Office official E.N. Cooper and, by feeding him confidential details of various cases, 'manage[d] to keep several dangerous Nazis and cleverly disguised spies at a safe distance from England'.[53] Through this connection he was also secretly able to help Jewish and other German exiles in Britain despite the fact that 'officially it was my duty to see that life was made as difficult as possible for these wretched refugees'.[54] Inevitably, given his anti-Nazi activities, by 1939 Putlitz was obliged to become a refugee himself.

Putlitz came from a long aristocratic lineage, his family estate in Brandenburg dating back to the twelfth century. As a diplomat, he was eventually obliged to join the Nazi Party, although he personally felt little but contempt for National Socialism.[55] The information he gave MI5 was passed through the German journalist Jona 'Klop' Ustinov (code-named 'Paul') who had worked for some years in London for the Berlin news agency, Wolffsches Telegrafen Bureau, and who had various contacts in German official and diplomatic circles. 'Klop' Ustinov, father of the actor Peter Ustinov, was a man of cosmopolitan background and liberal tastes, who had run into official trouble in 1935, when required to provide an 'Ariernachweis', proving that he had no Jewish ancestry. He refused – and was cast aside.[56] However, Ustinov had already chosen sides: earlier that year, he had become an MI5 agent, code-named 'U35'. One of his case officers, Dick White, later Director General of MI5, called him 'the best and most ingenious operator I had the honour to work with'.[57]

Putlitz records that he and Ustinov used to meet every fortnight:

> I would unburden myself of all the dirty schemes and secrets which I encountered as part of my normal daily routine at the Embassy. By this means I was able to lighten my conscience by the feeling that I was really helping to damage the Nazi cause for I knew [Ustinov] was in touch with Vansittart, who could use these facts to influence British policy.[58]

The Whitehall mandarin, Sir Robert Vansittart, was Permanent Under-Secretary at the Foreign Office, a post he held from 1931 to January 1938. He was a strong advocate of British rearmament, a conviction which put him at odds with the government he served, particularly after Chamberlain became Prime Minister. Vansittart was by then also operating an independent intelligence service (i.e. independent of MI6) focusing on Germany.[59]

The information Putlitz was able to disclose, according to an internal MI5 document, included the German intention to promote Otto Bene, the AO's group leader in London, to the post of German Consul General; the Foreign Office let it be known to the German authorities that they would not approve this.[60] As early as September 1936, Putlitz also foretold, *inter alia*, a war between Germany and Russia and indeed by February 1938 MI5 had sent the Foreign Office a summary of the views expressed by Putlitz, including his certainty that 'Britain was letting the trump cards fall out of her hands' by not adopting a firmer attitude towards Germany.[61] The details of German rearmament and German foreign policy passed on by Putlitz culminated in his disclosure of the plan to invade and occupy Czechoslovakia – some time before it happened. The MI5 officer Peter Wright later called it 'priceless intelligence, possibly the most important human-source intelligence Britain received in the pre-war period'.[62] While Vansittart undoubtedly passed this information to the government, it seems to have had little impact on government policy. At the beginning of 1938, Vansittart was appointed 'Chief Diplomatic Adviser' to the government, effectively consigning him to a policy backwater from which his advice could be more easily ignored. Vansittart's name and reputation were also well known in German émigré circles, although by 1939 his reputation probably far exceeded his influence on government policy. However, all that was to change with the approach of war.

Notes

1 Untitled memorandum, 23 November 1933, The National Archives [TNA], KV4/140.
2 Christopher Andrew, *The Defence of the Realm: The Authorised History of MI5*, London: Allen Lane 2009, pp. 190–210.
3 John Court Curry, *The Security Service 1908–1945: The Official History*, London: Public Record Office 1999, p. 142.
4 Andrew, *Defence of the Realm*, p. 191.
5 See circular letter from Vernon Kell to all Chief Constables, May 1934, TNA, KV3/58.
6 See 'The Fascist Movement in the United Kingdom, excluding Northern Ireland', report no. 1, June 1934, TNA, KV3/58.
7 'The Fascist Movement', report no. 5, 'Developments to the End of February 1935', TNA, KV3/59.
8 'The Fascist Movement', report no. 6, 'Developments from March 1935 to October 1935', TNA, KV3/59.
9 'The Fascist Movement', report no. 8, 'Developments from February 1936 to July 1936', TNA, KV3/59.
10 Andrew, *Defence of the Realm*, p. 192.

11 'Foreign Organisation of the NSDAP', 4 April 1935, TNA, FO371/18868.
12 Curry, *The Security Service 1908–1945*, p. 109.
13 'Memorandum on the Question of the Possibility of Proceeding against the Nazi and Fascist Organisations Established in the United Kingdom', 9 June 1936, TNA, FO371/19942.
14 See, for example, Circular Letter no. 12 from 'Landesgruppenleiter' Bene, 9 October 1934, TNA, FO371/ 17731.
15 See 'Nazi Matters: Specimen Circular London Group', 26 October 1934, TNA, FO371/17731.
16 Andrew, *Defence of the Realm*, p. 197.
17 *Ibid.*
18 'Note on the National Sozialistische Deutsche Arbeiter Partei in the United Kingdom', preliminary draft, n.d. [May 1935], TNA, KV5/108/1.
19 See, for example, John P. Fox, 'Nazi Germany and German Emigration to Great Britain', in Gerhard Hirschfeld, ed., *Exile in Great Britain: Refugees from Hitler's Germany*, Leamington Spa: Berg 1984, pp. 53–4. See also MI5 file on Thost, TNA, KV2/953.
20 Untitled minute (Wigram), 23 October 1936, TNA, KV5/109/16a.
21 'Extract from Cabinet Conclusions' 55 (36), 29 July 1936, TNA, FO371/19942.
22 Curry, *The Security Service 1908–1945*, p. 113.
23 *Ibid.*
24 On this, see also Charmian Brinson, 'The Gestapo and the German Political Exiles in Britain during the 1930's: The Case of Hans Wesemann – and Others', *German Life and Letters*, 51, 1 (January 1998), 43–64.
25 'Aufzeichnumg'. 28 April 1934, Politisches Archiv des Auswärtigen Amtes Berlin [AA], Inland II A/B, R99578.
26 *Ibid.*
27 See, for example, Geheimes Staatspolizeiamt report, 5 September 1934, Geheimes Staatsarchiv Preußischer Kulturbesitz, Berlin, I. HA Rep. 90 P No. 58, vol.1, pp. 54–5.
28 'Aufzeichnung', 28 April 1934, AA, Inland II A/B, R99578.
29 Geheimes Staatspolizeiamt report, as in note 27 above, p. 55.
30 *Ibid.*, p. 56.
31 *Ibid.*, pp. 55–6.
32 Untitled report appended to German Embassy London to Foreign Office Berlin, 28 May 1934, AA, Inland II A/B, R99578.
33 *Ibid.*
34 In one of three documents marked 'G.A. 5', 15 May 1934, AA, Inland II A/B, R99578.
35 Untitled report. as in note 32, above.
36 Otto Lehmann-Russbueldt to Kriminalpolizei Basel, 24 March 1935, Staatsarchiv des Kantons Basel-Stadt, Gerichtsarchiv KK2, 1936, vol. 15–16, l.c., [StAB], 137.
37 Wesemann wrote to Gumbel three times, on 15 March, 3 April and 30 April 1934, StAB, 276/16, 17 and 18.

38 Hans Wesemann to Kurt Caro, 2 June 1934, StAB, 253ZZ.
39 'Re Berthold Jacob', 4 April 1935, TNA, KV2/2834/44.
40 See transcript of Wesemann's interrogation of 11 July 1935, StAB, 687.
41 See, for example, German Embassy London to Foreign Office Berlin, 3 May 1934, AA, Inland II A/B, R99578.
42 *Ibid.*
43 See Max Braun, 'Wesemanns dunkles Treiben an der Saar: schon damals Entführungsversuch an Berthold Jacob geplant', *Pariser Tageblatt*, 28 March 1935, p. 1.
44 See, for example, Special Branch report 'Werner Kohlberg', 1 June 1938, Home Office, Aliens Department, K484.
45 See Jacob's statement, 19 September 1935, StAB, 714.
46 See Braun, 'Wesemanns dunkles Treiben an der Saar'.
47 A fuller account is given in J.N. Willi, *Der Fall Jacob-Wesemann (1935/36): Ein Beitrag zur Geschichte der Schweiz in der Zwischenkriegszeit*, Berne/Frankfurt a.M.: Lang 1972.
48 The letter is not held in Wesemann's MI5 file; however, its interception is recorded in the index to TNA, KV2/2834.
49 For example, in 'Re Dr Dora Fabian and Mrs M. Wurm', 5 April 1935, TNA, KV2/2834/48a.
50 'Re Berthold Jacob', 4 April 1935, TNA, KV2/2834/44.
51 'Summary of Information Concerning the Hitzmeyer [*sic*] Brothers', 7 May 1935, TNA, KV2/2834/84a.
52 StAB, KK2, 1936, vol. 15–16, no. 80, l.c., 254f.
53 Wolfgang zu Putlitz, *The Putlitz Dossier*, London: Allan Wingate 1957, p. 97.
54 *Ibid.*
55 *Ibid.*, p. 114f.
56 See Peter Ustinov, *Dear Me*, London: Heinemann 1977.
57 Tom Bower, *A Perfect English Spy: Sir Dick White and the Secret War 1935–90*, London: Heinemann 1995, p. 29.
58 Putlitz, *Putlitz Dossier*, p. 96.
59 See Robert Vansittart, *The Mist Procession: The Autobiography of Lord Vansittart*, London: Hutchinson 1958.
60 'MI5 Note on the Aggressive Policy of Hitler and Ribbentrop and consequent instructions to the Abwehr', n.d. [1942–43?], TNA, KV4/170.
61 *Ibid.*
62 Peter Wright, *Spycatcher: The Candid Autobiography of a Senior Intelligence Officer*, New York: Viking 1987, p. 87.

6

No more peace: Otto Lehmann-Russbueldt and German rearmament

Among those forced to flee Germany during 1933 were a number of political activists who had been arrested by the Nazis following the Reichstag Fire, but subsequently set free. The veteran pacifist Otto Lehmann-Russbueldt was released from prison only ten days after being arrested, an event which may have owed something to confusion about his identity, a quite plausible explanation in the chaotic circumstances of the time. Within three weeks he had escaped from Germany, crossing the German–Dutch frontier in bizarre and hazardous circumstances. On 30 March 1933, disguised as one of a group of psychiatric patients out on a walk, he was taken across the border by two Catholic priests belonging to the Peace Alliance of German Catholics (Friedensbund deutscher Katholiken). His daughter later recalled: 'My father later told me laughingly that he had walked over wagging his head and burbling to himself.'[1] It was in fact no laughing matter, a grotesque and dangerous prelude to the restless life of the political exile. After some six months in Holland, he moved on to Britain 'in order to continue my educational work on the nature of Prussian militarism' ('um meine Aufklärungsarbeit über den preussichen Militarismus fortzusetzen').

When he landed in Britain on 5 November 1933, Lehmann-Russbueldt was sixty years old, a lifelong pacifist and campaigner against the arms trade. He was by then officially stateless: in August 1933, his name had appeared on the first Nazi expatriation list, depriving their political opponents of their German nationality. He was travelling on a (provisional) Czech passport, acquired through the good offices of the Czech President, Tomas Masaryk, whom he had known for many years. He already had contacts with prominent figures in British public life, such as Lord Noel-Buxton, Lord (Robert) Cecil, the President of the League of Nations Union, and above all the well-known journalist Wickham Steed, a former editor of *The Times*, whom he had first met in Geneva in 1926 on the eve of Germany's admission to the League of Nations.

Lehmann-Russbueldt named as the object of his visit: 'To discuss questions of disarmament with Lord Cecil and others'– a response which the security services considered more compromising than any avowal of National Socialism. His MI5 file was opened within days.[2] In fact, he had come to Britain with the aim of alerting the British to the realities of the new regime in Germany and the renewed danger to peace posed by resurgent German militarism: 'I had made a resolution to fight, now more than ever, for the liberation of Germany from its eternal grave-diggers and particularly for the release of friends languishing in concentration camps.'[3] This resolve had an important corollary: like other political exiles, he wished to challenge the view that the German people overwhelmingly supported the Nazis, insisting on the existence of 'the other Germany' which represented more peaceful and progressive values.

His activities prompted renewed interest by MI5 in March 1934 when he was named as the source of documents made public by Wickham Steed. The documents described alleged German plans for poison gas attacks on the London Underground and the Paris Metro, which it was assumed would serve as air raid shelters in any coming war. Steed, who was well connected politically, passed the documents to the Foreign Office, which after some consideration saw fit to dismiss them as forgeries. Despite this verdict, Steed was convinced of their authenticity and proceeded to publish extracts from them in his journal *The Nineteenth Century and After*.[4] His article was widely reported in the national press, playing on British and French fears of vulnerability to the threat of biological weapons.

Initially, the British authorities, including MI5, were inclined to consider Lehmann-Russbueldt as a nuisance rather than a security threat. In a memorandum addressed to MI5's counter-espionage expert Captain Hugh Miller in May 1934, SIS's Major Valentine Vivian noted:

> The above-named person [Lehmann-Russbueldt] has come under notice as the purveyor of sensational information regarding Germany's aerial and gas warfare preparations via Wickham Steed. The information is supposed to come from Germany, but we suspect that he is in touch with German refugees in Paris.[5]

In fact, Lehmann-Russbueldt had been only an intermediary, having received the documents from Helmuth Simons, a bacteriologist and fellow-refugee living at the same address in Regent Square. The documents had originally been acquired in Germany by Dr Karl Meister, who had arranged a meeting at The Hague with Simons, a former business partner with whom he had remained in correspondence. Simons had travelled to Holland solely to receive the documents.

The documents concerned scientific experiments allegedly conducted by the Junkers concern in Dessau. While the Chemical Defence Research Department considered the scientific information to be bogus, MI5 attempted to investigate the authenticity of the documents by interviewing Dr Meister – who 'did not create a favourable impression'. He had refused to come into MI5's office, and agreed to talk at a London hotel, at a meeting arranged under the pseudonym Dr Herrmann. Meister claimed to have acquired the documents from a source whose name he consistently refused to divulge and who was referred to throughout the interview as 'X'. He also told MI5 that he had crossed the German border into Holland 'by foot and by tram' in an elaborate attempt to evade border controls. MI5 was sceptical of his story, commenting that these precautions 'strike one as being entirely unnecessary and bordering on the third-rate spy novel'. In conclusion, MI5 asserted confidently 'that it is merely a waste of time to continue this case from the point of view of chemical warfare, but on the other hand the activities in UK of Dr Simons and Dr Lehmann-Russbueldt will have to be further investigated'.[6] Captain Miller died shortly after as the result of an accident,[7] but not before requesting a postal intercept on Lehmann-Russbueldt.[8] By this time, MI5 had already opened a surveillance file on Wickham Steed, intercepting both his post and telephone calls.[9]

Steed, who had been *The Times* correspondent in Vienna for a decade before the First World War, was an expert on the German-speaking world. By the early 1930s, he had become alarmed at the potential threat to peace represented by Adolf Hitler. As a consequence, he had embraced German refugees and their causes. However, his relations with individual refugees were marked by a curious mixture of calculation and altruism. On the one hand, he hoped to acquire information that he could pass on to his intelligence contacts; on the other hand, he was capable of genuine friendship and acts of great kindness that lacked any hint of self-interest. He took an active interest in Lehmann-Russbueldt's work in Britain, supporting him financially and, after the death of his wife Lucia, in 1937, even provided a home for his young daughter Yvonne, also paying for her schooling. Lehmann-Russbueldt always retained the greatest respect for Steed, whom he called 'my protector and teacher in the ways of this contradictory people'.[10] Their friendship certainly outlived Lehmann-Russbueldt's ability to supply useful information.

MI5's early interest in Lehmann-Russbueldt resurfaced as a result of his research for the book *Germany's Air Force*, an exposé of secret German aerial rearmament in contravention of the Treaty of Versailles.[11] Preliminary details of Germany's secret aircraft programme, based on material supplied by Lehmann-Russbueldt and his fellow-campaigner Dora Fabian, had already appeared in the *Sunday Referee* in February 1934. The claims had also been raised in Parliament by the Labour member, F. Seymour Cocks, and emerged again that autumn in Dorothy Woodman's book *Hitler Rearms*, but the British government was inclined to dismiss the revelations as exaggerated. Against this background, Lehmann-Russbueldt intended his book to be a warning of the resurgence of German militarism and its threat to European peace. He also hoped the advance on the book would help to alleviate his own serious financial difficulties.

By the end of 1934, the manuscript was well advanced, but Lehmann-Russbueldt was anxious to delay publication, fearing for the safety of his wife and eight-year-old daughter who were then still living in Berlin. He was finally able to bring them to England, where they arrived on 1 July 1935 – the very day on which the book was published.[12]

Knowing the controversial nature of the book, Lehmann-Russbueldt was also concerned at the growing threat from the Nazi espionage network operating in Britain. In May 1935, his collaborator Helmuth Simons alleged that a Nazi agent, posing as an officer from Scotland Yard, had attempted to gain access to the flat to remove certain papers. As Lehmann-Russbueldt later wrote in the foreword to *Germany's Air Force*:

> The mere announcement of this book brought further Nazi police action against me. On April 21, 1935, a German spy pretending to be an official from the political department of Scotland Yard tried to gain entrance into my room to 'confiscate' certain papers. I was away, but a friend prevented the spy carrying out his intention. (pp. 25–6)

As he acknowledged in his foreword, the book was based on secret documents obtained by the journalist Dora Fabian, whose mysterious death was suspected by many refugees to be the work of Nazi agents. Refugee circles in London were indeed increasingly alarmed at the idea of Gestapo spies operating from the German Embassy. The unsolved mystery surrounding the deaths of Fabian and Mathilde Wurm gave rise to a flurry of rumour and speculation. The British security services took a more sanguine view. Two Special Branch officers who interviewed Simons considered his story to be a fabrication, commenting that he and Lehmann-Russbueldt 'both have a "persecution complex", see spies everywhere, and are constantly warning refugees to be on their guard', adding significantly: 'As far as is known they have not taken part in political propaganda inimical to the interests of this country.'[13]

At the time of his arrival in London, Lehmann-Russbueldt was already sixty years of age: an elderly man, in poor health, and apparently ill-suited to the rigours of life in exile. He cut a somewhat forlorn figure: an MI5 agent instructed to observe him in 1936 gave the following graphic if unflattering description: 'age 63, height 5'9", dark hair turning grey, small beard and moustache, number of warts on face, wears horn-rimmed spectacles, shabby appearance'.[14]

Shabby he may well have been. During these early years of exile, he lived a hand-to-mouth existence, his work hampered by constant financial problems. In his own words: 'I was in the middle of a flood of work, completely impoverished and living in the attics and basements of the refugee.'[15] Even the publication of *Germany's Air Force* had done nothing to alleviate this poverty, as the book's publishing history confirms. The German writer Karl Otten, who knew Lehmann-Russbueldt well, claimed that 'this book was virtually though not formally suppressed by the publishers at the request of the British government and probably only a bare hundred copies were circulated'.[16] Such a claim, while difficult to verify, seems highly likely. Certainly, sales of the book did nothing to improve the financial situation of its author.

Like many exiles, Lehmann-Russbueldt earned too much to starve but too little to live on. In Germany, he had relied heavily on his income from journalism. However, he had little success in placing his work with British journals, though one article of his did appear in *The Contemporary Review*, whose editor, the writer and historian G.P. Gooch, was well-disposed towards the refugees.[17] Most of his articles were published in German exile journals. Many of these were under-subscribed and short-lived; most of them could afford to pay contributors only a nominal fee, while some paid nothing at all. According to his own statement to the Home Office, Lehmann-Russbueldt had, 'from other sources', just enough to live but not enough to pay for secretarial services and research necessary to pursue his work. He was in fact forced to rely on a small grant from the Czech authorities and on the generosity of Wickham Steed, who paid him a modest monthly allowance.

However, his work, particularly on the international arms trade, had made his name widely known in peace circles. Towards the end of 1934, the National Peace Council, an influential body which coordinated the work of many smaller pacifist groups, had issued an appeal in support of his work. The Council agreed to raise the sum of £100 on his behalf. In the first six months, they had managed to raise only £45, though 'they [now] understood that another £20 would be sufficient'.[18]

Lehmann-Russbueldt was also planning to write a study of the armaments industry, a sequel to his book *Die blutige Internationale*, in which he was again collaborating with Helmuth Simons. Special Branch noted that Lehmann-Russbueldt was doing the writing, 'while Simons is procuring the data from books at the British Museum and other places'. Lehmann-Russbueldt's work in London was greatly handicapped by his limited command of English. Although he finally managed to read English with some ease, his spoken English stretched to little more than basic communication. Simons therefore had a vital function to perform – that of interpreter. He had accompanied Lehmann-Russbueldt on visits to British arms manufacturers. In 1935, they had visited a certain Major L.

at Imperial Chemical Industries, whom they questioned about the manufacture of explosives and munitions. Lehmann-Russbueldt asked most of the questions, framing them in German and relying on Simons to translate them into English. Interestingly, they had approached Major L. as a fellow-pacifist, but their attempts to elicit information were extraordinarily clumsy. Some of their questions were so indiscreet, requiring the disclosure of classified information, that L. considered the two men 'either fools or knaves'. In fact, he was so alarmed by the visit that he felt bound to report it to Scotland Yard.[19]

Though Special Branch was inclined to play down this incident, considering it an example of political naivety rather than espionage, Lehmann-Russbueldt remained an object of suspicion for MI5, which, during 1936, placed him under direct observation by section S11. The reports of the officer who was shadowing him indicate the tedious – and often pointless – nature of such surveillance. On 23 July, for example, he reported:

> Russbueldt at 10.45 am after purchasing two papers from the shop of the Librairie Internationale, Guildford Street, entered the Readers Room, British Museum, where he remained until 2.10 when he went to a Lyons café [...] He afterwards visited Woburn House and Jewish Board of Guardians, 127 Middlesex. He returned to the British Museum at 5.30 but was not seen to leave. Observation continuing.[20]

Meanwhile, Helmut Simons had left Britain. A pacifist and Communist, he had hoped to secure a post as a bacteriologist in Moscow,[21] but his application had been turned down – perhaps inevitably, at a time when the Soviet Union was convulsed by political suspicion of all foreigners, even foreign Communists, and especially German émigrés who were suspected of espionage. Simons was eventually able to emigrate to the United States, but his MI5 file remained open long after he had left Britain. In fact, like conjoined twins, he and Lehmann-Russbueldt have endured a lifetime together in MI5's Central Registry: after seventy-five years, they are still inseparable in one joint file.

During the early weeks of his exile in London, Lehmann-Russbueldt had found a room at a house in Gloucester Place, an address he left at the beginning of 1934 when he became a subtenant of his fellow-refugee Fritz Gross at a house in 3 Regent Square in Bloomsbury, later moving across the square to number 29. His frequent changes of address did not escape MI5 – which recorded each move, each time changing his postal intercept. Following the death of his wife Lucia in summer 1937, he had moved house again, this time moving in with the journalist Bernhard Reichenbach. Their shared accommodation at 19 Oppidans Road, in

Hampstead, was rather more spacious than Lehmann-Russbueldt had so far enjoyed in London, consisting of three rooms, a bathroom and a kitchen. Their flat became the meeting place for a group of refugees gathering information on developments in Germany. The driving force behind this informal group was neither Lehmann-Russbueldt nor Reichenbach, but the writer Karl Otten, an enigmatic figure, who had come to the attention of MI5 even before he had first set foot in Britain.

Notes

1 'Mein Vater erzählte mir später lachend, dass er immer mit dem Kopf gewackelt and vor sich hingelallt hat.' Quoted in Charmian Brinson and N.A. Furness, '"Im politischen Niemandsland der Heimatlosen, Staatenlosen, Konfessionslosen, Portemonnaielosen": Otto Lehmann-Russbueldt in British exile', in Ian Wallace, ed., *German-Speaking Exiles in Great Britain: Yearbook of the Research Centre for German and Austrian Exile Studies*, vol. 1, 1999, pp. 117–45.

2 The record of Lehmann-Russbueldt's arrival at Harwich, under the name Otto Lehmann, is the first item in his security file The National Archives [TNA], KV2/2001–6. The National Peace Council later appealed for support for his work.

3 Otto Lehmann-Russbueldt [O.L-R], 'Lebenserinnerungen', unpublished typescript, dated London 1940, held by his daughter, Yvonne Wells, p. 119.

4 See 'Aerial Warfare. Secret German Plans', *The Nineteenth Century and After*, July 1934; see also *Daily Herald*, 28 June 1934. Copies of both articles are in Lehmann-Russbueldt's security file.

5 SIS (Valentine Vivian) to MI5 (Capt. Miller), 6 April 1934, headed 'Otto Lehmann-Russbueldt, 3 Regent Square, WC 1', TNA, KV2/2001/1a.

6 MI5 to MI 3B, 1 May 1934, TNA, KV2/2001. The memorandum was copied to the Foreign Office.

7 See obituary, Captain H.M. Miller, *The Times*, 15 May 1934.

8 Request for postal intercept for Otto Lehmann-Russbueldt, 3 Regent Square, 2 June 1934, TNA, KV2/2001/21a.

9 The extent, let alone the purpose, of this surveillance is difficult to assess, since, Steed's file (PF 335690A) is one of many which have not been released and may even have been destroyed.

10 O.L-R, 'Mein Leben' (a hand-written continuation of 'Lebenserinnerungen', unpublished manuscript, Archiv der Sozialen Demokratie der Friedrich-Ebert-Stiftung, Bonn, p. 133.

11 See Otto Lehmann-Russbueldt, *Germany's Air Force: With an Introduction by Wickham Steed and an Appendix*, London: Allen and Unwin, 1935.

12 See Brinson and Furness, 'Im politischen Niemandsland der Heimatlosen, Staatenlosen, Konfessionslosen, Portemonnaielosen', p. 121.

13 See report Metropolitan Police Special Branch to MI5, dated 24 December 1935, TNA, KV2/2001.

14 Report dated 28 July 1936, TNA, KV2/2002/145a.
15 O.L-R, 'Lebenserinnerungen', p. 121.
16 See MI5 internal report, B.5b (M/S), 4 March 1938, TNA, KV2/1120/ 49a.
17 O.L-R, 'The Military and Political Strength of the Smaller Nations', *Contemporary Review*, CLI, February 1937.
18 Note, 6 April 1935, re. Home Office file forwarded to MI5, TNA, KV2/2001/45a.
19 Metropolitan Police Special Branch, 24 December 1935, TNA, KV2/2001/ 56a.
20 Report 28 July 1936, TNA, KV2/2002/145a.
21 MI5 to SIS, 10 March 1936, TNA, KV2/2002/88a.

7

Flying and spying: Claud W. Sykes, MI5 and the 'Primrose League'

In August 1938, at the height of the political crisis over Hitler's claim to the Sudeten border lands of Czechoslovakia, the British writer and translator Claud Walter Sykes, holidaying in Cassis-sur-mer, in the South of France, wrote a two-page letter to the German writer Karl Otten, living as a refugee in London. Beginning 'my dear Otten', Sykes's letter struck a friendly, even familiar note. It dealt briefly with two literary projects on which they were collaborating, Otten as writer, Sykes as translator, but made no reference to the grave political situation.[1]

The letter was intercepted by the GPO Investigation Branch and, like all such postal intercepts, was passed to MI5, which added it to the growing personal file it held on Karl Otten. Sykes's letter to Otten ended: 'Back home on the 8th. Meanwhile greetings to your wife and Lehmann.' He signed himself 'Yours ever, C.W.S'. On that same day, Thursday 8 September, MI5's section B5b wrote an internal memorandum headed 'Carl Otten Group':

> I have just heard from M/S who is returning from France on Thursday [...] that he has had a communication from Carl Otten [*sic*] referring to the matter of Groehl's difficulties with the passport authorities in Paris. It seems quite clear that there is no suspicion of M/S and Otten has merely warned M/S that the Home Office may make inquiries into his [i.e M/S's] bona fides.[2]

The Home Office did indeed make such inquiries. Their letter, also preserved in Otten's file, was addressed to Mr Claud W. Sykes, thus confirming that Sykes and the agent code-named M/S were one and the same person.

The reader may well ask at this point: who *was* Claud W. Sykes? Unfortunately, there is no simple or even single answer to this question. In replying to the Home Office, Sykes described himself as a British citizen, a journalist and translator, living in Letchworth. He was, however, much more than that: a man of many parts, each nestling within the next, like a *matryoshka* doll. Born in Ipswich in 1883, his father a former army officer, Sykes had initially pursued an acting career, doubtless a useful preparation for the different roles he was to play in later life.

During the 1930s, Sykes established himself as an author and translator, creating a distinct niche as a translator of books about First World War aviation, with English versions of various memoirs by German airmen, including such titles as *Zeppelin Adventures* (1932), *Wings of War* (1933), *Flying Section 17* (1934), *War Flying in Macedonia* (1935) and *An Airman Remembers* (1936), all of which appeared with the publisher John Hamilton.[3] Sykes was also the author of several books on the same theme, such as *German War Birds* (1931), which told 'the dramatic tales of air combat as fought by the top German flying aces of WWI' and *Richthofen: The Red Knight of the Air* (1932), recounting the career of the legendary German flying ace. These too were published by John Hamilton.

As Britain's leading publisher of aviation literature in the inter-war years, John Hamilton was tapping into a lucrative market. By the early 1930s, flying was being romanticised as the only form of individual combat in which the tradition of martial chivalry had survived amongst the mechanised carnage of modern warfare. Sykes's publications during this period show an interesting distinction between works he translated and those he actually wrote. Whereas the former all credited Claud W. Sykes as translator, all his authored works, whether factual or fictional, appeared under the pseudonym 'Vigilant'.

Sykes had first resorted to the disguise of a pen-name for the publication in 1930 of the book *Secrets of Modern Spying*, a title which announced his own fascination with espionage.[4] The book essayed a strong defence of the spy's profession:

> The word 'spy' has an unpleasant sound in many ears; to his profession is attached a stigma that often causes him to be despised by the masters he serves. [...] This is a wrong attitude of mind. The spy who goes alone into the enemy camp, where the mispronunciation of a word or ignorance of some trivial custom may betray him, deserves as well of his country as the soldier who serves in the field. (p. 9)

Many of the episodes described were already in the public domain, others seem to be written with inside knowledge, but whether the book is the work of a professional spy or a well-connected journalist is difficult to say.

Sykes gave further proof of his penchant for espionage in the three 'Lynx' novels, recounting the adventures of the fictional British air ace 'Lynx', which effectively married his interest in aviation with his fascination for spying. The three volumes, *Lynx V.C.* (1936), *Lynx Spyflyer* (1936) and *Lynx Counterspy* (1937), all appeared under his pseudonym 'Vigilant'. There is no evidence that Sykes ever took to the air, except in fiction, but throughout the 1930s flying and spying were inextricably linked in his imagination.

Files recently released by the Security Service confirm that by the mid-1930s at the latest Claud W. Sykes was an MI5 agent, charged with infiltrating German refugee circles in London, a task of growing importance for MI5. His work as a translator gave him a very plausible pretext for contacting German refugee authors in Britain. Many of his reports from this time have survived in the intelligence files, including reports on the activities of an informal group of refugees, known to MI5 as 'The Carl Otten Group' [*sic*], acknowledging the dominant role within it of Karl Otten.

A man in his mid-forties, balding and bespectacled, Karl Otten might have seemed a typical intellectual, but, like his antagonist Sykes, he was much more than he seemed, emerging from his MI5 file as a volatile and ambiguous figure with a taste for backstairs politics. He belonged to a literary generation which freely mixed poetry and political action. On the eve of the First World War, for example, he had been arrested in Strasbourg for distributing anti-war leaflets and held for fifteen months without charge. As a writer, he had twice achieved fame, which had twice proved transitory. He had first become famous as an Expressionist poet – so famous that in 1917 the key literary journal *Die Aktion* (*Action*) had devoted an entire issue to him. He was also known to the Prussian Secret Police, which in 1918 had impounded copies of his volume of anti-war poetry *Die Thronerhebung des Herzens* (*The Heart's Elevation to the Throne*). Otten's literary reputation had faded during the 1920s, but in the twilight of the Weimar Republic he had once more become famous as the author and scriptwriter of the film *Kameradschaft* (Comradeship), directed by G.W. Pabst, which in 1932 had become one of the first great international cinema successes. When the Nazis gained power, Otten's new fame had turned to notoriety. Anticipating arrest, he had fled to France, settling with his later wife Ellen Kroner in the artists' colony of Cala Ratjada on the island of Mallorca. On the outbreak of the Spanish civil war, the couple had fled once more, finally reaching Britain in September 1936.[5] By that time, Otten's name had already entered MI5's card index; his 'personal file' was to grow steadily over the next twenty years.[6]

A fervent anti-Nazi, Otten had wasted no time in London, gathering a group of like-minded refugees who received and distributed information about political and military developments in Germany. The group met in the flat shared by Otto Lehmann-Russbueldt and the journalist Bernhard Reichenbach at 19 Oppidans Road, Hampstead. Apart from Otten and the two occupants of 19 Oppidans Road, the group also included the aviation expert and former war pilot Hans J. Wolffsohn. Known to MI5 as the Carl Otten Group, it was known to its own members as 'The Primrose League', a name they adopted (much to their own amusement) because of the flat's proximity to Primrose Hill. MI5, less amused by the group's sobriquet, kept security files on all its members, though only those on Otten and Lehmann-Russbueldt have ever been released.[7]

Claud W. Sykes's earliest surviving intelligence report, dated 23 June 1937, describes a chance encounter with Otten, whom he met at the lending library run by the Austrian writer Fritz Gross, a former Communist who had been expelled from the KPD for 'Trotskyist tendencies' in 1932. (His former wife Babette had become the long-term companion of the Communist publisher Willi Münzenberg.) As a refugee in London, Gross had opened a German lending library in the basement of his Bloomsbury flat, which became a favoured meeting place for refugees: a salon of the dispossessed, where authors could meet and readers could browse.[8] It was also an obvious focal point for any spy intent on infiltrating refugee circles.

Sykes had clearly visited Gross before. His report, under the code name M/S, begins:

> I arrived to find Gross in conversation with a man who turned out to be Karl Otten, the writer of the scenario and words of the famous film *Kameradschaft*. 'Now you will hear something interesting,' Gross said to me, [adding to Otten] Herr – is trustworthy.[9]

M/S's report goes on to describe Otten as 'evidently a Trotskyist', adding: 'The general tone of the conversation showed both Otten and Gross to be so bitter against Stalinism that their former hatred of Hitler becomes a very minor consideration.'

M/S revisited Gross three weeks later – and again found Otten there, reporting back: 'I hope to be able to keep in touch with Otten, as I have promised to read a play he has written.'[10] Sykes did indeed keep in touch with Otten, whom he met again in the course of a further visit to Gross on 7 October. He reported: 'both Gross and Otten said they thought that the time for purely sectarian activity was at an end and that they would have to consider combining with any persons of an anti-Fascist nature [...] "whether communists or countesses"'.[11]

Thanks to M/S (alias Sykes), Otten's file was growing rapidly. On the afternoon of 20 October 1937, Sykes visited Otten at his home in Golders Green to discuss the translation of a play.[12] Though not named in this, or any subsequent report, the play in question was *Kein Held*, a five-act drama which Otten wrote in 1937–38, based on newspaper reports of a man who loses his memory and cannot even remember his identity, which Otten described as 'the struggle of the individual against the totalitarian system'.[13] Sykes, however, was less concerned with the dramatic than the political plot, reporting to his handler that Otten had 'already approached Paul Robeson via Dr. Harold Moody [...] to ask ROBESON if he will take the lead in this play'.[14] Robeson, the world-famous actor, concert-singer and political activist, had been monitored by MI5 for some years; Otten reminded Sykes that Robeson had recently offered his services free to the left-wing Unity Theatre.[15]

By now, Sykes had caught the interest of his handlers, one of whom wrote urging him to translate the play.[16] It was a request Sykes could hardly refuse. During 1938, he did indeed produce an English version, under the title *No Hero*, a typescript copy of which survives in Otten's *Nachlass*.[17] Though Robeson did not commit himself to appearing in *No Hero*, Otten continued to hold high hopes for the play, writing a long letter to Sykes regarding its future prospects:

> I wrote to the manager of Mr. Miller [i.e. Gilbert Miller] today to see what he thinks about the question of an American performance. With your translation I go to see Mr. Pommer for Charles Laughton, who knows all about the play – that time for the film rights.[18]

No more was heard of Charles Laughton, or Erich Pommer, or of film rights – and little more was heard of *No Hero*. A year later, Otten would describe it as 'a play waiting for a theatre'.[19] It is still waiting; while offered to more than one theatre, it was never performed or published.

Otten's relationship with Sykes had by then developed into one of trust and even friendship. Addressing Sykes as 'dear friend', Otten looked forward to extending their collaboration: 'So I beg you to propose me for this and the next play your conditions – a contract I think must be the right expression – or whatever you think suitable. Send it over as soon as possible.'[20] Sykes's response to the question of a contract is not on record.

The 'next play' mentioned by Otten was a radio play entitled *Mary Broad: The Girl from Botany Bay*, which was based on historical events: the dramatic escape of a group of convicts from an Australian penal settlement. The play itself has not survived but some idea of its style and content are contained in an internal reader's report for the BBC from which one can infer that Sykes had both translated the play and adapted it for broadcasting. Unfortunately, the finished script failed to bring the characters to life.

> Karl Otten and Claud W. Sykes have founded this play on an account by James Martin who escaped from Port Jackson, Australia in the eighteenth century and sailed with twelve others (including one woman) in an open boat to the island of Timor. It is a good subject, but there are really not enough details in the original narrative to give the characters life. [...] The play lacks guts.[21]

In the light of these comments, the BBC rejected the play.

In normal circumstances, Sykes the translator would merit barely a footnote in an overview of German exile literature. Translation, however, was clearly only a means to an end: this ostensibly 'literary' collaboration must be seen through the prism of political intelligence.

Having won Otten's trust, Sykes was soon able to delve deeper. At a meeting in March 1938, Otten had shown him a copy of Lehmann-Russbueldt's *Germany's Air Force* and pressed him to meet the author to discuss a new, and potentially explosive, book proposal:

> Lehmann-Russbueldt now wants to write another book on the same subject because he has recently got hold of a certain ROZINSKI, an ex-airman employed in the German Ministry of Defence until a few months ago when he escaped from Germany and got through to London, where he now lives.

Otten was reportedly anxious for M/S to meet both men in order to discuss publishing contacts. Sykes's MI5 handler Maxwell Knight sought urgent guidance in this highly sensitive matter:

> M/S has agreed provisionally to meet these two men on Friday next, 11th March. I should like to write to M/S early next week giving him some instructions as to how to proceed and therefore I should be grateful for any advice on the best line to take. Personally I am in favour of M/S meeting these two men so that he can give us his opinion as to the amount of confidential information [they have].[22]

On the evening of 11 March, M/S called on Otten, 'as per instructions', and was introduced to Lehmann-Russbueldt and his co-author Hans J. Wolffsohn. He reported:

> We then got down to business and Lehmann-Russbueldt and Wolffsohn presented me with a synopsis of the book they intend to write. I attach translation of this. [...] The book is not yet written, but the material is assembled and could be delivered in typescript in less than two months if he was interested. The political part is Lehmann-Russbueldt's work while the technical matter emanates from Wolffsohn.[23]

M/S inquired how Wolffsohn had managed to acquire the technical details and learned that he had devoted his life to aviation technology and had maintained contact with former colleagues. His report continues: 'Seeing from the synopsis that some of the material might be of interest, I began to think of ways and means to get the matter either in finished or unfinished form into your hands for a short period.'

Sykes therefore told them he had contacts with several publishers who might be interested, though stressing (quite plausibly) that no publisher would offer a contract, let alone an advance, until they had received a reader's report. He added that some publishers, such as his own, John Hamilton, might be reluctant to take a book which could risk spoiling their business with Germany. As a compromise, he suggested that publishers who knew him might be willing to accept the book 'if I could show them translations of important chapters [...] or if the authors could let me have their material for a few days so that I could write a report on it. They hailed this suggestion with joy'.

However, before Sykes could follow up his suggestion, the meeting was interrupted when Otten was called to the phone. When he returned to the room, he looked very agitated – he had just been told that German troops had crossed the border into Austria. Both Lehmann-Russbueldt and Wolffsohn were visibly shaken by the news and the meeting broke up shortly after. A few days later, the Ottens moved in with Lehmann-Russbueldt at 19 Oppidans Road, a move Sykes duly reported, enabling the GPO to re-direct the postal 'check' accordingly.

Having successfully penetrated the 'Primrose League', Sykes was instructed to find out their channels of information. He reported:

> On Friday June 3rd, I called upon Otten and found him alone. When alone, he becomes spontaneously confidential, but when his wife or Lehmann-Rußbueldt are present he is more reserved. I therefore learned some particulars which may be interesting. [...] Otten and his companions – a group of six in London – are directly working for Czechoslovakia now and are the London terminus of an intelligence service which has agents working in Germany. The letter-box is Groehl in Paris.[24]

The group's main source of information on developments inside Germany was indeed the journalist Karl Groehl (alias Karl Retzlaw) whom Otten had known since the Saar plebiscite campaign in 1935. Groehl was a former Communist who had been Head of Willi Münzenberg's propagandist publishing organisation until 1933. Since then, he had lived in Paris, but ran an extensive network of contacts inside Germany.

Sykes also learnt that the information supplied by Groehl, ostensibly acquired for the purposes of a book, was in fact being passed to the Czechoslovak legation, making use of Lehmann-Russbueldt's contacts there. Groehl, whom Sykes archly refers to as 'Mr Smith', frequently transmitted military information, some originating with the journalist Berthold Jacob in Strasbourg, but much of it smuggled out of Germany by agents whom Groehl met in France or Switzerland. However, since Groehl sent his intelligence reports to Otten by post, his letters were routinely intercepted by MI5.[25] In fact, in a particularly ironic twist, Sykes (at the request of Otten and his friends) had actually become Mr Smith's 'letter box', so that the letters went directly to him.

On 29 April 1938, Otten sent Sykes a letter concerning 'the visit of a friend', whom he asked Sykes to invite for the weekend in order 'to discuss our literary plans in peace and quiet'. The friend, whom Otten described as 'this extremely important man', was of course Groehl. Otten ended on a melodramatic note, instructing Sykes to 'burn this letter'. Sykes did no such thing; instead, he passed it to MI5.[26] Despite Sykes's letter to the Home Office, Groehl's visit came to nothing, because of difficulties with the French passport authorities.

Apart from the group's channels of information, Sykes was told to ascertain their ostensible sources of income: a subject of continuing interest to MI5, as a touchstone of ultimate political loyalty. On 9 June 1938, Sykes once more visited Fritz Gross, reporting back that he had 'managed to elicit some particulars about the financial resources of Oppidans Road'.[27] Gross had apparently been unusually garrulous, telling M/S that Lehmann-Russbueldt received a regular allowance from Wickham Steed, adding 'he also receives something from the Czechs'. As for Otten, he received a small grant from the Friends Emergency Committee, estimated by Gross to be about £1 per week, which, M/S commented, 'won't go far if he has to keep his wife as well on it'.

A week later, Sykes met Otten again:

> On 15.6.38 I called on Otten. After some discussion of the radio play he is writing [i.e. *The Girl from Botany Bay*] the conversation drifted to politics, and he asked me to look at a memorandum of some information about the German Air Force, which he said he had received directly from Germany and not via Groehl. I displayed great interest in it, and asked if I could take it home to copy some of the performance figures. He consented, provided that I send it back today. I can only therefore send you my translation of this document.[28]

On this occasion, Otten seems to have been unusually indiscreet, confiding to Sykes how Groehl's informants in Germany crossed the border – usually at Aachen or Saarbrücken – to transmit information to the outside world. He went on to say that 'he knew for certain that Hitler was planning a move against Czechoslovakia for the end of July or the beginning of August', but, as Sykes then noted, the arrival of Lehmann-Russbueldt 'prohibited any further confidences'.

As the political crisis gathered pace, Sykes began to visit Otten more regularly:

> On the evening of 20th July M/S called and had a talk with Otten [...] Apparently Lehmann-Russbueldt is the man who contrives to get in touch with British politicians and one of the connecting links is Professor Lindemann who is hand in glove with Churchill.[29]

Sykes's reports are remarkable documents, revealing his 'modus operandi', and the political conclusions he drew for his spy masters. Spying thrives of course on the exploitation of trust. In an internal memorandum, Maxwell Knight commented matter-of-factly: 'M/S has been in touch with Otten for some time and we have no reason to think that Otten does anything else but trust M/S implicitly'.[30]

What was it that inspired such implicit trust? Sykes was of course a former actor, who undoubtedly played his role with conviction. His specialist knowledge of aviation literature and his publishing contacts made him an apparently ideal translator for an exposé of German aerial rearmament. But he had an even more priceless asset. His literary credentials rested above all on his friendship and collaboration with James Joyce – a magical name in the pantheon of literary modernism. Sykes had first met Joyce in Zurich in 1917. Joyce was then engaged in writing the early chapters of *Ulysses*; what Sykes was doing is much less clear. He saw no active service in the First World War, and it is possible that he was in Switzerland to avoid conscription, which had been introduced in March 1916. He first met Joyce, whom he had often seen reading English newspapers in the library of the Museumgesellschaft, after answering an advertisement Joyce had placed regarding a film project. The project itself came to nothing, but their acquaintance flourished. Sykes's wife, Daisy Race, was a professional actress, who soon became friendly with Nora Joyce.[31] Joyce and Sykes met regularly to discuss subjects connected with Joyce's work, but their friendship might have passed unnoticed by literary historians had Sykes not also agreed to act as a typist for Joyce. In December 1917 and February 1918, he typed the first three episodes of *Ulysses*, working from Joyce's handwritten manuscript.

Sykes was supporting himself by teaching English but, as a professional actor, he longed to return to the stage.[32] In the spring of 1918, he and Joyce started The English Players, a troupe founded to perform plays in English, with Sykes as producer and director and Joyce as business manager. Their first production, Oscar Wilde's *The Importance of Being Earnest*, was performed in Zurich at the Theater zu den Kaufleuten on 29 April 1918. A month and a half later, Nora appeared as Cathleen in J.M. Synge's *Riders to the Sea*; Daisy Race was also in the cast, playing her mother.[33] The English Players continued to perform until late 1919.[34] After this short cameo, Sykes the actor makes his exit, reappearing a decade later as Sykes the author and translator.

Sykes's contacts with Otten intensified as the political crisis reached its climax towards the end of September.

> I took tea with Otten on 21.9.38, but found that both his wife and Lehmann-Russbueldt were present, which reduced the chances of getting anything interesting. Groehl has once more postponed his visit [...] since in the present situation he could not afford to leave Paris for even a single day.
>
> At the same time Otten is somewhat torn between the rival claims of literature and politics, especially as the Swedish branch of Fischer-Verlag [...] is bringing out a book of his. And he confided his desire to live in the country, where he would have more time for literature.[35]

Otten's 'desire to live in the country' was much more a desire to leave London, which the Munich crisis and its resolution had only strengthened. The conduct of the war in Spain had convinced him that the next European conflict would entail large-scale bombing of civilians. In his search for a safe refuge, he seemed to favour Letchworth, where he could be near his translator and 'dear friend' Sykes.

Barely a week later, Otten and his wife visited Letchworth to look at houses, also calling on Sykes. M/S reported: 'They both seem determined to get out of London as soon as possible, for they are tired of the ménage à trois with Lehmann and he really wants to devote himself to literature'.[36] Some 'chance remarks' by Otten led M/S to conclude that the 'Primrose League' must also be in 'very close touch with Winston Churchill'. Otten claimed, for example, to have been told that Chamberlain had lost the support of the Cabinet and that a National Government, including both Churchill and Eden, would be formed. Otten's source was gravely mistaken. Chamberlain was about to make his triumphal return to London to declare 'peace for our time': Churchill was to remain a voice in the wilderness.

While Chamberlain basked briefly in the glow of public approval, Otten – like many émigrés – regarded 'peace for our time' as an illusion. Sykes continued to maintain regular contact with him at this time, reporting that the 'Primrose League' was now supplying direct information to Winston Churchill, 'who seems to have taken the place of the Czech legation'.[37]

On 7 October, Otten and his wife again visited Sykes in Letchworth and reiterated their hope of moving there:

> They only stayed to tea as he wanted to get back to London [...] I gathered that he is preparing a memorandum for Wickham Steed on coming events in the Sudetenland [...] This memorandum is to be completed tomorrow and is then to be handed to Winston Churchill, who will then accuse the premier of having betrayed national interests. [...] It may depend upon Wickham Steed as to whether Otten goes to Letchworth to live or not. His wife wants to go, but he is debating whether it will not be too far for him if he still has to direct the League's operations. Everything will depend on his talk with Steed.[38]

In this case, Steed's influence prevailed, for only a month later M/S reported:

> I called on Otten on 16.11.38 and learnt that he is to move into a house on December 1st. His address will then be 52 Hampstead Way. It would appear that he is amply supplied with funds, for he is paying a rent of £100 a year, exclusive of rates and thinks nothing of spending £50 on redecoration.[39]

One source of Otten's new-found funds was undoubtedly Wickham Steed, whom Otten had known 'since my earliest days in England'.[40] Steed was a strong supporter of German refugees, though his motives were not entirely altruistic. Increasingly convinced of Germany's aggressive intentions, he had cultivated strong intelligence links with the Whitehall mandarin Robert Vansittart. He had indeed begun to pay Otten for political information from early 1939,[41] eventually giving him a monthly allowance of £7 from his own pocket.[42] Above all, he provided Otten with invaluable links to Randolph Churchill and to British intelligence.

Early in 1939, Section B5b reported wearily that 'M/S had another talk with Carl Otten [*sic*] on Jan. 12th, but unfortunately the time was taken up with literary discussions and there was not much opportunity for politics.'[43] Yet Sykes persisted, reporting shortly after:

> Otten was in a very excited state over the fall of Barcelona [...] it emerged that Otten had recently been in close touch with the Churchills. On 24th January he had a long interview with young Randolph Churchill. It appears that Otten is going to try to use the Churchills as a medium for explaining to the British people what Germany really is and what she means to do.[44]

Despite (or because of) the distraction of political events, Otten had continued to 'devote himself to literature'. At the height of the Munich crisis, agent M/S reported, 'I went round to see Otten last night. His wife was not there [...] and most of the time we were alone. He was full of a new novel he was writing'.[45] Otten was indeed completing the first draft of the novel *Die Reise nach Deutschland* (*The Trip to Germany*) – the third, and last, work of his that Sykes was to translate.

Otten's renewed belief in his literary vocation stemmed from an apparent change in his fortunes. In July 1938, *Torquemadas Schatten* (*Torquemada's Shadow*), his novel of the Spanish civil war on Mallorca, had been accepted for publication by Gottfried Bermann Fischer, who had just succeeded in re-establishing his publishing business in Stockholm after escaping Vienna in the aftermath of the Anschluss. Otten's advance on the novel was small (500 Swedish kroner), but it revived his belief in himself as a writer – and in writing as a contribution to political discourse. Replying to Bermann's letter of acceptance, he wrote:

> Since my next book, of which I am now preparing the final draft, deals with an English-German problem, it is possible that the English edition is of greater interest than the German. I must confess that up to now I have thought only about an English edition and have written the book completely with regard to English thinking.[46]

Otten's insistence on the primacy of an English edition confirms that his intention in writing the novel was unashamedly didactic: to warn the English of the true nature of National Socialism.

The Trip to Germany was very much a *Zeitroman*, seeking to engage with its time – and to influence it. The novel depicts Nazi Germany in the summer of 1938, seen through the eyes of a young Englishman who arrives in Cologne to stay with the Eilershoven family. The Eilershovens are liberal opponents of Nazism. The head of the family, Till Eilershoven, who is very much the author's mouthpiece, declares that Germany has become a police state, a dangerous mixture of 'blood feud, terror und cannibalism. And the source of all wars in Europe', predicting that the Nazis will plunge Europe into a new war within two years. This fateful prophecy, perhaps the book's best recommendation for publication, was strikingly out of step with the prevailing political mood of appeasement.

Otten's work on the novel – and his vain attempts to find a publisher – form a literary counterpoint to the Munich Agreement and the ensuing descent into European war. He was dismayed at the lack of urgency displayed by publishers, even when their readers commended the novel:

> It is vital for me to cast the book into the struggle before the catastrophe comes. [...] And how important it is to open the eyes of the English and the angels. To analyse away this tendency towards the conference table, for humiliation to the point of self-destruction, to drive out this capacity to eat one's hat and swing one's umbrella. I hope we won't come too late.[47]

Otten had naturally written the book in German, but pursuing his conviction that an English edition should take precedence, he sent the manuscript to Sykes, asking him to furnish an English version.[48] Aware of his dependence on the translator, Otten wrote to Sykes at some length, imploring him to be as faithful as possible to the style and spirit of the German text. He had, he wrote, sought 'a unity of style', adopting, even in the dialogue, a poetic, visionary language that he implored Sykes not to reduce to colloquial English.

> I must ask you now especially to carry over this principle of poetic unity, of poetic language and graphic power into the English version. And that's because I'm afraid of so-called 'modern colloquial English', which seems more impossible to me, the more I hear it. [...] This applies particularly to the dialogue – please bear in mind that this is not real dialogue but poetic questions and answers, behind which there lies much more than what they ostensibly deal with.[49]

Sykes's response, if any, has not survived.

While Sykes the translator was tackling the nuances of style and diction, Sykes the spy had been given a crucial assignment. Early in 1939, British and French counter-intelligence had agreed to collaborate in an operation against a German spy network targeting British and French operations in the Netherlands, run by a Gestapo agent called Kützner. Since the French already had a 'double agent' in place, the British were required to find a counterpart who would feed political disinformation to Kützner. On 10 February 1939, MI5 gave their French counterparts the name of the man chosen for this delicate task: 'a British citizen living in Letchworth under the name Claud W. Sykes', who was described as 'a well-placed German translator and Rotarian'.[50]

That Sykes was assigned this key role suggests that his infiltration of the 'Primrose League' had impressed his MI5 handlers. By May 1939, he was in direct contact with Kützner in Berlin, agreeing to provide information for an allowance of £40 per month. Sykes's work as a 'double agent' was able to survive the outbreak of war, but ended in November 1939 when his cover was apparently blown following disclosures made by an SIS agent captured in the Venlo incident.[51]

In the remaining months of peace, Sykes and Otten met less frequently. Sykes was doubtless distracted by his assignment for SIS, but in addition, the 'Primrose League' (which he had so successfully penetrated) had collapsed. Otten had long since fallen out with Lehmann-Russbueldt, whom he accused of making 'secret threats', an accusation which the latter attributed to Otten's 'sick imagination'.[52] Reichenbach had withdrawn from the group, while Wolfssohn too was keeping his distance, fearing that his involvement might prejudice his application for naturalisation. Otten was now dealing independently, passing information directly to the Foreign Office and the Churchills, contacts which were to culminate in his recruitment by British intelligence.

At the same time, Otten's literary fortunes had once more waned. The manuscript of *The Trip to Germany* remained unpublished. Its powerful prophecy that the Nazis would unleash a new European war was about to be realised, undermining the book's topicality and its impact as a political *Zeitroman*. It remained unpublished in Otten's lifetime.[53]

Despite the rejection of the novel, Sykes's career as a translator prospered. In 1940, he published two more translations from German: Heinz Halter's *Finland Breaks the Russian Chains* and Erich Wollenberg's *The Red Army: A Study of Soviet Imperialism*.[54] Both books had – in contrasting ways – a curious publishing history. Halter's book, recounting Germany's role in Finland's struggle for independence from Russia in 1917, was an example of Nazi historiography, first published in Germany in 1938; the English edition, published after the Soviet invasion of Finland, was appropriated for British anti-Soviet propaganda.

Wollenberg's *The Red Army* had first appeared in 1937, when Otten had recommended Sykes to translate it, which he did the following year.

Wollenberg was a German Communist who had been an officer in the Red Army under Marshal Tukhachevsky, but had become bitterly disillusioned with Stalinism following the 'show trials'. With its republication in 1940, *The Red Army* too became an adjunct to British anti-Soviet propaganda.

All in all, 1940 was a good year for Claud W. Sykes; in the summer, he finally became an MI5 'officer'. By then, Otten too was working for British intelligence, having been recruited to a secret department of the Foreign Office, responsible for devising and planning propaganda to the enemy. However, even after Otten became a 'watcher', he remained one of the 'watched': his MI5 file was not closed until 1956.

Notes

1 See The National Archives [TNA], KV2/1120/81a.

2 MI5 report B5b to B4b re. Carl Otten Group, TNA, KV2/1120/82b.

3 Rolf Marben, *Zeppelin Adventures*, London: John Hamilton 1932; Rudolf Stark, *Wings of War. An Airman's Diary of the last Year of the Great War*, London: John Hamilton 1933; Georg Haupt-Heydemarck, *Flying Section 17*, London: John Hamilton 1934; Georg Haupt-Heydemarck, *War Flying in Macedonia*, London: John Hamilton 1935; Hans Schroeder, *An Airman Remembers*, London: John Hamilton 1936. All 'Translated by Claud W. Sykes'.

4 *Secrets of Modern Spying* by 'Vigilant', London: John Hamilton 1930.

5 For more ample biographical details of Otten, see Richard Dove, *Journey of No Return: Five German-Speaking Literary Exiles in Britain, 1933–1945*, London: Libris 2000.

6 Otten first came to the notice of MI5 through his correspondence with Otto Lehmann-Russbueldt, one of the early items in Lehmann-Russbueldt's file is an intercept letter from Otten, dated 27 March 1936, giving news of Lehmann-Russbueldt's young wife, Lucia, who was then convalescing in Mallorca.

7 See TNA, KV2/1120–3 (Karl Otten); and TNA, KV2/2001–6 (Helmuth Simons (scientist)/Otto Lehmann-Russbueldt, alias Lehmann). Their original MI5 files were numbered PF 46464 (Otten) and PF 42816 (Lehmann [*sic*]). MI5 also held files on Reichenbach [PF 46549] and Gross [PF 42848], though these have not been released.

8 One regular visitor was Hans Flesch-Brunningen, whose fictional impressions of this meeting place are recorded in the novel *Untimely Ulysses*. See Vincent Brun (i.e. Hans Flesch-Brunningen), *Untimely Ulysses*, London: Jonathan Cape 1940.

9 M/S report to B5b, 29 June 1937, TNA, KV2/1120 /14b. Maxwell Knight's 'M' Section had, since late 1936, been known as section B5b. Knight's agents preserved strict anonymity, their reports being referenced M/H, M/Y, M11 – or in Sykes's case M/S. Only later, in August 1941, was B5b renamed M.S., but by then Sykes was no longer an agent, but an MI5 officer.

10 M/S report, 23 July 1937, TNA, KV2/1120/19a.

11 M/S report, 11 October 1937, TNA, KV2/1120 /27a.

12 Report 're. Carl Otten' [*sic*], 22 October 1937, TNA, KV2/1120/32a.

13 Otten to Val Gielgud, BBC Drama, 30 October 1939, Ellen and Karl Otten Archive, Deutsches Literaturarchiv, Marbach (DLA).
14 Robeson (1898–1976) had been living in Britain since the late 1920s, his activities regularly monitored by MI5 (file PF 44990). Dr Harold Moody (1882–1947), a Jamaican doctor and political campaigner, had founded the League of Coloured Peoples in 1931 in London (file PF 48318).
15 Robeson in fact appeared at Unity Theatre in 1938 in *A Plant in the Sun*.
16 MI5 (Noel Wallace) to Sykes, 14 October 1937, TNA, KV2/1120/30a.
17 The Otten *Nachlass* contains a German typescript of *Kein Held* dated 1937/38, and an English version under the title *No Hero*, dated 1938, 'translated by Claud W. Sykes', Otten Archive, DLA.
18 Otten to Sykes, 5 March 1938, Otten Archive, DLA.
19 See the autobiographical notes which Otten sent to the American Guild for German Cultural Freedom in April 1939, Otten Archive, DLA.
20 Otten to Sykes, Otten Archive, DLA.
21 Internal memorandum, 25 August 1938, BBC Written Archives Centre, Caversham.
22 B5b report 'Lehmann-Russbueldt and Rozinski' [*sic*], 4 March 1938, TNA, KV2/1120/49a.
23 Internal memorandum, B5b to B4b, 14 March 1938, attaching a verbatim report from M/S, TNA, KV2/1120/52a.
24 M/S report (undated) regarding visit of 3 June 1938, TNA, KV2/1120/66c.
25 Cf. letter B4b to Major Vivian, 2 November 1938/98a.
26 Internal report 're. Charles Groehl', 5 May 1938, which quotes Otten's letter to Sykes in full, TNA, KV2/1120/61a.
27 Cf. internal memo re Karl Otten Group, 13 June 1938, which quotes much of Sykes's report verbatim, TNA, KV2/1120.
28 Report M/S re Otten Group, 17 June 1938, TNA, KV2/1120/67b.
29 Report B5b (M/S), 22 July 1938, TNA, KV2/1120/35.
30 Internal report 're Lehmann-Russbueldt and Rozinski', 4 March 1938, TNA, KV2/1120/49a.
31 Brenda Maddox, *Nora. The Real Life of Molly Bloom*, London: Hamilton 1988, p. 143. Nora (b. 1884) was then 33, Daisy, a year younger.
32 See Richard Ellmann, *James Joyce*, New York: OUP 1959.
33 *Riders to the Sea* was performed on 17 June 1918 at the Pfauentheater, Zurich, as part of a triple bill, which also included Shaw's *The Dark Lady of the Sonnets*.
34 The Players produced Shaw's *Mrs. Warren's Profession* on 30 September 1918 and then performed Stanley Houghton's *Hindle Wakes* on 3 December 1918. In April 1919, they produced *The Mollusc*, by Hubert Henry Davis.
35 Report B5b (M/S), 23 September 1938, TNA, KV2/1120/87a.
36 Report B5b (M/S), 28 September 1938, TNA, KV2/1120/82a.
37 Report B5b (M/S), 18 November 1938, TNA, KV2/1120/102a.
38 Report B5b (M/S), TNA, KV2/1120/89b.
39 Report B5b (M/S), 18 November 1938, TNA, KV2/1120/102a. Otten's new address was duly added to the intercept list.

40 Otten to Steed, 19 December 1945, Otten Archive, DLA.
41 Steed to Otten, 15 March 1939, TNA, KV2/1121/145a.
42 Cf. Steed to Otten, 3 August 1939 and 6 September 1939, TNA, KV2/1122/200A, both letters enclosing a cheque for £7. See also Steed to Otten, 1 November 1939: 'If the allowance you have been offered can help you to keep body and soul together for a time, it will relieve the strain on my own limited resources', Otten Archive, DLA.
43 Memo B5b (M/S), 16 January 1939, TNA, KV2/1121/116a.
44 Report B5b (M/S), 30 January 1939, TNA, KV2/1121/122a.
45 Report B5b (M/S), 22 July 1938/71b.
46 Otten to Bermann Fischer, 4 August 1938, Otten Archive, DLA.
47 Otten to Volkmar v. Zuelsdorff, American Guild for German Cultural Freedom, 16 April 1939, Otten Archive, DLA.
48 The typescript of Sykes's English translation of the novel, *Thames and Rhine*, survives in the Otten Archive, DLA.
49 Otten to Sykes, 2 June 1939, Otten Archive, DLA.
50 See *Battleground Western Europe. Intelligence Operations in Germany and the Netherlands in the Twentieth Century*, ed. Beatrice de Graaf *et al.*, Apeldoorn: Het Spinhuis 2007, especially Chapter 1.
51 See Guy Liddell diaries, TNA, KV4/184–5, also quoted in *Battleground Western Europe*.
52 Lehmann-Russbueldt to Reichenbach, 9 June 1939, TNA, KV2/1121/181a.
53 It was finally published sixty years later: *Die Reise nach Deutschland von Karl Otten*. Hrsg. und mit einem Nachwort v. Richard Dove, Berne: Lang 2000.
54 Heinz Halter, *Finland Breaks the Russian Chains*, translated by Claud W. Sykes, London: John Hamilton 1940; Erich Wollenberg, *The Red Army: A Study in Soviet Imperialism*, translated by Claud W. Sykes, London: Secker and Warburg 1938, republished 1940.

8

'The Red Menace': keeping watch on the Communists 1933–39

As we have seen, MI5's long-standing preoccupation with the 'Red Menace' remained its primary focus at least up to 1935, and arguably until early 1939. MI5 files on suspects were grouped in specific categories such as 'Communists and suspected Communists, including Russian and communist sympathisers'; this was of course a catch-all category covering many whose sympathy with the Communists was strategic and highly contingent, melting away, for example, in the wake of the Nazi–Soviet Pact. On the other hand, many Communists routinely denied that they were Communists, or at least that they were party members. There was also a sub-series of files called 'Soviet intelligence agents and suspected agents', a category which embraced various suspected spies, such as the statistician Jürgen Kuczynski, the photographer Edith Tudor-Hart, the journalist Margaret Mynatt and the composer and musicologist Ernst Hermann Meyer.

'JK': the case of Jürgen Kuczynski

The economist and statistician Jürgen Kuczynski had been known to MI5 long before his arrival in Britain in 1936. In 1931, his name had appeared on a list of Communist functionaries, passed to MI5 by agents of the Secret Intelligence Service in Germany, so ensuring that a personal file was opened on him.[1] Kuczynski had entered Britain on the pretext of writing a book on British labour conditions which he intended to research at the reading room of the British Museum. In an interview with the Home Office, he explained that he was free to return to Germany, but as a Jew was denied access to research institutions there.[2]

JK (as he refers to himself throughout his memoirs) had indeed already established a promising academic career as an economist. Following a spell as a research student at the Brookings Institution in Washington in 1928, he also spoke good English. A promising academic, a committed Communist and a well-versed conspirator, JK was the ideal person to reinvigorate the party organisation in Britain. He was also a Soviet spy, having been recruited by Soviet intelligence in Berlin some years earlier. However, the security services seem initially to have had little inkling of this. In November 1936, Special Branch reported of Kuczynski that 'there is nothing recorded to his detriment', making the same comment about his wife Marguerite, who had accompanied him to Britain.[3] Over the next three years, MI5 built a case against JK with which they finally succeeded in achieving his internment in 1940.

JK was the son of a famous father. In 1934–35, he had made several visits to London to see his father Robert, who already held a Research Fellowship at the London School of Economics (LSE). A noted statistician, René Robert Kuczynski had published work which has been widely accepted as the basis of modern demography. Although not officially a member of the KPD, he was known to have Communist leanings, which had made him an intelligence target long before the Nazi takeover in Germany. As a leading member of the Deutsche Liga für Menschenrechte (German League of Human Rights) he had come to the attention of the authorities in 1926 as the chairman of the committee set up to campaign for the expropriation of the former Kaiser and the landowning aristocracy. Despite the failure of the campaign, the authorities had singled him out, placing him under surveillance the following year when he had led a vociferous campaign against the death sentence imposed on the anarchists Sacco and Vanzetti in the United States. Once the Nazis had inherited these intelligence records, Robert Kuczynski was a marked man. Fearing for his life, he left Germany in some haste, securing a lecturing post at the LSE.

Once established in London, JK set about reorganising the clandestine KPD group in Britain. The group was small, numbering roughly thirty or forty members. They consisted almost entirely of middle-class intellectuals, such as the economist Siegfried Moos and the composer Ernst Hermann Meyer. Thanks to JK, the Party group also came to enjoy good fraternal relations with the CPGB. JK was also a member of the editorial board of the Party's theoretical journal *Labour Monthly*, whose editor Rajani Palme Dutt he had known for some years. Kuczynski also had important contacts with the Left Book Club, set up by the publisher Victor Gollancz. It was the Club which published his short treatise on labour conditions in Britain, Germany and the Soviet Union, some 50,000 copies of which were distributed to Book Club members. JK was also in great demand as a speaker to Left Book Club groups, contacts which he cultivated in the cause of the Popular Front.

As political organiser of the Party group in Britain, JK made regular short trips to the Party headquarters in Paris to receive the latest directives of the Comintern. He went there roughly every three months or (in his own phrase) 'whenever the laws of conspiracy allowed'.[4] His travels did not escape the notice of the security services. Early in 1938, MI5 asked Special Branch to check whether JK and his father 'are at present in this country', to which Special Branch replied with reference to JK: 'Alien paid many visits to France during 1937'.[5] In October 1938, MI5 raised no objection to a Home Office proposal to grant JK permanent residence in Britain.

In 1934, Robert Kuczynski had moved into 12 Lawn Road Flats, a new block of flats in Belsize Park inspired by the ideals of Walter Gropius. Completed only in 1934, the Lawn Road Flats complex was designed to meet the needs of modern communal living, proving highly attractive to progressive intellectuals. It was also an object of great interest to MI5, which noted that it had become a focal point for those with Communist sympathies and perhaps also a centre of Soviet intelligence. When JK first came to Britain, he stayed briefly with his father; his younger sister Brigitte, by this time also reputedly a Soviet spy, was living in Flat number 4 with her English husband A.G. Lewis, known to MI5 as a member of the CPGB.[6] JK stayed only a matter of weeks with his father before moving a stone's throw away to 36 Upper Park Road.

The Soviet intelligence presence in Lawn Road Flats was not confined to the Kuczynski family. Among the other residents was the Austrian Communist Arnold Deutsch, who became the most notorious – and successful – Soviet spy then living in London. In 1934, Deutsch had been sent to London to put in place a Soviet spy network, a task he accomplished with speed and efficiency. As a cover for his espionage activity, Deutsch registered to study psychology at London University, finding a home in the newly built Lawn Road Flats. Many of Deutsch's neighbours there were refugees, some of whom also had links to Soviet intelligence. However, Deutsch's recruitment policy, approved by the Centre (Soviet intelligence headquarters), was to seek to cultivate high fliers from Oxford and Cambridge with Communist sympathies, before they entered the upper echelons of the government and civil service.[7] Deutsch was later identified as the main recruiter of the 'Cambridge Five' (Kim Philby, Donald Maclean, Guy Burgess, Anthony Blunt and John Cairncross). However, his first recruit to the Soviet intelligence network in London was the young photographer Edith Tudor-Hart.

Code name EDITH: the case of Edith Tudor-Hart

Even in the ambiguous world of espionage, Edith Tudor-Hart seems an ambivalent figure, a woman of many faces. Her MI5 file still lists her as 'Edith Tudor-Hart alias Suschitsky, White, Betty Grey (*sic*), code name EDITH'.[8] Suschitzky was not an alias: she was born Edith Suschitzky in Vienna in 1908. Her family background was highly politicised. Her father owned a Socialist bookshop in the working-class suburb of Favoriten and also ran the radical publishing house, Anzengruber Verlag. Her brother Wolfgang was in no doubt that 'the foundations of her social conscience were laid by our father'.[9]

Edith originally trained to be a Montessori kindergarten teacher: she first came to Britain in 1925, at the age of sixteen, to gain practical experience as a kindergarten teacher, and returned periodically in the following years. In 1929, she studied photography under the renowned Walter Peterhans at the Bauhaus in Dessau. She attended the Bauhaus shortly after the Swiss architect Hannes Meyer had been appointed as its Director. Under his leadership, the institution took a decisive turn to the Left. Meyer emphasised the social mission of the Bauhaus, placing its established doctrine of the social utility of the applied arts into a Marxist framework.[10] Suschitzky's brief time at the Bauhaus proved decisive in her artistic development: photography became a means of cultural propaganda.

By 1930, Suschitzky was once more in London, living with Alexander Tudor-Hart, a Communist medical student at St. Thomas's hospital. She was first brought to the attention of MI5 in October 1930, when a Special Branch watcher reported that she took part in a demonstration in support of the Workers Charter (a CPGB initiative intended to retain and regain working-class support) in Trafalgar Square, where she was 'noticed to be in conversation with a number of prominent Communists'. The report closed with her description:

> Height 5'6"
> Slim build
> Pale complexion
> Eyes blue-grey
> Blond bobbed hair.[11]

Little else was known about her at the time. A letter from Valentine Vivian of SIS to Captain Liddell at Scotland Yard even stated that 'There is nothing on record to show that she has Communist tendencies'.[12] In fact, Edith Suschitzky was already a Communist activist: in 1927, she had joined the CPGB under the pseudonym 'Betty Gray'. MI5 had not yet penetrated her alias, but based on the rather flimsy evidence of her presence at a Communist demonstration, she was ordered to leave the country. Intercepted letters on her file reveal that she tried to enlist the support of the Mayor of Vienna, Karl Seitz, and the Cambridge economist, Maurice Dobb, in order to remain in Britain, but 'after repeated warnings', she was finally expelled early in 1931.

She returned to Vienna, where she became a photographer for the Soviet news agency Tass, a rite of passage followed by other Comintern agents, but her career as a press photographer came to an abrupt end in late May 1933. As the Dollfuss government moved to consolidate its power, banning the KPÖ and arresting some 800 of its activists, Suschitzky was arrested as a courier for the now illegal party. How she came to be released is not known, but her arrest forced her into exile. Alexander Tudor-Hart travelled to Vienna in August 1933, marrying Edith Suschitzky in a ceremony at the British consulate. This was not a marriage of convenience, though it did conveniently give her British nationality, thus allowing her to return to London a few weeks later.

The couple moved into a flat in Brixton, but separated within two years: by August 1935, they were no longer living together, although they both remained under Special Branch observation. Forced to find a livelihood, Edith Tudor-Hart (as she now was) became a successful photographer, setting up a photographic business which she ran from her flat at 158a Haverstock Hill, NW3. MI5 watchers considered her profession to be merely a cover for her political activity. However, for Tudor-Hart, photography was much more than a 'cover'; the camera was 'the eye of conscience', her images of working-class London providing the hard evidence to endorse her political ideology.[13]

By then, she was already working as a Soviet agent under the rather transparent code name EDITH, having been recruited early in 1934 by Arnold Deutsch, whom she knew from Vienna. Deutsch himself later claimed that, as early as 1931, he had introduced Edith to a Soviet intelligence officer in Vienna. However, the Soviet spymaster owed the first of his Cambridge recruits, Kim Philby, to a recommendation by Edith Tudor-Hart.

Tudor-Hart's photographic studio on the corner of Haverstock Hill and Lawn Road, two minutes' walk from the Lawn Road Flats, was quickly identified by MI5 as 'a rendezvous of persons interested in communist matters'.[14] It was indeed a meeting place for party comrades. Among those who frequented the studio were Brian Goold-Verschoyle, a Soviet agent who was later to disappear in the Soviet Union, and his lover, Charlotte Moos, who had come to London as a refugee in 1934. Moos had originally contacted Tudor-Hart in the hope of finding some work in her dark room, but although there was little work to be done, Tudor-Hart was a generous friend. Moos, according to her own later statement, visited the flat frequently, mainly to take a bath or wash her clothes, 'also sometimes to have a good meal'.[15] Her visits were noted by the two plain clothes men who regularly observed the comings and goings at the studio from their vantage point across the road.

Following the birth of her son in 1936, Tudor-Hart began to specialise in child portraits, but continued her activity as a photographer of social conscience. She was a member of the Workers Camera Club, contributed photographs to *Picture Post* and helped to organise the 'Artists against Fascism and War' exhibition in 1935, under the auspices of the Artists

International Association.[16] She was undoubtedly a highly successful photographer. In January 1938, Special Branch reported that her photographic business had been transferred to 17 Duke Street, W1, 'and it appears to be a flourishing one'.[17]

In the course of that year, Edith Tudor-Hart was more than once brought to the attention of MI5. In March, she was directly implicated in the Woolwich Arsenal spy plot (MI5's most successful counter-intelligence operation of the 1930s) when a Leica camera used by the Percy Glading group to photograph documents taken from the Woolwich Arsenal was linked to her by sales receipts showing that she had originally purchased it. However, when questioned by Special Branch detectives, she simply denied any involvement, claiming that her connection was completely innocent. For whatever reason, neither MI5 nor Special Branch chose to pursue the matter.

Later that year, Special Branch reported that a group of the Austrian Communist Party had been established in London, the leader of which was alleged to be Engelbert Broda, an Austrian scientist, now a refugee, who had arrived in Britain in April 1938. Tudor-Hart, it was reported, had been delegated by the Central Committee of the CPGB to liaise between it and the new group. The report stated that Broda's address was kept secret from other group members, even Tudor-Hart, who knew only his telephone number and communicated with him by that means.[18]

Despite such reports, and despite continuing Special Branch surveillance, MI5 made little attempt to follow up these leads. It is striking that while MI5 paid ever closer attention to Jürgen Kuczynski – and succeeded in having him interned in January 1940 – they seemed to have little interest in Edith Tudor-Hart, whom Nigel West has described as 'a key figure in Soviet espionage operations in Britain'.[19] It may well be that MI5 underestimated her importance to Soviet intelligence, considering her a low-level agent, little more than a willing go-between; they were clearly unaware of her role as a talent-spotter and recruiter. They learned only much later that it was Tudor-Hart who had made the first approach to recruit Kim Philby, possibly the most prolific British traitor ever, whom she then recommended to Arnold Deutsch.[20] She knew Philby through his first wife Litzi Friedmann, a long-standing friend of hers from Vienna; she introduced him to Arnold Deutsch on a park bench in Regents Park.

'Alias Mander, Meinhardt, Minotti, Minetti': the case of Margaret Mynatt

When the Communist journalist (Bianca) Margaret Mynatt arrived in Britain in 1934, MI5 was unusually slow in adding her to its black list of 'Communists and suspected Communists'. In almost every respect, her circumstances were indistinguishable from those of other political refugees from Germany. Like them, she spoke next to no English, had few, if any, English contacts and was virtually penniless. There was, however, one crucial difference between her and other political refugees: she possessed British nationality.

Mynatt's family background was unusual. She was born in Vienna in 1907 to an Austrian-Jewish mother and a British father, John Charles Mynatt, a musician who chose to be known professionally as Giovanni Carlo Minotti. He was soon to abandon his family, leaving his daughter nothing but his name and his British nationality. Margaret Mynatt had moved to Berlin in 1929, where she worked as a journalist, joined the KPD and became part of the circle around the playwright Bertolt Brecht, assisting in the creation of *St Joan of the Stockyards*. She had fled Germany shortly after the Reichstag Fire in order to avoid probable arrest, arriving in London via Prague and Paris in 1934.[21] It is likely that, as a British subject, she had passed relatively unnoticed into Britain, raising something of a question mark against MI5's procedures for identifying political undesirables.

Mynatt had found life hard in her early months in Britain, managing to find occasional work as a teacher of German and as a researcher. It will be recalled that one of her more sensitive assignments from 1936 to 1938 was to collect material for the American journalist Clara Leiser who was investigating the still unexplained deaths of Dora Fabian and Mathilde Wurm in 1935. Mynatt had also made early contact with the CPGB, an unusual step, since émigré Communists were normally instructed to steer clear of the local party. The initial cause of MI5's interest in her was her involvement with the Communist-inspired Relief Committee for the Victims of German Fascism, and in particular letters she had written to the brilliant Communist propagandist in Paris, Willi Münzenberg, and his associate Otto Katz,[22] both of whose names were prominent on MI5's black list. All correspondence to and from the Committee's Litchfield Street address was being intercepted by the Security Service in connection with the recruiting of volunteers for the Spanish International Brigade.[23]

Mynatt's work for the Relief Committee was only the tip of the iceberg. She also performed various other clandestine duties for the Party, acting as a trusted courier for the Comintern. It was a role for which Mynatt, as the holder of a British passport, and lacking any family or other personal commitments, was ideally suited. Her work as a courier involved her in flying regularly to the Soviet Union and carrying money from there to fellow couriers elsewhere in Europe for Communist parties declared illegal within their own countries. So secret was this activity that when, on one occasion, Mynatt's plane was involved in an air crash in Finland, her chief concern was that she should not be taken to hospital lest the nature of her mission be disclosed.[24]

Judging by the sparseness of the early part of Mynatt's 'personal file', MI5 seems to have been initially unaware of her role as a courier or of her other Comintern commitments, a failure which perhaps reflects the competence of Comintern clandestine operations rather than the incompetence of MI5. However Mynatt continued to interest MI5, and in 1940 it is noted in her file that 'a reliable informant' had described her as a 'highly respected and trusted Comintern official'.[25] At much the same time, a report by Claud Sykes, who by then had become an MI5 officer, describes her as the 'chief GPU officer in the KPD'; the report was based on information from a refugee informer (the ex-Communist Hans Wistuba).[26] However, the chief reason why Mynatt became the focus of MI5 attention was the leading role she played in the Czech Refugee Trust Fund where she was responsible for the preparation of materials for Czech Refugee Trust Fund (CRTF) members appearing in front of the Alien Tribunals. Chapter 14 charts MI5's growing concern at Communist influence within the Trust Fund, culminating in the dismissal of Mynatt and her friend Yvonne Kapp in June 1940.

'Confused and contradictory': the case of Ernst Hermann Meyer

'Information about Dr. Ernst Hermann Meyer is confused and contradictory.'[27] So ran a narrative report on Meyer written as late as November 1942. MI5 may well have contributed to its own confusion: it listed Meyer for some years as an Austrian[28] and noted at different times that he (probably) was or (possibly) was not a member of the KPD. The only possible conclusion is that, in this instance, MI5 was not paying proper attention.

The composer and musicologist Ernst H. Meyer was born and brought up in Berlin. He joined the KPD in 1931, playing a minor role in the Communist-dominated 'Kulturfront'; his name was not among those passed to MI5, perhaps because for some time it was not known to the Gestapo. Having lived through the early months of the Nazi regime, Meyer left Berlin in great haste in July 1933. According to his own story, he was warned by a friend that the Gestapo was already waiting for him at his home in Fasanenstrasse in Berlin's West End. He left Berlin immediately with no more than the clothes he was wearing and the money he had in his pocket, leaving behind his possessions, his house and his wife Ilse. He did not return to his native city until 1948.

Meyer was among the few refugees who, having been forced into exile, chose to come to Britain. He arrived at Harwich from the Hook of Holland on 21 July 1933, giving his occupation as 'student of music science' and claiming that he wished to pursue research into early English chamber music, notably the seventeenth-century composer Henry Purcell. It was no empty claim. Meyer had studied music at the University of Heidelberg, completing a doctorate in 1930 on chamber music by seventeenth-century North German composers; he went on to conduct extensive research into early English music, his authoritative book on the subject finally appearing in 1951.[29] During his final years in Germany, he had also become a pupil of the Communist composer Hanns Eisler.

Meyer's arrival in Britain prompted only routine interest from MI5; a report by Section M2 in October 1933 noted succintly: 'This man is a German refugee, believed to be a party member'. This belief was based on Meyer's contacts with Lord Marley's Relief Committee for the Victims of German Fascism. There was little further information to confirm or deny it. In fact, Meyer had been instructed to pretend that, while he had left-wing sympathies, he was not a Communist, a pretence he maintained with some success until the outbreak of war. One later MI5 report admitted: 'Nothing is known of Meyer's activities between 1935 and September 1939'.[30] In fact, his activities in Britain were neither secret nor obscure, and it is possible to piece together his biography during the four years leading up to the Second World War.

After a period of initial adjustment, Meyer began to be active in the field of workers' education. He became friendly with the Communist composer Alan Bush, a Professor at the Royal Academy of Music. Bush had studied philosophy and musicology in Berlin and was well acquainted with the cultural situation there prior to 1933. He was sympathetic to refugees, cultivating links with both Meyer and his Austrian counterpart Georg Knepler. Though their friendship probably dated from 1934, Bush became Meyer's principal contact with the CPGB, drawing him into the cultural activities of the British party. Meyer was known within the CPGB by the name Peter Baker, an alias given to him by Alan Bush in order to disguise his connection to the Party.[31] Bush was the conductor of the London Labour Choral Union and Chairman of the William Morris Musical Society, a precursor of the left-wing Workers Music Association (WMA). Meyer became involved in both organisations; from about 1935, he began lecturing for the Workers Educational Association (WEA). When the WMA was set up in 1936, in response to the continuing advance of Fascism, Bush became its Chairman.

By this time Meyer was well established in London. His wife Ilse had followed him to London at the end of 1933. From 1936, they lived at 52 Parliament Hill, in a flat owned by the Communist film director and producer Ralph Bond. During the 1930s, Bond was making a name as a documentary film-maker; he was also known to MI5 as a member of the CPGB. Through John Grierson, Bond had been offered a job as production manager at the GPO Film Unit, a role which enabled him to give Meyer the opportunity to write and edit music for GPO documentary films.

Meyer worked for the GPO Film Unit from 1937 to August 1940, composing and arranging the music for several documentary films, including most notably *North Sea*, the story of an Aberdeen trawler which is damaged during a storm, runs into trouble and is assisted to safety by the Wick coastguard radio station. *North Sea* (1938) was a pioneering example of the now familiar drama documentary, using dramatic development and characterisation within a documentary format. The film was directed by Harry Watt, a stalwart of the documentary film movement. Watt had made his name as co-director of *Night Train* which, with music by Benjamin Britten and words by W. H. Auden, remains the best-known film to emerge from the 1930s documentary movement.

Meyer's work for the GPO Film Unit brought him some recognition from his fellow-professionals. He had become established in Britain – to the extent that he even considered taking British nationality, after having completed the necessary five years of residence. However, external events intervened, with the outbreak of war and the consequent suspension of naturalisation procedures.

MI5's rather dilatory investigation of Ernst Hermann Meyer only changed pace in September 1939. At the same time, the Service also began to take further interest in the case of Jürgen Kuczynski and his fellow-residents in the Lawn Road Flats. This renewed interest in Communists, not least German Communists, came with the announcement of the Nazi–Soviet Pact in late August 1939 – less than a fortnight before the outbreak of war. The surveillance of left-wing refugees was to remain a continuous item on MI5's agenda throughout the war years – and well into the post-war period.

Notes

1 The National Archives [TNA], KV2/1871/3a 'MI1c forwarded a list of functionaries of the central communist organisations', 24 June 1931. MI1c was a cover name for the Secret Intelligence Service (SIS), originally adopted during the First World War. Although the name SIS was commonly used after 1919, the cover name MI1c continued in use up to the outbreak of the Second World War, see Keith Jeffery, *MI6: The History of the Secret Intelligence Service 1909–1949*, London: Bloomsbury 2010, pp. 50, 162.

2 TNA, KV2/1871/74a.

3 Special Branch report re the Kuczynski family, 11 November 1936, TNA, KV2/1871/15a. Marguerite Kuczynski, as Jürgen's wife, was thereby deemed equally suspect and so shares an MI5 file with him.

4 Jürgen Kuczynski, *Memoiren: Die Erziehung des J.K. zum Kommunisten und Wissenschaftler*, Berlin/Weimar: Aufbau, 2nd edition 1975, p. 286.

5 Special Branch to MI5, 23 February 1938, TNA, KV2/1871/26a.

6 David Burke, *The Spy Who Came in from the Co-op: Melita Norwood and the Ending of Cold War Espionage*, Woodbridge: Boydell Press 2008, Chapter 7. Burke has stated the intention of writing a book about the Lawn Road Flats.
7 Christopher Andrew, *The Defence of the Realm: The Authorized History of MI5*, London: Allen Lane 2009, pp. 169–72.
8 TNA, KV2/1012–14.
9 Suschitzky, Wolf, ed., *Edith Tudor-Hart: The Eye of Conscience*, London: Nishen 1987, p. 8.
10 Frank Whitford, *Bauhaus*, London: Thames and Hudson 1984.
11 Special Branch to SIS (Valentine Vivian), 31 October 1930, TNA, KV2/1012/2a.
12 Letter from SIS (Valentine Vivian) to Scotland Yard (Capt. Liddell), TNA, KV2/1012/6a.
13 See Wolf, *Tudor-Hart, The Eye of Conscience*.
14 Extract Special Branch report, 9 September 1935,TNA, KV2/1012/24a.
15 Charlotte Moos, statement to the Governess of Holloway Prison, 27 April 1940, TNA, KV2/1241.
16 The AIA was set up in 1933 to promote 'the unity of artists for peace, democracy and cultural development'. From its inception, it was involved in aiding artists displaced by political persecution in Germany and Austria. Beginning in 1935, it held several large group exhibitions, the first being 'Artists against Fascism and War'.
17 Extract Special Branch report, 14 January 1938, TNA, KV2/1012/32a.
18 Extract Special Branch report, 23 July 1938, TNA, KV2/1012/35a.
19 Nigel West and Oleg Tsarev, *The Crown Jewels: The British Secrets at the Heart of the KGB Archives*, London: Harper Collins 1998, p. 273.
20 *Ibid.*
21 See '1996 Foreword' to Yvonne Kapp and Margaret Mynatt, *British Policy and the Refugees, 1933–1941*, London/Portland: Frank Cass 1997, pp. xv–xvi.
22 Dated 1 December 1936 and 24 February 1937, TNA, KV2/3364, 1A and 2A.
23 See Special Branch report, 27 January 1938, TNA, KV2/3364.
24 Charmian Brinson interview with Yvonne Kapp, 1994.
25 Special Branch Report, 6 May 1940, TNA, KV2/3364/53x.
26 M/S Report, *c.* 16 March 1940, TNA, KV2/3364/47b.
27 TNA, KV2/3502/91a.
28 Some mistakes die hard. This mistake has been copied into the summary written for Meyer's file, when it was finally released on 4 April 2011, TNA, KV2/3502–3.
29 E.H. Meyer, *Early English Chamber Music: From the Middle Ages to Purcell*, London: Lawrence and Wishart 1951 (reprinted 1982).
30 Narrative report on Meyer, November 1942, TNA, KV2/3502/91b.
31 Report B5b ('Conquest') to Mr Hollis, B4a, 24 April 1941, TNA, KV2/3502/35a.

9

'Peace for our time'

In early October 1938, the British Prime Minister Neville Chamberlain returned to Britain after signing the ill-fated Munich Agreement, which effectively dismembered Czechoslovakia. Standing outside 10 Downing Street, triumphantly waving 'a piece of paper', signed by himself and 'Herr Hitler', Chamberlain announced that he had achieved 'peace for our time'. Historians, with the benefit of hindsight, have dealt harshly with Chamberlain, but it is worth noting that his stance commanded wide support among the British public at the time.

Peace was, of course, short-lived. On 16 March 1939, the German army marched into the remainder of Czechoslovakia, shattering the illusions of even the most ardent advocates of appeasement and setting the stage for the Second World War. In the same month, the British government finally abandoned the policy of 'appeasement', issuing a declaration that Britain was ready to support Poland in the event of a German invasion. This declaration marked an about-turn in government policy – everything the British government did subsequently was designed to *prepare* for war, not to prevent it. In April, the introduction of military conscription was announced – the first time in British history that such a measure had been introduced in peacetime.

Among the signs of impending war was the growing number of German-speaking refugees arriving in Britain. The Nazi persecution of Jews in the months after the Anschluss had forced a stream of refugees to leave Austria. By the end of 1938, the stream had become a flood, as the horrors of the 'Kristallnacht' pogrom caused a mass flight of Jews from Greater Germany.[1] Those who stayed behind were mostly those who lacked the will or the means to emigrate or simply failed to master the bureaucratic obstacles to emigration in time.

As the political situation deteriorated and other avenues of escape closed, Britain became the goal of desperate refugees, seeking either a permanent refuge or a staging post on the way to the United States. Up to 1938, the guiding principle of British immigration policy had been that Britain was a country of temporary refuge, not of permanent settlement. Officially, this policy did not change. In July 1938, the British government reintroduced the visa requirement for Germans and Austrians wishing to come to Britain. However, as the situation deteriorated, the government bowed to pressure from groups representing the refugees by relaxing the entry regulations for particular groups, most notably by waiving the visa requirement for unaccompanied children. In the following months, over 10,000 children left Greater Germany and the former Czechoslovakia on special trains: the so-called 'Kindertransport'.

There are differing estimates of the total number of refugees who fled Greater Germany between 1933 and 1939. The most reliable figure is probably still that given by Sir Herbert Emerson, the League of Nations High Commissioner for Refugees, who estimated in his final report to the League Assembly that a total of 400,000 refugees had left Germany, Austria and Czechoslovakia since 1933. The great majority of these, amounting to 360,000–370,000, were Jewish refugees fleeing racial persecution; the overall number of 'political' refugees may therefore have been between 30,000 and 40,000 (roughly eight to ten per cent of the total).[2]

The final number of refugees reaching Britain has been the subject of keen debate amongst academics, though the best estimate – based on Home Office statistics issued in 1943 – seems to be that by September 1939 some 78,000 refugees were living in Britain.[3] How many of these were 'political refugees' remains a matter of conjecture, though a reasonable estimate seems to be some 6,000–8,000 (i.e. about eight to ten per cent of the total).

In the last two decades, historians like David Cesarani, Tony Kushner and Louise London have criticised British government policy towards refugees, accusing both the government and its agencies, including MI5, of being anti-alien and therefore also anti-Semitic. Their critique poses the question: how far did MI5 press the government to pursue policies which were anti-Semitic in effect, if not in intent. There is little doubt that anti-Jewish prejudice existed in MI5, as in the other government departments with which they collaborated. We have already noted Guy Liddell's implicit anti-Semitism in a report following his visit to Berlin in March 1933, which lent credence to stories of official corruption in 'Government institutions where the Jews had a firm foothold'. Moreover, MI5 files contain further examples of casual anti-Semitism, some of which are sufficiently notable to be quoted elsewhere in this study. However, they reflect very much the social attitudes of the day at a time when, for example, many tennis and golf clubs routinely barred Jews from membership.[4] Such prejudices were widespread and even deemed acceptable, not least among the social class from which MI5 exclusively recruited. As to MI5 itself, it certainly seems to have had few Jewish officers, although one of its outstanding recruits during the Second World War was Victor Rothschild, heir to the banking dynasty.[5] However, his work in counter-sabotage did not involve contact with German refugees.

Whatever the actual extent of anti-Semitism in MI5, there is no sign that such sentiments actually motivated its surveillance of refugees, which was driven by its traditional suspicions of Germany and Germans. In August 1939, it advocated the wholesale internment of 'enemy aliens' (some ninety per cent of whom were Jewish) in the case of war, on the grounds that they represented a possible danger of Nazi espionage; MI5 argued that it lacked the resources to distinguish those 'enemy aliens' who might be spies from those who were not. German Jews were evidently considered no less German for being Jewish.

While attitudes within the security services began to harden against the Nazis, hostility to Communists remained unchanged. The Nazi–Soviet Non-Aggression Pact, completed in August 1939, merely confirmed MI5's inveterate anti-communism. It expressed particular concern about the wave of political refugees entering Britain from Czechoslovakia in the aftermath of the Munich Agreement. Many of them arrived under the auspices of the CRTF, which had been inaugurated – as a gesture of atonement for the British role in dismembering Czechoslovakia over the heads of its people – in September 1938 in order to administer funds provided by the government to support refugees from the Sudeten border areas of Czechoslovakia; its remit was rapidly extended after the German annexation of Bohemia and Moravia.

Among the political refugees rescued from Czechoslovakia were also many Austrians and Germans who had found asylum there after escaping their native countries and who were now forced to flee for a second time. Of the 8,000 refugees in the care of the CRTF in September 1939, some ten per cent were Reich Germans. They included a group of Social Democrats and an even larger group of Communists, numbering about 280, among whom were leading Party functionaries such as Wilhelm Koenen of the KPD and his Austrian counterpart Hans Winterberg, as well as prominent cultural figures like the artist John Heartfield and the writer Max Zimmering. In 1939, the British government thus found itself in the paradoxical position of acting as host to a substantial group of left-wing political activists.

MI5 was well aware of this paradox, regarding many of the new arrivals with alarm. In November 1938, the Labour MP Ellen Wilkinson submitted a list of German and Czech Communists to the Home Office, requesting on their behalf 'visas without delay'. The list comprised thirty-two names, including those of Koenen and Heartfield.[6] Both men had been known to MI5 for some time. Koenen had indeed been refused entry to Britain as long ago as 1932. A Communist deputy to the Reichstag, he had fled Germany for Prague in 1933, following trumped up allegations that he had been involved in the Reichstag Fire.

Despite the 'strong objections' of MI5, the Home Secretary authorised the admission of all thirty-two persons to Britain for an initial period of two months.[7] Koenen arrived in Britain on 12 December 1938, initially staying with D.N. Pritt. In a note to the Home Office, Kenneth Younger of MI5 particularly deplored the admission of Koenen, whom he described (rather fancifully) as 'formerly chief of the GPU in France, who is now assisting in the formation of a London bureau of the Comintern'.[8]

MI5 did not give up. In the following months, and especially after the outbreak of war, it sent the Home Office repeated memoranda, recommending that various leading Communists (including Koenen) should be interned. It stressed 'the danger of allowing Communist émigrés to enter the UK as "refugees from Nazi oppression"', contending that some of them were not even genuine refugees, but trained Comintern agents, versed in the dark arts of espionage.[9] In a letter to Alexander Maxwell, concerning a report on the Czech Refugee Trust Fund, Vernon Kell even claimed to have 'very recent and extremely reliable information to show that the German Intelligence Service has been, for a long time past, collaborating with the Soviet Intelligence'.[10] Little more was heard of this claim but – as outlined in chapter 14 – the CRTF was to remain a particular thorn in the side of MI5.

As the government reversed its policy in March 1939, the security services also began to prepare for war, beginning, for example, to assess prospective intelligence sources amongst the refugees. In April, SIS informed MI5 'that we have ascertained a considerable amount about Otten, Groehl and half a dozen other refugee organisations which are supplying information. *The whole matter has assumed great importance* [author's emphasis] – We hope to have a conference of officers here (i.e. at SIS) on the matter shortly after Easter.'[11]

Only a fortnight later (on 19 April) Valentine Vivian, head of Section V of SIS, addressed Guy Liddell at MI5 ('my dear Liddell') to report that SIS had compiled a list of 'alien refugees [...] likely to be useful to us for *propaganda purposes* in time of war and for whom exemption [from internment] would be requested, provided you consider them suitable'. The list was short, comprising only four names, one of which was Karl Otten.[12] Shortly after, SIS sent MI5 a list of 'German Emigré Sources', prominently marked 'Secret'.[13] Both organisations were intrinsically suspicious of all intelligence emanating from émigrés, seeking to evaluate the émigrés' own sources of information, as well as their likely motives, their political affiliations and their British contacts. These contacts included journalists like Wickham Steed, political figures such as Lord (Robert) Cecil, Lord Marley and the Labour MP, D.N. Pritt, as well as academics like Professor R.W. Seton-Watson, an expert on Czechoslovakia and a firm opponent of Chamberlain's policy of appeasement, and Professor Frederick Lindemann, friend and scientific adviser to Winston Churchill. Most of these had already earned a surveillance file of their own, though Pritt's file is the only one to have been released.[14] MI5's watch on these and other 'friends in need' is the subject of chapter 16.

During 1938–39, MI5's structure and recruitment also revealed clear signs of the approaching war. In July 1938, the Service had boasted twenty-six officers; six months later the number had risen to thirty and by July 1939 to thirty-six, secretarial and Registry staff also increasing in proportion. At the end of 1938, MI5's two divisions were increased to four,[15] the new additions being C Division, responsible for vetting candidates for sensitive positions, and D division, dealing with security in military establishments. B Division, which continued to deal with counter-espionage and counter-subversion, included Maxwell Knight's 'M' section, known as B5b,[16] as well as section B4a, responsible for monitoring Communists and Trotskyists, headed by its new 'Communist expert', Roger Hollis. Section B4a in fact consisted solely of Hollis and his secretary. All this changed with the outbreak of war.

Notes

1 See Bernard Wasserstein, *Britain and the Jews of Europe 1939–1945*, Oxford and New York: Oxford University Press 1979, pp. 7–10.

2 See A.J. Sherman, *Island Refuge: Britain and Refugees from the Third Reich 1933–1939*, London: Frank Cass, 2nd edition 1994, pp. 269–70; and Werner Röder, *Die deutschen sozialiatischen Exilgruppen in Großbritannien 1940–1945: Ein Beitrag zur Geschichte des Widerstandes gegen den Nationalsozialismus*, Bonn-Bad Godesberg: Neue Gesellschaft 1973, pp. 15–19.

3 Louise London, *Whitehall and the Jews 1933–1948: British Immigration Policy and the Holocaust*, Cambridge: Cambridge University Press 2000, pp. 11–12.

4 Cf. Tony Kushner, 'Clubland, Cricket Tests and Alien Internment 1939–40', in David Cesarani and Tony Kushner, eds, *The Internment of Aliens in Twentieth Century Britain*, London: Frank Cass 1993.

5 Christopher Andrew notes that Rothschild joined MI5 at the recommendation of Guy Liddell, thereby hoping to absolve Liddell from any hint of anti-Semitism (Andrew, *The Defence of the Realm: The Authorized History of MI5*, London: Allen Lane 2009, p. 190).

6 Memo B4, 18 November 1938, The National Archives [TNA], KV2/2798/54a.

7 TNA, KV2/2798/54a and 103a.

8 Draft minute for Home Office file from KGY (= Kenneth Younger), KV2/2798/62a.

9 Memo dated 30 April 1940, TNA, KV2/2798/115b.

10 Kell to Maxwell, 30 January 1940, TNA, KV2/2714/17a.

11 SIS (Section V) to MI5 (KGY=Kenneth Younger), 6 April 1939, TNA, KV2/1121/154a.

12 SIS (Vivian) to MI5 (Liddell), 19 April 1939, TNA, KV2/1121/165b.

13 SIS to MI5 (KGY), 3 May 1939, TNA, KV2/1121/164.

14 MI5 kept files on Steed (PF 35690A), see TNA, KV2/1120/89; Pritt (PF 48156), see released file for relevant period at TNA, KV2/1062; Seton-Watson (PF 52661), see TNA, KV2/1121/164; and on Lindemann (PF 24412), see TNA, KV2/1120/71B. Re Lord Cecil, see M/S report 14 October 1938, TNA, KV2/1121/89b and 91a.

15 See Andrew, *Defence of the Realm*, p. 134.

16 Knight's office was known as B5b from 1937; after Sir David Petrie's reorganisation in 1941, 'M' section became known as B1F.

Part II

Secrets, lies and misinterpretations

10

'A state of confusion which at times amounted almost to chaos': MI5 1939–41

When war broke out, MI5 embarked on a rapid – and largely unfocused – recruitment policy which was to contribute to a temporary descent into what its own rapporteur called 'a state of confusion which at times amounted almost to chaos'.[1] During the early months of the war, the intelligence situation remained febrile. MI5's operations had acquired new urgency, but no increased clarity. The relationship between MI5 and other intelligence agencies had sometimes been uneasy: responsibilities often overlapped with those of rival agencies such as SIS or Radio Security Services (RSS) – or were even disputed. For example, SIS and not MI5 was responsible for wireless interception. Moreover, the demands of war threw up new agencies, which were sometimes regarded as operational rivals. After the fall of France, the Special Operations Executive (SOE) was created in July 1940, with responsibility for subversion and sabotage behind enemy lines.[2] Another wartime creation was the Political Warfare Executive (PWE), formed in August 1941 as a clandestine department of the Foreign Office, responsible for planning and devising propaganda to enemy countries.[3] There was, however, one agency with which MI5 continued to work closely. It is striking that many reports filed during the early war years derive from Special Branch, without whose support MI5 would simply have lost oversight of many of its suspects.

The early months of war witnessed a frantic recruitment drive by MI5. In July 1939, the Service had a complement of 36 officers; by January 1940, this had risen to 102, a substantial increase, but far fewer than necessary to fulfil the demands of wartime.[4] Among its earliest recruits was William Robson-Scott, who had first-hand experience of Nazi Germany. He had been a *Lektor* at Berlin University from 1933 to 1937, before transferring to Vienna, where he completed his doctorate in 1939. Returning to Britain shortly before the war, he was appointed to a lectureship in German at Birkbeck College, London, before being – to quote his obituary – 'immediately seconded to the War Office' (a common euphemism for MI5). His knowledge of German and Germany made him a valuable recruit for MI5, fitting easily into the surveillance of German émigrés. Not all recruits were so compatible.

By May 1940, MI5's administration was close to collapse. John Curry noted that some of those recruited in such haste at the outbreak of war were unsuitable, or had little idea of their duties. Curry's internal history of MI5, written in the relative calm of 1945–46, was of course a retrospective view. Fortunately, we also have an eyewitness account of these testing times in the diaries of Guy Liddell, Director of B Division.[5] These diaries, hailed as the 'single most significant insight into the wartime workings of the Intelligence Service' (*The Guardian*), are indeed a unique record. In May 1940, Liddell became Director of B Division in succession to Brigadier 'Jasper' Harker, thus assuming control of British counter-intelligence. His diaries, dictated every evening to his secretary, cover the entire period of the Second World War, being the only example of the 'operational diary' of a senior figure in the intelligence apparatus.

Liddell's Diaries reveal much about the policies and day-to-day work of MI5 at an operational level, but they are also an eloquent record of the ideological mindset of the Security Service and the political priorities which Liddell had helped to foster. By 1940, he had spent nearly two decades in the business of counter-espionage, years which had unmistakably shaped his world view, in which the greatest threat to the British Empire was posed by international communism. This guiding principle was reinforced by the Nazi–Soviet Pact, an alliance which emphasised the potential threat to British security posed by Communists – not least German Communists.

Within MI5, sections B4a and B4b were responsible for monitoring Communist activity, dealing with British and foreign Communists respectively. However, the two sections worked closely together, for although alien Communists were rarely admitted to the CPGB, they relied on the British Party for advice and assistance and followed the same general policy.[6] During the first period of the war, the work of B4b consisted chiefly in obtaining as much information as possible about alien refugees who were suspected of being Communists or Communist sympathisers. This involved close collaboration with the Home Office and with Chief Constables of districts where aliens were registered. Their investigative work was undoubtedly hampered by the administrative 'chaos' already noted.

These were difficult times not only for MI5. Throughout the 1930s, Communists had believed that the only true enemy of Fascism was the Soviet Union. The Nazi–Soviet Pact had therefore come as a devastating shock to party members and supporters, demanding of them an intellectual somersault. The CPGB had initially announced its support for the war. The Party's general secretary, Harry Pollitt, even published a pamphlet entitled *How to Win the War*, calling on members to support the war effort.

A month later, the Party reversed its position, adopting the ideological line dictated by the Comintern: that the war was a conflict between two 'imperialist' powers which the working class had a duty to oppose.

The Nazi–Soviet Pact was particularly painful for German Communists, who had been among the earliest opponents of Nazism and were also among its first victims. In common with the CPGB, German Communists in Britain had initially declared the conflict to be an 'anti-Fascist war'. Now they were required to move from outright opposition to Nazism to a policy of accommodation with it.

By early 1940, an open letter written by Walter Ulbricht, the exiled KPD leader in Moscow (and later leader of the German Democratic Republic), was circulating in Britain. The Ulbricht letter, reaffirming the Party line that this was an 'imperialist' war, became a significant yardstick of loyalty to the Party. Communist propaganda in support of the Party line merely confirmed the worst suspicions of MI5, which could plausibly claim that Communists were spreading 'defeatism' by calling for strikes in vital war industries, thereby subverting the British war effort. It was this very claim which eventually led to the publication of the *Daily Worker* being suspended in January 1941.

In the meantime, MI5 had even more pressing concerns: some of its intelligence links were beginning to unravel. The most notable case was Wolfgang zu Putlitz who had been posted to The Hague as Head of Legation in May 1938. 'Klop' Ustinov had been meeting him regularly in Holland to receive information for transmission to Vansittart. However, the penetration of the SIS station in Holland had placed Putlitz in imminent danger of being exposed.[7] In January 1939, he had taken special leave to visit London, where he met Vansittart, who had offered him sanctuary in the event of war.[8] In fact, Putlitz escaped from Holland by plane on 14 September 1939.

During these early months of the war, there was one significant windfall for MI5 which affected particularly its surveillance of German-speaking refugees. Two years earlier, in October 1937, the Soviet intelligence officer Walter Krivitsky had defected. Krivitsky had been an important figure in the 'Fourth Department' of Soviet Military Intelligence, rising to become control officer in The Hague, where he had adopted the cover of an antiquarian. Fearing for his life, Krivitsky had fled to the United States at the end of 1938. Brought to London in January 1940, he was interviewed at length by a team comprising Liddell, the Soviet expert Jane Archer and Valentine Vivian of SIS. MI5 considered the interview very valuable, concluding that Krivitsky gave them 'for the first time' an insight into the methods of the Russian Secret Intelligence Service and their operations in Europe and against Britain (although Krivitsky had defected over two years earlier, in 1937, and had, in any case, not been responsible for Soviet operations in Britain). It assessed Krivitsky's views as 'factually correct, honest and reliable'. His debriefing also served to illuminate details of some cases already under investigation by B Division.[9] Several refugees described on file as 'Soviet agents' were among those denounced by Krivitsky.

Liddell's Diaries are most revealing about the attitude of the Security Service towards their political 'masters'. It was often impatient with the actions of elected politicians and even government ministers, whose judgement it considered questionable and whose interventions it perceived as damaging. Such reservations also extended to the actions of senior civil servants. Liddell's diary records his tacit contempt for the views of civil servants, like Sir Alexander Maxwell, Permanent Under-Secretary at the Home Office, and indeed for those of John Anderson, the Home Secretary, whose attitude was notably more liberal than that of MI5. The intense rivalry between MI5 and the Home Office was most evident in their different attitudes to the question of internment.

Notes

1 John Court Curry, The *Security Service 1908–1945: The Official History*, London: Public Record Office 1999, p. 145.
2 With the founding of SOE in early 1940, SIS lost responsibility for conducting subversive warfare.
3 The PWE combined the Political Intelligence Department of the Foreign Office and the departments of the BBC and the Ministry of Information concerned with overseas propaganda.
4 Christopher Andrew, *The Defence of the Realm: The Authorized History of MI5*, London: Allen Lane 2009, pp. 134, 222.
5 Nigel West, ed., *The Guy Liddell Diaries*, vol. I: *1939–1942*, vol. II: *1942–1945*, London: Routledge 2005.
6 'The Work of F2b (formerly B4b) in Wartime', The National Archives [TNA], KV4/57, p. 8.
7 Cf. West, *Liddell Diaries*, vol. I, pp. 20–1.
8 See Wolfgang zu Putlitz, *The Putlitz Dossier*, London: Allan Wingate 1957, p. 163.
9 Curry, *The Security Service 1908–1945*, pp. 190–2. See also West, *Liddell Diaries*, vol. I, pp. 62–6.

11

The internment of 'enemy aliens'

With the outbreak of war, all German and Austrian refugees in Britain were transformed overnight into 'enemy aliens', and therefore regarded as potential enemy agents. During the First World War, the British government had introduced general internment of 'enemy aliens' and MI5 had advocated a similar policy in any new conflict, 'largely because it saw no practicable alternative'.[1] However, the government initially decided against mass internment. Instead the Home Office announced a policy of review, under which 'enemy aliens' were to appear before specially constituted tribunals that were required to place them into one of three categories, according to the degree of risk they were judged to represent: 'A' (to be interned), 'B' (exempt from internment, but subject to restrictions) and 'C' (exempt from internment and restrictions).

MI5 was dismayed: in its world view, all Germans were *ipso facto* potential spies. Although some ninety per cent of German and Austrian refugees in Britain were Jews, MI5 considered them no less German for being Jewish. Against the background of war, MI5's attitude towards 'enemy aliens' was extremely hawkish, as a diary entry by Guy Liddell confirms:

> I discussed this morning with Eric Holt-Wilson and Patrick Cooper (of the Ministry of Supply) the Home Secretary's suggestion that tribunals should be set up to deal with enemy aliens. My personal feeling is that enemy aliens should be interned and they should be called on to show cause why they should be released. From an MI5 point of view, it would be far preferable to have them put away.[2]

All German and Austrian refugees should therefore – so MI5 believed – be interned and required to demonstrate their loyalty to the British cause: that is, they should be assumed guilty until proven innocent. However, this view did not prevail. Liddell noted: 'I was told however that it had already been decided by the Committee of Imperial Defence that internment of all enemy aliens was impossible and undesirable and that there was nothing to be done.' For the moment, the Home Office had won the day. Guy Liddell complained in December 1939 that, as a result of the government's policy, about four-fifths of MI5's time was spent dealing with the problem of aliens.[3]

The Aliens Tribunals began their work in October 1939 and by the end of the year had reviewed some 70,000 cases. The great majority of these, some 64,000, were placed in category 'C'. A few thousand were classified as 'B', and therefore subject to minor restrictions, although left at liberty, but only 569 'enemy aliens' were placed in category 'A' and therefore interned as a risk to British security. Overwhelmingly, however, Austrian and German refugees were left to continue their daily lives as normal, a state of affairs which lasted several months.

Frustrated in its desire for mass internment, MI5 concentrated on securing the internment of key individuals. Following the disclosures by Walter Krivitsky in January 1940, MI5 was more convinced than ever of the need to intern 'leading foreign communists', lobbying the Home Office to this effect:

> MI5 sent to the Home Office a memorandum on the attitude of MI5 towards Communism. This described the collaboration between the German and Russian intelligence services, and stressed the dangers of allowing Communist émigrés to enter the UK as 'refugees from Nazi oppression' when some of them are in reality agents of the Comintern who have been carefully trained in illegal work. It was suggested that the leading foreign Communists should be immediately interned, and a list of them was given.[4]

Among the Communists on this list were Jürgen Kuczynski and Eva Kolmer, leading lights of the Free German League of Culture and the Austrian Centre respectively. Their cases illustrate both the extent and the limits of MI5's power. Decisions about who was interned or not lay with the Home Office; MI5 could only lobby or recommend – which it certainly did, though not always successfully. MI5 did, however, have one important right. Under the tribunals' terms of reference it was able to submit confidential evidence in cases of particular concern. The individuals concerned were unaware of such evidence and therefore unable to challenge it.

In late 1939 Jürgen Kuczynski appeared before a tribunal, together with other members of the Kuczynski family. He was interned on 20 January 1940 'on the recommendation of the tribunal', although the tribunal's decision was heavily influenced by evidence submitted by MI5. This evidence rested largely on the (correct) assertion that JK was a Communist, citing his support for the World Committee against War and Fascism and his friendship with the 'well known Communist' R.P. Dutt. For good measure, MI5's note added: 'Recently we received a report (which is still under investigation) to the effect that he is assisting in the running of a G.P.U espionage system at Bloomsbury House, the refugee centre.'[5] D.N. Pritt, writing to the Home Office in support of JK's release, ridiculed this 'supposed espionage system in Bloomsbury House': 'I have heard an infinite variety of stories in my time, but never have I heard it suggested that that collection of timid and highly respectable Jews had anything to do with espionage.'[6]

MI5 clearly had no evidence of Kuczynski's real espionage activities, nor those of other members of the family, but its statement that Kuczynski was a member of the KPD sufficed for the tribunal to order his internment. He was sent to Seaton Camp in Devon, which before the war had been a Warner's holiday camp.

At this stage, Kuczynski's detention, some months before the introduction of mass internment, was an exceptional measure. However, he had influential supporters, many of whom wrote to the Home Office to appeal for his release. They included not only Communists such as Will Lawther of the National Union of Mineworkers and the 'Red Dean' of Canterbury, Hewlett Johnson, but also the Liberal MPs Geoffrey Mander and Sir Richard Acland, Labour MPs Harold Laski and George Strauss, and of course the reliable D.N. Pritt.[7]

If MI5 was insulated from British public opinion, the Home Office was not, writing to MI5 of 'the great pressure which is being brought to bear in this case', and asking to be informed 'as early as possible' of the results of investigations the Security Service was conducting into Kuczynski. Memoranda continued to be exchanged between the Home Office and MI5 between February and April 1940 on this subject. Sir Alexander Maxwell at the Home Office noted that the Tribunal's only reason for interning Kuczynski was that he was a Communist, 'but this is not in itself a reason for internment. Unless MI5 have some information beyond what appears in these files, Kuczynski ought to be released without further delay'.[8] Milicent Bagot of MI5 wrote to Valentine Vivian of SIS on 2 April: 'We have a great deal of information about this man taking an active part in anti-British propaganda but we are having some difficulty in convincing the Home Office.' Could Vivian please provide her with additional ammunition, Bagot added, since the Home Office was pressing for Kuczynski's release.[9] Shortly after, the Home Secretary Sir John Anderson wrote to Labour leader Clement Attlee, who had asked a question about Kuczynski in the Commons, informing him that Kuczynski would be released.[10] He was indeed freed on 19 April 1940.

Kuczynski had made good use of his time in internment, having given a series of lectures to fellow-internees, many of whom were Nazis, who at this early stage of internment represented a majority of the prisoners.

His lectures were reportedly 'compelling', engaging his fellow-prisoners and above all impressing the camp commandant, whose report to MI5 was a glowing character reference:

> This man was released yesterday, and if the Director of Enemy Propaganda wants the services of an extremely able man, I think he will find few better than Kuczynski. [...] He left this camp respected alike by the camp officers and the internees, even I think by the Nazis. I repeat, he is a very able man intellectually, and a thoroughly good sort personally. He should be made use of.[11]

MI5 was furious at his release, complaining bitterly that it had been 'over-ruled' by the Home Office. It continued to regard Kuczynski 'as a very dangerous person' and requested a letter intercept on his new address, 6 Lawn Road Flats.

The situation of 'enemy aliens' took a turn for the worse as the war situation suddenly deteriorated. On 10 May 1940, Winston Churchill replaced Neville Chamberlain as Prime Minister. On the same day, Germany attacked Holland and Belgium: in an atmosphere of near panic as the Germans overran the Low Countries, the British government began the large-scale internment of 'enemy aliens'. On 15 May, it ordered the arrest of all 'B' category male refugees, followed, at the end of the month, by the order to intern 'B' category women. Anti-German sentiment was widespread and was further inflamed by newspapers such as the *Daily Mail*, which published wild rumours that the refugees constituted a 'fifth column' which would sabotage British defences and smooth the path for an invasion of Britain.[12]

Worse was to come, following the evacuation of the British Expeditionary Force from Dunkirk and the fall of France: the French surrendered on 22 June. As fears of invasion grew, the government reversed its previous policy, ordering the mass internment of German and Austrian refugees, including 'C' category refugees officially listed as 'victims of Nazi persecution'. The hawks of MI5 had won the day, though it was to prove something of a Pyrrhic victory. The attempt to arrest many thousands of refugees in such a short time resulted in administrative chaos, causing a major diversion of time and effort from the business of fighting the war.

During these first weeks, the introduction of mass internment bore every sign of improvisation. 'Enemy aliens' were arrested by local police and taken to hastily designated local camps. In Edinburgh, for example, the Donaldson School for deaf and dumb children was cleared to act as a temporary holding centre. Elsewhere, several racecourses were pressed into service, including York, Lingfield and Kempton Park, where internees were accommodated in the Tote building and even in the stables. At Prees Heath in Shropshire, where the internees lived under canvas, the conditions deteriorated quickly due to torrential rain. They were even worse at Warth Mills, a derelict cotton mill near Bury in Lancashire, where poor food was matched by squalid and unsanitary conditions. These improvised locations served as transit camps while more permanent accommodation was prepared. The largest transit camp, which continued in use for over a year, was at Huyton, near Liverpool, where the newly built Woodfall Heath housing estate was hastily converted into a camp. The living conditions were fairly primitive. Although the houses had been completed, they had been left empty. The lack of beds or any other furniture meant that prisoners had to sleep in straw sacks on stone floors.

Camps were subject to military jurisdiction. Prisoners found themselves behind barbed wire, guarded by armed soldiers. For several weeks, they were denied newspapers and thus also denied any news of the war: even worse, they were unable to contact family and friends – even to say where they were. Food was often scarce and accommodation woefully inadequate. Conditions only began to improve once internees were moved to more permanent camps, mostly on the Isle of Man.

The introduction of mass internment did not deflect MI5 from its campaign to secure the internment of prominent Communists. In July 1940, as mass internment reached its peak, it once again took up the Kuczynski case with the Home Office: 'We presume that Jürgen Kuczynski is included in the general internment of enemy aliens.'[13] But, despite the supposedly damaging evidence MI5 continued to compile against Kuczynski, they presumed wrongly. Protected by his eminent British friends, he remained at liberty then, and indeed for the rest of the war.

At the same time, MI5 had turned its attention to the case of Eva Kolmer, the Secretary of the Austrian Centre – the main organisation representing Austrian refugees. Young, attractive and resourceful, with a host of English friends and contacts, Kolmer had quickly become the public face of the Austrian Centre and its main link to the British authorities. She was also an object of great suspicion to MI5, which made repeated requests to have her interned. Indeed the correspondence on the desirability of interning Kolmer, like that regarding Kuczynski, runs throughout her Security file.

On 1 May 1940, well before the implementation of mass alien internment, MI5 wrote to the Home Office on the possible internment of Communist refugees and, in a letter that clearly indicated official differences in attitude, drew a distinction between the Communist rank and file and the leadership:

> As regards Communist refugees, knowing your point of view on this matter, I did not advocate any measure of general internment at the present time. The particular persons whom I recommended for internment are all persons who may be regarded as potential leaders and organisers of foreign Communists in the UK. I feel that if these few persons are interned the danger of our having to compete with an organised movement among Communist refugees will be greatly reduced [...] I trust that with these summaries in your possession you will feel the necessity of issuing internment orders in each case.[14]

One of the summaries related to Eva Kolmer who 'in her position at the Austrian Centre [...] has had unbounded opportunities for spreading Communist propaganda among refugees throughout this country', and was indeed doing so, as MI5 had learned 'from a variety of sources'.[15]

A further MI5 letter requesting Kolmer's internment was sent to the Home Office on 6 June,[16] but the Home Office, far from ordering Kolmer's internment, was seriously considering a request she had made, as a representative of a refugee organisation, to visit interned Austrians in the camps. She had indeed been allowed to visit Seaton Camp at the beginning of 1940 but in this case, her application – submitted at the height of the internment furore – was turned down. With reference to her application, MI5 noted pointedly:

> We have twice recommended that this woman should be interned [...] If the Home Office care to accept our recommendation, Miss Kolmar [*sic*] will have ample opportunity to carry on her work among refugees inside an internment camp.[17]

In July, MI5 returned with further allegations against Kolmer – 'now regarded as one of the most efficient Communist agents amongst Austrians in this country'[18] – only to be told that the Home Office 'have insufficient evidence on which to intern [her]'. In fact, like other officials of the Austrian Centre, Kolmer was never interned, a source of great chagrin to MI5.

Despite this, the process of mass internment continued unabated. Also interned were some four thousand Italians, who were transformed into 'enemy aliens' after Mussolini's belated declaration of war, on 10 June 1940. Prime Minister Churchill, when asked *which* Italians should be interned, had given the brutal and much quoted reply: 'Collar the lot!'

Meanwhile, the internment of Germans and Austrians was proceeding steadily. By the beginning of July, many internees had been dispersed to camps on the Isle of Man, most of which had become more permanent facilities. At the height of the internment crisis some 25,000 men and 4,000 women had been interned, but even as the process reached its peak, the tide was already beginning to turn.

One of the most infamous measures of the whole internment episode was the deportation of several thousand men to Australia and Canada. In fact, only one ship, the *Dunera*, went to Australia. The shameful mistreatment of prisoners on board by the crew and the military escort, who deprived them of food and looted their luggage, caused a major scandal. The commanding officer and two of his subordinates were eventually brought before a court martial.

Of four ships which set sail to take internees to Canada, only three arrived. On 2 July 1940, the former cruise liner *Arandora Star* was transporting 1,200 German, Austrian and Italian internees across the Atlantic when it was torpedoed and sunk by a German submarine with the loss of some 650 lives. Public and parliamentary disquiet at this incident was so great that deportations effectively ceased shortly after. By the end of July, plans were being made for the phased release of internees, as the government issued a White Paper, setting out various categories under which prisoners could apply for release.[19] The first releases began in August 1940 and by the end of the year almost a third of 'enemy aliens' had been freed. MI5 bitterly opposed both the scale and speed of such releases, but was unable to do much about it.

'By the time of the fall of France', so John Curry recorded, 'the organisation of the Security Service as a whole was in a state which can only be described as chaotic.'[20] Curry attributed this chaos largely to understaffing, and a consequent inability to deal with the problem of internment, but a further reason was certainly inadequate leadership. On 10 June 1940, the day Italy declared war on Britain, the Director of MI5, Major-General Sir Vernon Kell, was summarily dismissed from the Service he had founded and moulded very much in his own image. He was summoned by Sir Horace Wilson, head of the Civil Service, and told 'it had been decided to make certain changes' in the management of MI5. Kell's deputy, Sir Eric Holt-Wilson resigned in protest; the unfortunate Kell was dead within two years. Churchill appointed Jasper Harker, head of 'B' Division, as Kell's successor, a job for which he was manifestly unsuited.

MI5 continued to argue for the need to maintain mass internment, but Harker proved a less than skilful advocate for this viewpoint, advising the Security Executive, for example, that German and Austrian domestic servants should not be released, because 'experience had shown that [they] were not always as harmless as they appeared'.[21] Harker too was removed and replaced by Sir David Petrie, who became Director General in April 1941.[22] Harker himself was not dismissed but became Petrie's Deputy.

Throughout the internment crisis, MI5 was therefore in a state of disorganisation and low morale. Faced with the steady release of internees, it tried to salvage what it could from the situation, dispatching MI5 officers to conduct interrogations within the camps. Claud Sykes, for example, had already visited Huyton Camp and various camps on the Isle of Man as early as July 1940, returning there in November. As we shall show, many of the informers from within the refugee community were recruited at this time.

MI5 also did its best to delay the process of release as long as possible on the grounds that some of those set free posed a security threat. There were, however, limits to MI5's ability to intervene: the Home Office still remained the 'releasing authority'. The Security Service found an unlikely ally in Sir Herbert Emerson, the League of Nations Commissioner for Refugees, who, following a visit to internment camps on the Isle of Man, took the view that 'some men have been released who would have been better in internment'. This view was enthusiastically endorsed by MI5's Theodore ('Ted') Turner: 'Our experience confirms [this] statement. It is hoped that under the new arrangements to refer *all* applicants for release to MI5, recurrences of these unfortunate happenings will be rare.'[23] Turner, head of the newly created 'E' Division (Aliens Control) also sat on the 'Swinton Committee', which eventually agreed 'that the point had now been reached where every application for release should be thoroughly considered by the Security Service, even at the risk of some delay.'[24] By then it was too late. In March 1941, MI5 had managed to appoint Major Armitage as Senior Intelligence Officer on the Isle of Man, to whom Camp Intelligence Officers had to report and through whom all applications for release were to be channelled. Armitage wrote some 'Notes for Intelligence Officers' which included advice on how to spot 'likely informants' among the internees, though he had to concede that 'not many are now left'.[25] The numbers of internees had indeed declined dramatically: by August 1941, a year after the first releases, only 1,300 refugees remained in captivity. Many of those released, including some Communists, were drafted into British war industries.

MI5's efforts to delay the process of release were therefore largely unsuccessful, but in one respect they did prevail: in keeping known Communists interned far longer than the average. It also managed to ensure that specific internees – the most urgent or intransigent cases – were transferred from the Isle of Man to Camp 001 in London where special interrogations took place.[26]

As early as November 1939, 'batches from different camps' were brought to London on a weekly basis, and 'questioned at intervals' by MI5 officers.[27] At this point, these 'batches' comprised Category 'A' internees of whom the Security Service was particularly watchful. There were decided advantages in conducting interrogations at the Oratory Schools, so MI5 informed MI6, which 'consist in the psychological effect and the presence of a fairly reliable stool-pigeon'.[28] To save on escorts to and from London, internees were brought up in groups from the Isle of Man and elsewhere, arriving on a Tuesday and returning on a Friday (for reasons of efficiency the Home Office enjoined MI5 to clear as many cases as possible between Tuesday and Friday).[29]

While some of the approximately 600 enemy aliens in category 'A' had received their 'A' classification for good reason, others had been woefully miscategorised. The Jewish refugee Heinz-Alex Nathan was one of these, having had the misfortune back in 1935 to be implicated, in the eyes of the British authorities, in the case of Dora Fabian and Mathilde Wurm. At the request of MI5, Nathan was arrested on 12 September 1939 and interned in Seaton Camp before being interrogated at the Oratory School on 6 December by the formidable MI5 officer, Lieutenant-Colonel Robin 'Tin-Eye' Stephens. It is evident from the transcript of the interrogation that Stephens concluded that Nathan (as an ex-Communist) was politically unreliable, a 'shifty customer' and even a 'suspected Gestapo agent'. Since, moreover, as a homosexual and a schoolmaster, Nathan had to be denied any 'opportunities for perversion', Stephens recommended his continued internment.[30] As a result of MI5's intervention, Nathan remained interned until August 1943, far longer than the average Jewish internee.

Another internee about whom MI5 was particularly uneasy was the prominent Communist Wilhelm Koenen, who had been brought back from Canada to the Isle of Man in December 1941 and transferred to the Oratory Schools following representations for his release by MPs Eleanor Rathbone and D.N. Pritt. On 26 February 1942, Koenen appeared before the Home Office Advisory Committee under Cecil J.B. Hurst who reported back to MI5 that Koenen 'was an interesting fellow'.[31] The Committee had asked for assurances that Koenen would stand loyally by the Allied cause, regardless of the state of relations between Germany and the Soviet Union, and having received such an assurance, had recommended his release. MI5, it was noted further, would not oppose Koenen's release if he gave an undertaking not to take part in politics while in Britain; this Koenen gave.[32] Unsurprisingly, he spent the remainder of his time in Britain involved in the activities of the KPD in exile (though not in British politics).

Ludwig Baruch, who had lived in Britain since 1928, most recently working for the Donegal Tweed Company, was also interned in Camp 001 following his return from Canada in late 1942. This was indeed his second confinement there, his first having been in 1939, so that he was able to compare conditions then with those he had experienced earlier. In a letter to his fiancée, intercepted by MI5, he wrote:

> The place is awful, although not quite as bad as it was 3 years ago. It is like a prison and I did not see the sun whilst there, only the reflection on the high grim walls [...] The worst was the lack of food, I have not felt so terribly hungry for many a day. I rather not talk about hygiene, especially the conditions of the blankets.[33]

Though it was noted in an unknown hand that other Camp 001 internees had made the same allegations regarding food and hygiene, these were officially denied by the Intelligence Officer.[34]

MI5 did have its successes, however, such as Ludwig Max Warschauer, who was interrogated at the Oratory Schools over several weeks in summer 1942. Warschauer had previously played a leading role in Hutchinson Internment Camp, setting up the highly successful Technical School and the Language School and becoming the Camp Commander's right-hand man. Although Jewish, he generally denied his Jewishness. Warschauer made two applications for release and in August 1941 he appeared before the Advisory Committee which recommended he be released as actively friendly to the Allied cause. MI5 thought differently and transferred him to the Oratory Schools. Under interrogation, Warschauer admitted that, although he had come to Britain ostensibly as a refugee, he had in fact been sent there for industrial espionage purposes by the German Intelligence Service. But he had not attempted to carry out this mission, he insisted. Warschauer remained in internment for the rest of the war, when he was informed he would be repatriated to Germany – a fate against which, as a 'Jewish refugee', he protested strongly though unsuccessfully.[35]

In the last thirty years, after four decades of silence, much has been written about the internment of 'enemy aliens' in the Second World War. While historians are generally united in considering internment an arbitrary and unnecessary measure that failed to achieve its stated objectives, little has been said about the role of MI5 in this sorry episode, mainly because the relevant files have only recently become available. A reading of the files suggests that MI5's political judgement was wrong, its advice to government frequently mistaken and its attitude unbending. MI5 historians have reached different conclusions. John Curry's in-house history glosses internment as merely a contributory factor to the administrative chaos within MI5 in 1939–40. Christopher Andrew, writing an official history over sixty years later, is more circumspect, but views internment from the same perspective. Both accounts leave the impression that – like the courtiers of Louis XVIII – MI5 has forgotten nothing and learned nothing.

Notes

1 Christopher Andrew, *The Defence of the Realm: The Authorized History of MI5*, London: Allen Lane 2009, p. 222.

2 Nigel West, ed., *The Guy Liddell Diaries*, vol. I *1939–1942*, vol. 2 *1942–1945*, London: Routledge 2005, entry for 30 August 1939, p. 12.

3 Andrew, *Defence of the Realm*, p. 222.

4 Internal memo, dated 30 April 1940, The National Archives [TNA], KV2/1010.

5 'Observations of MI5 on Case of Kuczynski, Jürgen', 27 December 1939, TNA, KV2/1871/15a.
6 Extracts from letter to Home Office (HO) from D.N. Pritt, dated 22 January 1940, TNA, KV2/1871/68a.
7 For the long list of Kuczynski's supporters, see 'HO file K4790 re Jürgen Kuczynski, 13 February1940', TNA, KV2/1871/68a.
8 Copy of letter from Maxwell, 16 March 1940, HO File re Kuczynski, TNA, KV2/1871/73h.
9 Bagot to Vivian, 2 April 1940, TNA, KV2/1871/75a.
10 Extract from HO file, Sir John Anderson to Mr Attlee, 8 April 1940, TNA, KV2/1872/79a.
11 TNA, KV2/1872/85ab.
12 Cf. G. Ward Price in *Daily Mail*, 24 May 1940.
13 Draft minute, MI5 to HO, 8 July 1940, TNA, KV2/1872/79a.
14 Extract from letter 're foreign Communists', MI5 to HO [Sir Alexander Maxwell], 1 May 1940, TNA, KV2/2517/ 85b.
15 Draft minute, MI5 to HO, 8 July 1940, TNA, KV2/1872/79a.
16 Letter not present in file but referred to in internal MI5 correspondence, 27 June 1940, TNA, KV2/2517/93a.
17 See internal MI5 documentation, *ibid.*
18 Draft minute (White to HO), 30 July 1940, TNA, KV2/2517/96a.
19 'German and Austrian Civilian Internees: Categories of Persons Eligible for Release from Internment and Procedures to be followed in applying for Release', Cmd. 6217, July1940. A slightly revised version of the White Paper was issued in August in response to initial reaction.
20 John Court Curry, *The Security Service 1908–1945: The Official History*, London: Public Record Office 1999, p. 163.
21 Andrew, *Defence of the Realm*, p. 230.
22 Kell and Harker both had the title of 'Director'; Petrie became MI5's first Director-General.
23 Confidential memo from Sir Herbert Emerson, 15 January 1941; note by T.F. Turner, 6 February 1941, TNA, KV4/335/16a.
24 Minutes of the Home Defence Security Executive, item 2, 'Camp Intelligence', 23 April 1941, TNA, KV4/335/27a.
25 'Notes for Intelligence Officers', n.d., TNA, KV4/335/41b.
26 'Camp 001', housed at the Oratory Central Schools in Stewart Grove, Fulham Rd, London SW3, was used only for interrogating male internees; female internees were questioned at Holloway Prison.
27 'Internees', internal MI5 memorandum, 13 November 1939, TNA, KV4/324/6a (i).
28 S. Bingham (MI5) to SIS, 26 June 1941, TNA, KV4/324/46c.
29 HO to MI5, 30 May 1941, TNA, KV4/324/41a.
30 See 'Nathan, Heinz Alexander. Interrogation 6.12.39', TNA, KV2/1743/40a, and 'Observations of M.I.5 on the case of Heinz Alexander Nathan', 10 December 1939, TNA, KV2/1743/41a.

31 Cecil Hurst to MI5, 5 March 1942, TNA, KV2/2799/162a.
32 'Interned Enemy Aliens Tribunal, Category 19', 3 March 1942, TNA, KV2/2799/165a.
33 Intercepted letter from Baruch to fiancée Miss H. Froom, 21 November 1942, TNA, KV4/325/96a.
34 Denial dated 7 December 1992, in *ibid.*
35 MI5's reports on Max Ludwig Warschauer are contained in TNA, KV2/1139–42. Warschauer also reappears in semi-fictional form as the sinister Schlick in Richard Friedenthal's novel on life in Hutchinson Camp, *Die Welt in der Nussschale* (The World in a Nutshell), Munich: Piper 1956.

12

'The largest Communist sideshow in London': the Free German League of Culture

The Freie Deutsche Kulturbund or Free German League of Culture (FGLC) was founded in London in December 1938 by German refugees from Hitler as, to quote its constitution, 'a German, anti-Nazi, antifascist non-party refugee organisation', aiming to preserve and advance Free German culture. The first – high profile – honorary co-presidents of the League were the artist Oskar Kokoschka, the theatre critic Alfred Kerr, the world-famous author Stefan Zweig and the film director Berthold Viertel. Of these, only Kokoschka remained in his position throughout the seven years of the League's existence. The emphasis on cultural rather than political aims reflected the restrictions on overt political activity imposed on refugees by the British government. For the League, and its Austrian counterpart, the Austrian Centre, cultural associations were also a surrogate for political activity: politics by other means.[1]

The League quickly attracted the attention of MI5 which, together with Special Branch, kept it and its leading activists under close surveillance.[2] From the outset, the intelligence services perceived Communist influence within the League. A Special Branch report in December 1939 described it as 'an organisation which aims to arrange lectures and other events on artistic and literary matters but is more or less recognised to foster communist sympathies among refugees and British subjects.'[3] MI5 was more reductive, calling it 'a communist front organisation', a phrase repeated in various reports.

The truth was more nuanced: the League was founded as a typical product of the Popular Front period, its activities calculated to appeal to the widest possible audience. The composition of the Executive Committee elected to run the business of the League was significant: of eight members, only three – the actor Gerhard Hinze, the composer Ernst Hermann Meyer and the Secretary Hans Schellenberger, a former teacher – were known members of the KPD. The elected Chairman was the artist Fred Uhlman, a known Social Democrat.

At its peak, the League had some 1,500 members. Membership was open to anyone who agreed with its aims, but it was largely unsuccessful in increasing its numbers despite various attempts to publicise its programme and broaden its appeal. However, its policy of open recruitment made it easy for Special Branch and MI5 to infiltrate informers into the organisation. Most of the reports on the League in MI5 files came from informants within the refugee community. They included the self-styled Austrian aristocrat Josef Otto von Laemmel (code-named 'Kaspar'), ex-communists like the journalist Rudolf Moeller-Dostali as well as the politically unaligned like Karl Otten.[4] However, perhaps the most prolific informant on the League was the writer Kurt Hiller who wrote a series of reports denouncing it as a 'camouflaged Communist organisation'. Ten years later – and several years after the League had ceased to exist – he was still damning it as 'a Russian invention'.[5]

An early target of Hiller's was Jürgen Kuczynski, the KPD's British organiser, who was remarkably frank in his support for the Party line, his comments soon finding their way back to MI5:

> Today I got the opportunity in the Coffee Corner of the Kulturbund [...] to meet Dr. K[uczynski]. A political discussion developed of which I would report the following: The Stalinist Treaty policy with Germany [i.e. the Nazi-Soviet Pact] is, according to Kuczynski, the only way of ensuring a new and free Germany for the future. Europe must be prevented above all from falling under an English domination.

Advocating an end to the 'imperialist' war, Kuczynski had allegedly continued:

> The people of the belligerent countries have it in their power to decide when peace shall be reached. For, if munitions are exhausted, no one can go on fighting. [...] With his last remark [...] he wished, no doubt, to hint at the possibility of sabotage and strikes etc. in important war industries.[6]

Kuczynski's lack of discretion is surprising, particularly in a man who had already been interned once, but despite his outspoken rhetoric the League itself remained circumspect. On the outbreak of war, it sent an open letter to *The Times*, thanking the British people for their help and hospitality 'in this grave hour'.[7] In a memorandum to the Ministry of Information, it went further, offering its services to Britain in any capacity. MI5 remained sceptical, warning that the Kulturbund 'is in close touch with the CPGB [...] Offers of help, therefore, from this organisation should be treated with reserve'.[8]

In its internal communications, MI5 was even more dismissive:

> The largest Communist sideshow in London appears to be the KULTURBUND [i.e. the FGLC] which is very well camouflaged. Pretending to cater for cultural activities, this organisation has acquired a façade of respectable names such as the writer Heinrich Mann, but these persons are kept in total ignorance of the KULTURBUND's real purpose.[9]

The report listed it among 'organisations which should be watched' – as indeed it was. An (unnamed) MI5 agent, posing as a journalist interested in refugee matters, paid a visit to the League three weeks later. The young woman who welcomed him was 'very quick to tell me about the support they had received from the Ecclesiastical Commissioners and prominent personages in the Church, including, of course, the Bishop of Chichester', though he found her statements 'a little too pat'.[10]

An early report by Kurt Hiller attacked the political neutrality of the Kulturbund as a mere façade to hoodwink the authorities – and its English friends:

> Last Sunday the Kulturbund held an Anglo-German Friendship evening. 80 English people were invited and many Germans were present. [...] The programme was outstandingly neutral. E.H. Meyer and Käte Forster played music from Beethoven and Schubert, Agnes Bernell[e] sang one or two songs, [the artist] Kurt Lade did some quick sketches. Then the English actor Walter Hudd, who is one of the patrons of the Kulturbund, read from a book by a German author who goes under the pseudonym Jan Petersen who is at present interned in Canada [...] As I have said, yesterday's meeting was of a purely harmless nature and was obviously intended to further the friendship of the English guests to whom, by the omission of everything revolutionary and communistic, they wished to demonstrate free German culture.[11]

Among Hiller's subsequent targets were the main officers of the League, including its Chairman, the Austrian writer Hans Flesch:

> According to what I have heard [...] Dr. Flesch is not a party member. [He] can perhaps be described as a kind of ideal Communist [...] In all his remarks, lectures and discussions, this political outlook of his is quite apparent. Further, Flesch is an enthusiastic friend of the Soviet Union and a fervent admirer of Stalin. [...] His chairmanship of the Kulturbund results in his being a catspaw of the Communists who use him as they do many others, as window dressing.[12]

One pointer to government policy against Communists and Communist sympathisers at this time is provided by the BBC, for which Hans Flesch worked as a translator/announcer with the German Service. Flesch was interned in 1940 – even though his work for the BBC officially gave him exemption. Once released from internment, Flesch was dismissed by the BBC, supporting himself and his wife by working as a kitchen-hand in a Lyons Corner House (an experience which he called 'Germany's biggest humiliation'), and later in a Walls ice-cream factory. After some months, he applied to the BBC for reinstatement and was told that he could resume his old job in the German Service – provided he resigned as Chairman of the League. In the circumstances, Flesch unwillingly agreed to do so: 'It made my heart ache, but on the other hand I was happy to be rid of the responsibility. In the middle of the war there began for me a very quiet time.'[13]

The crucial argument that MI5 deployed against the League was that it used lectures and other cultural events to spread Communist propaganda. In fact, its lecture programme, while anti-fascist, was fairly catholic in its appeal, perhaps deliberately so. Nonetheless, informants such as Hiller were able to single out lectures by suspect figures like John Heartfield and Jürgen Kuczynski who certainly gave a Marxist interpretation of their subject matter. In March 1941, Kuczynski gave what was described as a brilliant lecture on 'Dichtung und Wahrheit der Statistik' (Fact and Fiction in Statistics), using his material for propaganda ends. According to what MI5 called 'a reliable source' (actually the ever-present Kurt Hiller), Kuczynski was also able to inspire his audience: during subsequent discussion, the meeting was transformed into 'a committee of enthusiasm for the Soviet Union.'[14]

Hiller also reported on other leading figures in the League, such as Helmut Herzfeld, better known as the artist John Heartfield. Heartfield had adopted an English pseudonym during the First World War in protest against Prussian militarism. He had been a founder member of the KPD in 1919 and, together with George Grosz and Raoul Hausmann, had helped to found the Dada movement in Berlin. In the 1930s, he became widely known as the German pioneer of photomontage, a technique he used particularly in cartoons ridiculing Hitler and the Nazis.

When he arrived in Britain in December 1938, Heartfield was stateless, having been expatriated by the Nazis. He had been rescued from Prague with the help of the British Committee for Refugees from Czechoslovakia, entering Britain on an interim Czech passport. His name was already known to MI5 and his entry was not automatic: 'The name of Helmut Herzfeld appeared on the list of Communist refugees from Czechoslovakia who were at first refused admission to this country and subsequently allowed to come for two months only.'[15] In fact, Heartfield was to remain in Britain until 1950.

Heartfield was arrested and interned in July 1940, but spent barely six weeks in internment (though passing through three separate camps). His case was raised in the House of Commons and, following parliamentary questions from the MPs Ellen Wilkinson and Eleanor Rathbone, he was released on 26 August on medical grounds. (He suffered from a rare form of epilepsy.) His release displeased MI5, which recommended that he be re-interned, advice the Home Office declined to follow.[16]

The charismatic Heartfield was well known among his fellow-refugees for his overtly political, anti-Nazi photomontages, but as an avowed Communist, he had difficulty in publishing his work in Britain; only isolated examples appeared in *Picture Post*, *Lilliput* and the Cooperative-owned newspaper *Reynolds News*. However, this left him free to play an active role in the League. He created stage designs for the League's Little Theatre, designed book covers for its publications and regularly gave lectures on art, such as 'Wie ich den Dadaismus erlebte' (My experience of Dadaism).[17] In addition, he wrote articles for the League's journal *Freie Deutsche Kultur* (Free German Culture), including a lengthy tribute to his role model, the caricaturist Honoré Daumier.[18]

In June 1941, the League held an exhibition in celebration of Heartfield's fiftieth birthday, displaying a selection of his photomontages from the *Arbeiter-Illustrierte Zeitung*. Heartfield himself gave the introductory address, describing the evolution of photomontage from photography. Among those in the audience was Kurt Hiller, who reported that Heartfield had demonstrated 'how he and his fellow-workers had always used [photomontage] in the service of the truth (as the Communists understand it) and how great a part this could play in social and revolutionary struggles'.[19]

The allegation that the League was a Communist front entered the public domain in May 1941 when a statement by the Trades Union Council contending that the League was controlled by Communists appeared in the (trades union-controlled) *Daily Herald*.[20] The story's publication caused English supporters of the League to mount a staunch defence of its independence and cultural importance, answering the story with a letter of protest, signed by E.M. Forster, Storm Jameson, Ralph Vaughan Williams and others, which appeared in *The Manchester Guardian*, *Reynolds News* and *New Statesman*. The argument was short-lived, undercut by the Nazi invasion of the Soviet Union, transforming that country overnight into a war ally.

Another prominent figure in the League who was regularly monitored by the security services was the actor Gerhard Hinze: 'Born 2/1/1904; height about 6'1" [1m86]; well built, hair fair, turning grey (brushed back); eyes grey; complexion fresh; now clean shaven; smartly dressed.' Such was the description of Hinze given by Sergeant G.R.A. Smith of Special Branch who added: 'I know this man well.'[21] He certainly did. Hinze had been under surveillance as a suspected Communist since his arrival in Britain. When he arrived at Harwich on 17 May 1938, he was initially refused leave to land, but was finally given a visa for one month 'on condition that he does no work, paid or unpaid'.[22] That he was permitted to land at all was only due to the late intercession of the Labour MP, Ellen Wilkinson, who agreed to stand as his guarantor.[23]

Hinze was a founder member of the League, a member of its Executive Committee and Chairman of the Actors' Section. MI5 kept him under close observation, reporting that he was living 'with a woman who is alleged to be one half Russian and who is not married to him. [...] It seems that Hinze lives on his 'wife's' earnings and on what he can get from Bloomsbury House.'[24] Questions of propriety soon gave way to those of security. In common with other refugees, Hinze was required to appear before an Aliens Tribunal, which placed him in Class 'B' – presumably because of his sojourn in the Soviet Union. On 12 May 1940, the government began the process of general alien internment, beginning with those in Class 'B'. Hinze was arrested on 16 May, police swooping on his home at 31 Boundary Road, London NW8.

Hinze was interned on the Isle of Man, being held in Central Promenade Camp, Douglas, but surveillance did not end there. An MI5 agent, almost certainly Claud Sykes, who visited the camp, reported:

> A Communist called Hinse [*sic*] and the notorious Colonel Kahle (GPU chief in Madrid during the Spanish Civil War, according to information I received at various times) gave a lot of trouble in the camp, according to [Martin] Sander, and everyone was relieved when they went off to Canada. They should be carefully watched there.[25]

Hinze was deported to Canada on the former troopship *SS Ettrick*, which sailed from Liverpool on 3 July, the first such ship to make the crossing since the sinking of the *Arandora Star*. Among others travelling on the *SS Ettrick* were the prominent Communist Hans Kahle and the atomic scientist Klaus Fuchs.

Like others from the *Ettrick*, Hinze was initially held in Camp L, outside Quebec City. In October, the men were dispersed to different camps. Hinze was moved to Camp A at Farnham in Quebec province, where he formed a highly active drama group. He organised a reading of Goethe's *Faust*, and directed a performance of R.C. Sheriff's *Journey's End*, followed by Chekov's *The Proposal*, in which the leading role was played by the young actor Anton Diffring, whose later roles would include a portrayal of the Nazi architect of the Final Solution, Reinhard Heydrich.

During this time, Hinze's MI5 file continued to grow. In Farnham Camp, he was reported to be on friendly terms with the former Communist member of the Reichstag Wilhelm Koenen; with Koenen and others, he presented a letter to the Camp Commandant protesting against being interned together with Nazi Germans. As a result, they were transferred to Camp S, a detention centre for Italian Fascists, and released only after representations in the House of Commons by Ellen Wilkinson.

Hinze was finally released from Camp S on 5 November 1941 and shipped back to Britain. Fifty internees from this shipment, including Hinze, were supposed to be re-interned on the Isle of Man while their cases were reviewed, but were actually released in Liverpool by mistake.[26] Hinze was later officially released under Category 19 of the government White Paper, covering those who had 'consistently taken a public and prominent part in opposition to the Nazi system'.

Once freed, Hinze lost no time in resuming his role at the League. His file contains a report on a meeting of the Actors' Group in January 1942, chaired by Hinze, which concerned 'efforts being made to affiliate members of the actors group to Equity'. The (anonymous) informant reported:

> Hinze made it clear that, as far as the FDK [i.e. the League] was concerned, this represented a first-class opportunity for penetration of Equity by alien Communists and pressed the point that every effort must be made by all Party sympathisers to approach and, if possible, infiltrate into British Trade Unions.

The report continued:

> As regards Hintze [*sic*] himself, it is stated by a source not given to exaggeration that he is a very good-looking man of his type, with a great deal of personal charm, good manners and intelligence. Source considers he is well-versed in Communist tactics and rates him as one of the most intelligent members [...] of the Kulturbund.[27]

Appearing before the Interned Enemy Aliens Tribunal on 1 January 1942, Hinze had denied that he was a Party member, insisting: 'I was never an organised communist [...] I am not a member of the Communist Party'.[28] The security services clearly dismissed such evasion. A Special Branch report over a year later reiterated that Hinze was a member of the German Communist Party in Britain, having joined it in 1930, and noted his association with 'Dr. Ernst H. Meyer and other prominent communists in Berlin'.[29]

MI5 had paid only fitful attention to Ernst Hermann Meyer since his arrival in Britain, considering him a suspected Communist whose main interest was in music. Shortly after the outbreak of war, his name appeared as a signatory to the League's declaration, offering its services to the British government, prompting a flurry of interest from the security services. Meyer had been a founder member of the League; he was to remain a key figure throughout its seven-year existence.

Although Meyer was a member of the Executive Committee of the League, his most influential role was as Chairman of the Musicians' Section. As such, he was responsible for programming and organising musical performances, thus commanding the outstanding asset in the League's cultural portfolio: the German classical musical heritage and its unique place in the European concert repertoire. The League's musical programme was extensive, offering both regular concert performances and an accompaniment to many of its other events. Music enabled it to unite its disparate membership around cultural common ground, reminding exiles of their musical heritage. Equally importantly, music was an international language, speaking to a British public across the divide of exile.

The power of music to inspire and reassure its audience is exemplified by the daily lunchtime concerts organised by Dame Myra Hess at the National Gallery, which continued throughout the war and were recognised as an important boost to public morale. In recognition of this unique contribution to the war effort, Myra Hess was made a Dame of the British Empire in 1942. Moreover, the most popular composers for these concerts were Bach, Mozart and Beethoven: respect for the German musical tradition evidently transcended the state of war between Britain and Germany. The League's early concerts were held at its clubhouse in Upper Park Road, but they proved so popular that many subsequent concerts were held at larger outside halls, particularly the Wigmore Hall, which became a favourite venue for refugee audiences. Meyer was particularly skilful in the use of music as cultural propaganda. In May 1941, for example, the League put on a concert of music by Mahler at the Wigmore Hall to mark the thirtieth anniversary of the composer's death. The propaganda value of the concert was of course that Mahler was a banned composer in the Third Reich.

After the Nazi invasion of the Soviet Union in June 1941, the League's musical programme increasingly shaded into overt political propaganda. Meyer had come to the attention of Special Branch in October 1941 as the conductor of a choir of thirty, 'singing songs of freedom' at the Austrian Centre. Thereafter, he regularly came to notice as the organiser of 'brilliant concerts and similar activities to publicise the FDKB [i.e. the League] and to secure influential support from "intellectuals"'.[30] One such concert noted by Special Branch was 'the great international concert, entitled 'Music of the Allies', held at Wigmore Hall on 22 February 1942,[31] an event allowing the Free Germans to stake their claim to a place in the international alliance against Nazism.

Throughout 1942, the League's cultural agenda provided an eloquent counterpoint to political events. In June, for example, it mounted an ambitious event at the Hampstead Everyman Theatre to mark the first anniversary of the German invasion of Russia. There were readings of literary texts, ranging from Pushkin to Mayakovsky, and of political speeches by Churchill and Stalin. The performance was punctuated by the music of Rimsky-Korsakov and Khachaturian, and ended with the playing of both the British and Soviet national anthems.

Meanwhile Special Branch was pursuing a different narrative. In August 1940, Meyer had joined the Realist Film Unit, a production company set up by Ralph Bond to make documentary films for the Ministry of Information and other official bodies. The Unit, based at 47 Oxford Street, had already incurred the suspicion of Special Branch which reported, 'there seems little doubt that it is a rendezvous for communists', adding that Ralph Bond 'is now earning a princely salary through film work for the Ministry of Information.' It concluded: 'There is very little doubt that

Bond and Meyer are in very close political contact [and are] both connected with the Realist Film Unit. This film centre also houses Ivor Montagu, the well-known Communist.'[32]

MI5 began to receive regular reports on Meyer's work with the Unit from a source listed as GMH, who can be identified as the film-maker G.M. Hoellering. If MI5 was seeking proof of Communist influence, Hoellering's reports must have been a disappointment. They were consistently bland, providing little more than a list of Meyer's film credits. Among Meyer's credits were the soundtrack for a film by Paul Rotha, and the music for two films by the documentary film-maker Len Lye.[33]

Hoellering's reports amply confirm that Meyer enjoyed the confidence and respect of his professional colleagues. In fact, his reputation continued to grow: in May 1942, the Ministry of Information asked him to direct a public information film called 'Mobilise your Scrap', and approached MI5 for security clearance for Meyer to visit a metal salvage dump. MI5 raised no objection, 'provided Meyer does not come into contact with any [...] confidential or secret information or material'.[34] The film, for which Meyer also wrote the music, later appeared under the title 'Dustbin Parade'.

MI5, however, was far more interested in Meyer's political role within the KPD in Britain. In 1940, Meyer had escaped internment – purely by luck, he maintained, though it was almost certainly because of his film work for the Ministry of Information. In the absence of other leading cadres, such as Wilhelm Koenen or Hans Kahle, who had both been interned, Meyer became, almost by default, the leader of the KPD in Britain (a position he ceded to Koenen when the latter finally returned from internment in Canada).

MI5's heightened interest in Meyer made him the subject of frequent reports, but despite this MI5's William Younger complained plaintively that 'we do not know a great deal about this man'.[35] There was no lack of information: indeed, there may have been too much. During 1940–41, MI5 received numerous reports on Meyer, emanating from informants like Hiller, 'Kaspar' and Hoellering.

However, the most knowledgeable was undoubtedly an informant codenamed 'Conquest', who knew Meyer personally – apparently as a fellow-member of the William Morris Musical Society. According to 'Conquest', Meyer was a secret member of the Society's Executive Committee, 'in fact, so secret that he is never circularised of meetings but is invited only through Alan Bush'.[36] Meyer was not only a close friend of Bush's, but was 'absolutely dominated' by him, and would undertake nothing connected with Communist Party activities without Bush's approval. 'Conquest' also reported that Meyer was known in the Party as Peter Baker. However, while acknowledging Meyer's musical talent, 'Conquest' found the idea that he was 'the supreme political leader' of the KPD in Britain 'very surprising', suggesting that he lacked the necessary personal attributes.

> Source ('Conquest') has met Dr. Meyer on several occasions and while Dr. Meyer has appeared to him as being a Marxist, and a very able one, his general conduct has not struck him as being a 'leader'. He is an extremely timid little man, apparently more interested in music than anything else. He is a Master of Arts and a Doctor of Music and has written several books on musicological matters.[37]

Apparent proof of Meyer's role as 'supreme political leader' came to light as the result of a break-in, when an (unnamed) source acquired a list headed 'The Central Committee of the German Communist Party in Great Britain', which described Meyer as the leader of the clandestine Party.

> The source [name redacted] admitted he had procured this information by breaking into the room of Siegbert Kahn at [the Czech Refugee Trust hostel] Canterbury Hall and copying the list of the Central Committee which was in his room.[38]

As a result, MI5 intensified its interest in Meyer. Millicent Bagot, sitting at the centre of MI5's web of information, announced 'extensive action including B8 observation on this man'; Meyer's letters were also intercepted.[39]

In January 1942, Meyer became Chairman of the Free German League of Culture, following the resignation of Hans Flesch.[40] That year was to be one of intense political involvement. As the KPD in Britain moved onto the public stage, Meyer too stepped out of the political shadows, coming to the notice of Special Branch as a speaker at various public meetings organised by the League. One such meeting was held at Conway Hall in June 1942 to protest at the destruction of the village of Lidice, at which Meyer took the Chair;[41] another was a meeting of protest at the Nazi persecution of the Jews, held at Stern Hall on 1 December 1942.

Despite such public appearances, Meyer's profile remained indistinct, the subject of conflicting information. 'Kaspar' professed to know that he was a candidate for party membership, though GMH asserted that he was not a member of the party at all. Another [anonymous] source asserted that he had been a member of the party since 1931, while yet another informant [name redacted] insisted that Meyer was an agent of the GPU. Unsurprisingly, a narrative report on Meyer in November 1942 concluded that 'information about [him] is confused and contradictory'.[42]

Meyer continued to combine music with politics. On 31 January 1943, he chaired a rally held by the League at the Stoll Theatre under the programmatic title *We Accuse! Ten Years of Nazi Fascism*. The rally consisted of speeches, recitations and political songs, performed by 'the Massed Choirs of the London Cooperative Society, the Free German League of Culture and the Free German Youth'. Meyer conducted the choirs in singing political songs, including Alan Bush's 'Britain's Part', his own 'Spring Rising', with words by the Communist poet Honor Arundel and Khachaturian's 'Song to Stalin', then much in favour at political meetings.

The FGLC choir was an important instrument of musical propaganda, used for example, at a meeting to celebrate the twenty-sixth birthday of the Red Army on 19 February 1944. Meyer not only ran the FGLC choir from 1940 to 1945, but also conducted the Clapham Cooperative Singers, with whom he rehearsed every Tuesday evening. This choir was well-known in left-wing cultural circles, winning a choral competition held by the Workers Music Association in June 1942. Significantly, these choral activities were those that Meyer recalled most fondly in his memoirs over thirty years later.[43]

As the war in Europe approached its end, MI5 withdrew attention from refugee organisations – though not from Communists. In March 1945, just six weeks before the end of the conflict, it prevented Meyer giving a lecture on music to British troops, telling the Commanding Officer that 'it would be inadvisable to give Meyer employment as a lecturer to troops on general subjects and we feel that he is the type of man it would probably be wiser not to employ at all.'[44]

In the immediate post-war years, the League slowly withered away, as its leading activists (including Heartfield and Meyer) began to return to Germany, many of them to the Soviet Zone of Occupation (the later GDR). Early in 1946, it was decided to dissolve the League. A successor organisation, the Heinrich-Heine-Bund, briefly offered a comparable, if greatly reduced, cultural programme to the still sizeable German refugee community in London, but after less than a year, this too was wound up. MI5, now focused on the demands of the emerging Cold War, had long since lost interest.

Notes

1 For the Free German League of Culture, see Charmian Brinson and Richard Dove, *Politics by Other Means: The Free German League of Culture 1939–1945*, London: Vallentine Mitchell 2010.

2 MI5's organisational files on the Free German League of Culture have not been released to The National Archives (TNA). The following account is based largely on various 'personal files' which *have* been released, notably those on Jürgen Kuczynski (KV2/1871–80), John Heartfield (KV2/1010–11), Gerhard Hinze (KV2/2364–65) and Ernst Hermann Meyer (KV2/3502–3). The file on Hans Flesch-Brunningen (i.e. Hans Flesch) (PF 49007) has been destroyed, although a few items have been cross-posted to other files in the public domain.

3 Special Branch report dated 6 December1939, TNA, KV2/2364.

4 These, and others, are dealt with more fully in Chapter 15.

5 Kurt Hiller, *Rote Ritter: Erlebnisse mit deutschen Kommunisten*, Gelsenkirchen: Ruhr Verlag 1951, p. 95.
6 Report, dated 12 February 1941, source Hi, TNA, KV2/1872/128a.
7 *The Times*, 5 September 1939.
8 MI5 minute to Home Office (HO), 18 September 1939, TNA, KV2/2364/4a.
9 TNA, KV2/1872/92ab.
10 Report re Kulturbund', dated 21 June 1940, original in O.F. 42/9, a file dedicated to the FGLC, not released, copy in John Heartfield's file (PF 47198), TNA, KV2/1010/25b.
11 Unnumbered report B.8 (Sykes) (Source Hi), dated 3 February 1941, TNA, KV2/3502.
12 Report re Dr Hans Flesch (Source Hi), dated 14 March 1941, TNA, KV2/1010/31b. The original copy of this report was on the file held on Hans Flesch (PF 49007), which has been destroyed. Information on Flesch is therefore limited to such cross-postings.
13 Hans Flesch-Brunningen, *Die verführte Zeit: Lebenserinnerungen*, Vienna and Munich: Brandstätter 1988, p. 112.
14 MI5 internal memo: 'note re meeting of the Kulturbund on 7.3.41', TNA KV2/1010/31a.
15 Extract from letter to SIS, forwarded 20 February 1939, TNA, KV2/1010/8b.
16 Memo from MI5 to HO, 1 December 1940, TNA, KV2/1010/28a.
17 *FDKB Nachrichten*, 28 December 1939.
18 John Heartfield, 'Daumier im "Reich"', *Freie Deutsche Kultur*, February 1942.
19 Report, 20 June 1941, Source Hi, TNA, KV2/1010/35b.
20 *Daily Herald*, 3 May 1941. The story's appearance in the *Daily Herald* suggests it can be traced back to the Social Democrats: the SPD journalist Victor Schiff was a well-regarded staff writer at the paper.
21 Special Branch report, 23 March 1944, TNA, KV2/2364/62a.
22 Special Branch report, Harwich, 18 May 1938, TNA, KV2/2364/1a.
23 Richard Dove interview with Joan Rodker, 5 August 2009. Cf. also Hinze to Under-Secretary of State, Aliens Department, 8 September 1941, Gerard Heinz Papers, privately held.
24 Report M11 to B5b, WAY (=William Younger). 25 February 1940, TNA, KV2/2364/7a.
25 'Extract from M/S report following his trip to the Isle of Man', TNA, KV2/2364/15a. M/S was almost certainly Claud W. Sykes.
26 MI5 internal memorandum, E5 (5), TNA, KV2/2364/28a.
27 Report by W.A. Younger (M11) to L/B2, 12 January 1942, TNA, KV2/2364/33a.
28 Transcript of Interview with the Interned Enemy Aliens Tribunal on 1 January 1942, TNA, KV2/2364/33b.
29 Special Branch Report to MI5, 17 May 1943, TNA, KV2/2364/53a.
30 Special Branch report, 27 July 1943, TNA, KV2/3502/96.
31 Extract from Special Branch report, 16 April 1942, TNA, KV2/3502/78a.
32 Special Branch report on Ralph Bond, 29 December 1941, TNA, KV2/3502/58b.

33 Film Report, source GMH, 13 September 1941, TNA, KV2/3502/52a.
34 MoI application and MI5 reply, 11 March 1942, TNA, KV2/3502/71a.
35 B5b (Younger) to B4b (Bagot), 12 June 1941, TNA, KV2/3502/43b.
36 'Conquest's' comments make it easy to deduce that he was a fellow-member of the Executive Committee, though it has not been possible to identify him.
37 Report from B5b (London) ('Conquest') to B8c (Sykes), 9 June 1941, TNA, KV2/3502/43ab.
38 Report E3 (extract), 18 February 1942, TNA, KV2/3502/66b.
39 Bagot to B2, 24 January 1942, TNA, KV2/3502/59a.
40 Special Branch report, 21 January 1942, TNA, KV2/3502/67a.
41 Agent's report, 14 June 1942, TNA, KV2/3502/86b.
42 Narrative Report, November 1942, TNA, KV2/3502/91b.
43 Ernst H. Meyer, *Kontraste. Konflikte: Erinnerungen, Gespräche, Kommentare*, Berlin: Verlag Neue Musik 1979, pp. 201–2.
44 MI5 to Captain Pulley, Eastern Command, 13 March 1945, TNA, KV2/3503/112a.

13

The Austrian Centre – and 'the great Eva'

Of all the organisations founded by the German-speaking exiles in Britain, the Austrian Centre was probably the most successful, both in terms of its number of members and in the range of facilities and services it offered.[1] It was established in March 1939 as a charitable, non-profit-making and non-political body, with the ailing Sigmund Freud as its first Honorary President, to be succeeded by the former Austrian ambassador to Britain, Sir Georg[e] Franckenstein. It was run by a committee that, in the initial period at least, included representatives of a wide range of political affiliations; however, as in two Austrian precursor organisations, Austrian Self-Aid and the Council of Austrians (founded in spring and autumn 1938 respectively), the Communist contingent played a particularly active role, among them Franz West, Willi Scholz, Jenö Kostmann, Georg Knepler and Eva Kolmer. In this, a strategy also observed in the formation of the Free German League of Culture (see chapter 12), they were following the Comintern's Popular Front policy.

The Austrian Centre was set up with a wide-ranging remit to foster Austrian culture and offer welfare and educational services to the refugee population as well as to 'serve as a bridge between the Austrians and the English in this, our host country'.[2] Overt political activity among the refugees in Britain was not permitted, especially in the early years of exile. However, the overriding political goal of the Centre, which was made explicit after 1941 through the mouthpiece of a further formation, the Free Austrian Movement (FAM), was the reestablishment after the war of an independent and democratic Austria (i.e. the nullification of the Anschluss). With a membership of 2,000 by June 1939, only three months after its formation (a figure that would soon rise to 3,500), the Austrian Centre offered the Austrian refugee population, *inter alia*, a meeting place, a library, a range of periodical publications (including the weekly newspaper *Zeitspiegel*), a theatre (the *Laterndl*), any number of concerts, lectures, exhibitions and courses, a small publishing house, facilities for shoe mending and tailoring, and a restaurant where members could eat Austrian dishes at a reasonable cost. Starting out in a house in Paddington, 124 Westbourne Terrace, London W2, the Centre soon expanded into two neighbouring houses, into further premises in other parts of London and, beyond London, to other British towns. At the same time, it developed an active affiliated youth group, Young Austria, which boasted a membership at its height of around 1,000.

As is discussed more fully in chapter 16, most of the refugee groups in Britain at this time had their native British champions who could smooth the way for and promote the concerns of their protégés. The Austrian Centre was outstandingly successful in attracting British patrons who included MPs like Geoffrey Mander and Eleanor Rathbone; peers of the realm such as Lord Strabolgi and Lord Lytton; churchmen of all denominations, including the helpful George Bell, Bishop of Chichester; ex-ambassadors like Sir Walford Selby; and leading representatives of British cultural and intellectual life such as the president of the Royal Society, Sir William Bragg. These friends and supporters, some of whom had had pre-war connections with Austria, others of whom regarded Austria as a victim of and therefore a separate entity from Germany, were regularly called upon to lend support or intercede in one way or another. Their patronage frequently irritated the British authorities in whose view, following the Anschluss, the refugee Austrians were to be regarded as on a par with their German counterparts.

There was, therefore, often a gulf between the well-connected British patrons and the authorities, the latter being scarcely as well disposed towards the Austrian 'enemy aliens' as the former. Indeed, up until June 1941, when the Soviet Union entered the war, relations between the British authorities and the Austrian Centre were particularly guarded. It was this turning point in the war, and the keenness of the Communists thereafter to support the Allied war effort, that made possible the launch of the FAM by the end of 1941 with overtly political aims such as, on the domestic level, the revocation of the 'enemy alien' status for Austrians and, internationally, the promotion of Austria's right to self-determination after the war. The FAM, like the Austrian Centre, proved exceptionally successful in enlisting native British support, an endeavour formalised in the formation of the 'Friends of Austria' in late 1942.

The differences between the British authorities and the British patrons in their views on the refugee Austrians were replicated, arguably, in the deep divisions between one British government department and another: the more liberal Home and Foreign Offices, on the one hand (although these, too, frequently differed in their approaches), and the far more hard-line Security Service on the other. It should be noted that the MI5 organisational files on the Austrian Centre have recently been released as have the personal files on a number of their leading lights – Eva Kolmer, Wilhelm Scholz, Jenö Kostmann and Franz West, amongst others, though not Georg Knepler – permitting an insight into MI5's view of the protagonists themselves and the organisation in which they were engaged.

The MI5 file on Franz West (i.e. Weintraub) opens with a Special Branch report from February 1940 recording that during the illness of Eva Kolmer, the then secretary of the Austrian Centre, West had taken over her duties.[3] This fact was reiterated in a later MI5 report on West as evidence of his importance within the Austrian Centre hierarchy; he had, in addition, been working on a voluntary basis for Austrian Self-Aid from May 1939 and was taken onto the Austrian Centre's paid staff in July 1939, while in September 1940 he was described as secretary of the Centre's Information and Advice Department. Prior to emigration, West had already been a member of the Austrian Communist Party for some years and had been 'prosecuted repeatedly' in Austria for political activities. According to an informer, West's visa for Britain had been obtained by Eva Kolmer who 'needed his help in building up the Austrian Communist organisation here' [in Britain]. West's rise within the Austrian Centre, of which he soon became president, and the leading role he played in the other Free Austrian organisations were carefully documented by MI5. West had been 'reported by various sources as one of the Communist officials of the Centre responsible for spreading subversive propaganda' and, being also 'extremely intelligent and politically active', needed to be watched.[4]

To the serious displeasure of MI5, in 1940 neither West nor his colleague Willi Scholz were interned, being exempted because they held an official position within a refugee organisation. They were therefore both free to support Eva Kolmer in the campaign against the British government's policy of internment, as was noted sourly by MI5.[5] Born in Graz, Scholz had started out as a Social Democrat but by 1934 had turned to the Communist Party. MI5 described him as 'well known to Eva Kolmer [...] who, soon after the founding of the Austrian Centre [...] gave Scholz a post in the domestic administration of the Centre'.[6] The Security Service kept a watchful eye on Scholz who soon took over from Eva Kolmer as general secretary of the Austrian Centre as well as reportedly acting as propaganda expert for the Central Committee of the Austrian Communist Party.[7] In July 1941, shortly after the Soviet Union entered the war, Milicent Bagot of MI5 asked Special Branch to forward her any details they had on Scholz's political activities.[8] Back came the following unequivocal reply:

> In company with Eva Kolmer [...] Scholz commenced to oust all non-communists from positions of importance on the Council of Austrians and also on the Management Committee of the Austrian Centre. Their object at that time was to sabotage the British war effort in the factories in order that England would be forced to sue for peace, and to work for the revolution which was to follow the conclusion of the war. Since the German attack on Russia, however, this attitude has changed to one of cooperation.[9]

Like his fellow Austrian Centre functionaries, Scholz remained an object of suspicion to MI5 throughout his years of exile and indeed beyond.

Unlike West and Scholz, Jenö Kostmann was interned not merely once but twice, on the second occasion being deported to a camp in Canada. He was an experienced journalist and veteran of the Austrian Communist Party who after his return to Britain was appointed editor of *Zeitspiegel*, the newspaper published by the Austrian Centre for the Austrian refugee population. An MI5 memorandum in Kostmann's file, dated 15 October 1942, reflected on the rather convoluted official reasoning behind granting Kostmann the necessary permit: 'The Ministry of Labour is going to grant Kostmann his permit, as it would appear to be a good thing that the *Zeitspiegel* should thus reveal its political colour.' Until recently, it was noted further without a hint of irony, Kostmann had been employed as a fire-watcher at the headquarters of the Communist Party of Great Britain.[10]

At around the same time, MI5 recorded that Kostmann was serving as Agitprop Leader of the Austrian Communist Party in Exile,[11] and that he was on the executive of a new Austrian Centre-based group, the 'Jewish Organisation for War Work'. The declared object of the organisation was to mobilise Austrian Jews to take part in work of national importance, though MI5 thought otherwise: 'As a branch of the Austrian Centre the main object is obviously to influence the Jewish refugees in this country from Austria with KPÖ-ideology.'[12] It was probably of greater concern to MI5, however, that copies of Kostmann's 1942 pamphlet, *Restive Austria*, had reportedly been sold in a factory engaged in war production in the north of England at the instigation of a British Communist Party member. Kostmann's booklet sought to present Austria as the first victim of Nazi aggression, some eighteen months before the Moscow Declaration turned this into official Allied policy. 'No doubt many copies of this pamphlet are being distributed throughout the country in a similar manner,' so it was surmised grimly.[13]

The MI5 file on the Austrian Centre's very active Cultural Secretary Georg Knepler has not been released,[14] nor have a large number of cross-references to Knepler emerged from the organisational files or from the files of his comrades. Given that Knepler was responsible for the Centre's extensive cultural programme as well as being a committed Communist, the relative absence of references is perhaps surprising. It may in part be explained by the manner of Knepler's arrival in Britain, several years earlier than most of the Austrian cohort, ostensibly as a musician rather than as a political exile, and of independent means (he was supported by his father Paul Knepler, librettist to Franz Lehar and Oskar Straus). He was also extremely well connected, this too being at least in part due to his father's influence. The few traces that have emerged indicating Security Service interest in Knepler include a mention in MI5 officer William Robson-Scott's appendix to an MI6 report on the Austrian Centre noting that: 'It is not clear whether he is a member of the C.P. but he is certainly on familiar terms with other C.P. members.'[15] Further indications are to be found in his Home Office file in which, in early 1941, an MI5 request to see Home Office records on Knepler was entered, followed by a minute from Milicent Bagot of 21 January 1941: 'Seen, thank you. This alien has been reported by several sources as an active Communist connected with the Austrian Centre.' Other references there to the attentions of British intelligence include a mention of an obviously adverse MI5 report on Knepler of 1 April [1941?] as well as one of a Special Branch report of 1 August 1944.

The most prominent functionary in the Austrian refugee organisations in Britain was undoubtedly the 25-year-old Eva Kolmer,[16] initially the secretary of both the Council of Austrians and the Austrian Centre, and later of the FAM, as well as co-founder of all these organisations. A large proportion of MI5's organisational files on the Austrian Centre are devoted to her activities and connections while her personal file stretches to no fewer than eight volumes. The daughter of a well-known Viennese professor of medicine, Kolmer was at the time of her emigration in 1938 a medical student in Vienna. She was also a known Communist and therefore particularly endangered in Austria after the Anschluss (she arrived in London within a couple of weeks, on 25 March 1938). Before the end of the year, she had published, under the pseudonym Mitzi Hartmann, a book dealing with recent events in Austria entitled *Austria Still Lives*. The resonant title, with its assertion of Austrian national and cultural identity, symbolised the resolve of Kolmer herself – and that of the Austrian Communist Party – to restore Austrian independence.

Kolmer's bent for organisation was equalled, at least, by her talent for networking. Possessing an excellent knowledge of English and some useful pre-existing British contacts, she went on to forge a large number of further contacts which were to benefit her and the Party. Her acquaintance with François Lafitte, for instance, then a young researcher with Political and Economic Planning, bore fruit in 1940 when she collaborated in his book *The Internment of Aliens*, supplying him with information from inside the internment camps. Moreover, if Kolmer was the most prominent activist in the early development of the Austrian Centre, she was also the post-war chronicler of its achievements which were, to no small degree, also hers.[17] It is no wonder, then, that she became the object of intense interest from the Security Service.

The MI5 files on the Austrian Centre and on Kolmer contain substantial evidence both on MI5's opinion of Austrian Self-Aid, the Council of Austrians, the Austrian Centre and the FAM as well as on the fundamental disagreement between MI5 and the Home Office as to the danger they – and Eva Kolmer herself – presented. Initially, at least, the Home Office official E.N. Cooper, who was in general sympathetic to the refugees, appears to have held Kolmer in high regard, noting after a meeting with her in October 1939 to Sir Robert Vansittart at the Foreign Office:

> I have always considered Miss Kolmer, whom I have known for some time, to be a trustworthy person of moderate views, anxious only that the Austrians in England should show their appreciation of the asylum that has been granted to them by refraining from any political activity which would bring them into conflict with the Authorities here, and that the work of the Committee should be confined to promoting the economic, cultural and social welfare of its members.[18]

It would not be long, though, before reports from disgruntled non-Communists, who soon found themselves forced out of the Free Austrian organisations, reached the ears of the British authorities. The Monarchist Graf Strachwitz, for example, had left the Council of Austrians after a disagreement,[19] and there had been a further dispute with another right-winger, Dr B.P. (Paul) Wiesner, himself the lessee of the Centre's premises, who had tried but failed to wrest the Council leadership from the Communists in January 1940.[20] For the time being, Professor Hertz had remained as chairman, but he too was having to deal with complaints that the Communists were taking over. Hertz himself resigned later in January 1940 (to be replaced by the Socialist Professor Walter Schiff). By the following month, February 1940, Hertz was reporting to Georg Franckenstein that most of the Monarchists had by then left the Council, leaving behind them a preponderance of left-wing members.[21] Another of the non-Communist members to be ousted from the Council and Centre was the Austrian Centre's first librarian, Josef Otto von Laemmel, who turned informer under the pseudonym of Kaspar.

Clearly, by late 1939, both Home Office and Foreign Office were well aware of the political dissensions within the Austrian Centre (which, in the light of the official constraints placed on political activity by refugees, would scarcely have served as a recommendation). Yet the manner in which Eva Kolmer, in a visit to the Home Office, presented the situation was little short of masterly. Giving no hint of her own political affiliation, she reported with regret that the Council of Austrians' original decision to refrain from political activity had been breached by both Monarchists and Communists. Graf Strachwitz had been anxious that the Council in London should associate itself with Austrian Monarchist activities in Paris, a stance that had led to continual wrangling in London and to the demand from 'the left-wing element' on the Committee for Strachwitz's resignation.

It had now been decided, so Kolmer reassured Cooper, that the Council of Austrians would from then on be kept free of political activity and that no political meetings would be held on Centre premises. In a final sally, well calculated to influence the British authorities – which had adopted a deliberate policy of even-handedness towards all the refugee groups – against Strachwitz, Kolmer had reported on his claim of 'working in close cooperation with the Foreign Office'; if, so Strachwitz had allegedly threatened his fellow-refugees, the Council of Austrians and Austrian Centre did not promote the restoration of the Austrian monarchy, they would be regarded by the Foreign Office as suspect (i.e. of being aligned with the Communists). It was following this interview with Kolmer that the Home Office had concluded, as noted above, that she was 'a trustworthy person of moderate views'.[22]

This was, of course, scarcely the view of the Security Service. A letter from SIS to MI5 dated 21 November 1939, attaching notes on activists Eva Kolmer, Wilhelm Scholz and others, reported on a claim from one of their sources that the 'Communists working in the Austrian Centre are not just single members of that Centre but a coordinated group working systematically under direct control of Moscow'.[23] This would have been a serious allegation at any time, but particularly so in wartime and in view of the Nazi–Soviet Pact. Indeed numerous reports found their way to MI5 at this time on the Communist ascendancy in the Centre, and from several informers.

One of these informers, 'Ariel', submitted a report on the situation at the Austrian Centre in January 1940 in which he maintained that, while admirable charitable work was being undertaken there, the decision to depoliticise the Centre had never been carried out. It was, he continued, 'an imperative necessity that the Austrian Centre should be depoliticised, not only in word but in actual fact'. Eva Kolmer, 'the driving force of the organisation' was 'an ardent communist' and the Austrian Centre itself 'constitutes a great danger for the Austrian emigrants', all the more so since the Communists at the Centre were disguising their true allegiances.[24]

In addition to informer reports, the Centre's and Eva Kolmer's post was regularly intercepted so that MI5 was well aware of the problems Kolmer was experiencing in sending publications to the internment camps and in particular copies of Lafitte's blistering critique of the government's current internment policy, *The Internment of Aliens* (1940).[25] Similarly, the Security Service would have known full well from intercepted mail of her efforts to address the problem of Nazis and anti-Nazis being confined together in the same internment camps (e.g. in Huyton).[26] They were undoubtedly also aware that at the end of 1940 Kolmer had asked one of the Austrian

Centre's most faithful British supporters, Margery Corbett Ashby, to underwrite an additional bank account for the Centre, a request that filled Corbett Ashby, who failed to understand the necessity for this, with some anxiety.[27] Letters referring to all these issues, intercepted and copied before being resealed and dispatched to the recipient, are present in Eva Kolmer's MI5 file, together with numerous adverse intelligence reports on her. Yet at the same time there are many intercepted letters there from her British friends and patrons testifying to their regard for her: from the MP Graham White,[28] for example, or from Lord Lytton.[29]

All in all, Eva Kolmer presented British – largely male – officialdom with a considerable dilemma: for she was an attractive, cultured, persistent, intelligent, well-dressed woman of good family and as such, and in the face of her excellent British contacts, she proved very difficult for them to place or indeed to deal with. E.N. Cooper at the Home Office appears to have been rather captivated by her and was criticised for this by MI5 (see below). At the Foreign Office, it was Geoffrey Harrison, as the official responsible for Austrian affairs, who had most dealings with her; in 1942, after Kolmer had repeatedly phoned the Foreign Office for an appointment to discuss a commemoration of the Anschluss, a colleague of Harrison's noted wryly: 'Mr Harrison had better see Miss K. and defend himself as best he can.'[30] And even William Robson-Scott at MI5 betrayed a certain ironic admiration of Kolmer by referring to her on occasion as 'the great Eva'[31] or 'the great lady herself'.[32]

Despite this, however, throughout much of 1940, MI5 repeatedly applied to the Home Office for Eva Kolmer to be interned but was frustrated on each occasion. In August 1940, the Security Service requested Kolmer's Home Office file as a 'very urgent' matter, but here too they were disappointed: first the file apparently went missing, then it was found but was still not dispatched to MI5;[33] thereafter, the file was reportedly in the hands of the Assistant Under-Secretary of State at the Home Office[34] (and therefore not available to MI5).[35] In October 1940, Milicent Bagot at MI5 wrote emphatically to Frank Newsam that since the Home Office still had the file, could they please indicate what they intended to do about Kolmer 'whose internment we have several times recommended'. This had become all the more pressing since, following the publication of the second Home Office White Paper in August 1940,[36] Eva Kolmer, as secretary of the Austrian Centre, would now be entitled to recommend the release of internees. 'As we regard this woman as a political intriguer with anti-British sympathies, we do not consider her a proper person for such a position.'[37]

While the correspondence continued in similar vein, MI5 stepped up its surveillance of Kolmer in order to gather some more damning evidence against her. Personal observation of her movements 'by our regular watchers and by a female assistant' was soon called off as fruitless, however, since the latter failed even to identify her. It seemed probable, MI5 reflected, that as secretary of the Centre, Kolmer's work would have largely kept her inside, hence the surveillance problem for the watchers outside.[38] On 23 November, the Security Service gave vent to its frustration with the Home Office in this matter:

> Eva Kolmer boasts of the special protection she enjoys at the Home Office owing to her friendship with Mr Cooper. *Though she is in every way undesirable* on account of her activities in this country, *all our warnings regarding her have been persistently disregarded.*[39]

It must have been especially galling for MI5 that Eva Kolmer, who had already been permitted to visit Seaton Camp at the beginning of 1940 in her capacity as a refugee official, was granted leave to visit the Isle of Man internment camps at the end of the year. All that the Security Service could do was to step up surveillance of her movements there.[40] Kolmer, in fact, complained at her treatment, for instance at being compulsorily searched, such that Lord Lytton, under whose patronage she had visited the camps, would feel it necessary to apologise to her (in an intercepted letter) for the unsatisfactory nature of her visit.[41]

As a next move, in January 1941 MI5 applied directly to Sir Cecil Hurst, who chaired the Home Office's Interned Enemy Aliens Tribunal, with a further case for Eva Kolmer to be interned (in which much was made of her efforts to send *The Internment of Aliens* to the internment camps, leading to 'alarm and dissatisfaction' there, and her friendship with the 'known Communist Party member' François Lafitte). Furthermore, it was alleged that Kolmer had supplied the names and addresses of Austrian Centre members to the Swedish Communist Party, which as a result was now supplying them with (undesirable) newspapers. Bypassing their customary Home Office correspondents such as Cooper, whom they now deemed unreliable, MI5 emphasised once again their conviction that 'Eva Kolmer is a danger to the security of this country and should be interned'.[42]

However, this line of action failed to go MI5's way either. Firstly they were instructed by Hurst to draw up a fuller case against Kolmer,[43] and secondly, when this had been accomplished, Tribunal members considered the case still 'too nebulous' for the Home Secretary to order internment. Instead, what was needed, so Hurst suggested in late April 1941, was a 'reorganisation of the Austrian Centre so that it may become what it was originally intended to be, a cultural centre for Austrians of all shades of opinions'.[44]

By then, with the Nazi–Soviet Pact still intact, MI5's case against both Kolmer and the Austrian Centre was taking on an extremely serious aspect, as exemplified by a six-page report on the Austrian Communist Party in Great Britain, with the informer 'Kaspar' as its source, which concluded:

> For anyone who has eyes to see it is clear that the Austrian Centre with its subordinate organisations is nothing more or less than a camouflaged body of the Austrian Communist Party, and that from the outset Eva Kolmer has built up this organisation on the instructions of the C.P. It would be an unpardonable sin of omission for anyone who desires the ultimate victory of England not to draw attention to the great danger inherent in the activities of this woman and her collaborators. These activities are aimed at the destruction of the British Empire, however cleverly they may be disguised. Only by interning all leading communist members of the Centre and by continuing the Centre itself as a real non-political charitable institution under reliable non-political leadership can this danger be effectively met.[45]

No action was taken, however, either against Kolmer or the Austrian Centre, despite the gravity of these allegations; and, in any case, only a few weeks after this, Germany invaded the Soviet Union and the political landscape changed completely, especially for Communists. Thus, on 6 August 1941, Cooper of the Home Office was writing to Sir Norman Kendal, Assistant Commissioner of the Criminal Investigation Department at New Scotland Yard, of the decision that 'at the moment no steps should be taken either to intern Eva Kolmer or to insist on a re-organisation of the Austrian Centre [,] the possibility of which we have had under consideration'. The Centre and Kolmer should of course still be watched, and indeed 'if the Centre indulges in any anti-British activities, now that Russia and this country are united in fighting the common foe, we should be on much stronger ground in taking action against it and in interning the principals if necessary'.[46]

That it never came to a compulsory closure or reorganisation of the Austrian Centre was almost certainly the result of the Free Austrians throwing themselves enthusiastically behind the Allied war effort, following the German invasion of the Soviet Union. Kolmer, too, remained at liberty, MI5 finding it well-nigh impossible to draw up a case that would convince the Home Office. Nevertheless, they continued to be irritated by the whole situation and in particular at E.N. Cooper who outraged them by contending on 12 July 1941 that, 'as the Home Office did not see fit to intern Miss Kolmer during the period when her Comintern sympathies gave a pro-German or at least an anti-British twist to all her activities', there could scarcely be grounds for interning her now.[47] This amounted, in T.F. Turner's view, to nothing less than 'a confession of dereliction of duty' from the Home Office.[48] Moreover, even more annoyingly, MI5 had to concede that, in the light of recent developments, the Home Office decision was probably the only possible one:

> I suppose the reason why one finds Cooper's minute so overwhelmingly irritating is that, with lapse of time, I believe the decision is right and that it would be a bad move at this stage to intern Eva Kolmer. I believe you are aware that the Home Secretary has recently decided that any internee with a Communist background who claims to have suffered a change of heart by reason of the German attack on Russia is to have the right of having his case reviewed by yet another Committee, on this occasion presided over by Mr Macaskie, K.C. The first fruits of this decision was [*sic*] the recommendation for the release of the six Czech Communists of the Beuer Group [...] So long as that opinion holds the field, I think it is useless to press for the internment of Eva Kolmer.[49]

What becomes clear in this particular exchange and elsewhere is the importance attached by the Home Office to public opinion (obviously a factor that MI5 was not obliged to consider). As MI5 went on to note regarding the Home Office's position in this matter: 'The attitude of seeking to avoid "unfriendly critics" is typical of all that is worst in the Home Office and is responsible for most of their weakest decisions.'[50] Tellingly, Roger Hollis of MI5 had noted in March 1941:

> When I saw Sir Cecil Hurst and Miss Sutherland on 26.2.41 he pointed out that, if the Home Secretary made an order for the internment of Eva Kolmer, there would be an outcry in some quarters and a general pulling of strings and that the Home Secretary must be very sure of his ground.[51]

Although, from the time of the ending of the Nazi–Soviet Pact and the new mutual assistance pact between Britain and the Soviet Union, the Security Service still continued to keep a wary eye on the Free Austrian organisations, undoubtedly much of the urgency had gone out of the situation. On 9 September 1941, Roger Hollis recorded that a Communist posed 'a continuing danger', certainly, but 'not a particular menace at the time of a war emergency'. It should be noted, he continued, that 'the Communists have not formed part of the Fifth Column in any country which has been invaded'. For this reason, the Security Service considered that 'Communists should not be put on the same suspect list with other enemies of the country' because 'the need to deal with the Communists will come at a different time'. For this reason also, so Hollis concluded, he did not believe that Eva Kolmer should be on the suspect list.[52]

The founding of the FAM at the end of 1941 created a fresh flutter of Security Service interest, admittedly, with reports being submitted by the usual informers on the interrelationships between the Movement's constituent groups and, in particular, the growing Communist predominance, mirroring earlier developments in the Austrian Centre and other Free Austrian organisations.[53] MI5 also retained its interest in the Austrian Communist Party group in exile[54] as well as in any reports of links between the Austrians and exile groups of other nationality such as the Czechs[55] or the Germans.[56]

Of course, MI5 continued to maintain its surveillance of Eva Kolmer, demonstrating almost as much interest in her plans to leave Britain as in her activities in Britain. As for the Austrian Centre, short reports in the MI5 organisational file chart the progressive termination of its activities. It was decided at an extraordinary general meeting – despite considerable opposition – that the Centre should be dissolved on 15 January 1947.[57] The Finsbury Park Branch (one of several Centre branches in London) had already turned itself into an autonomous 'Anglo-Austrian Friendship Club' with a membership of 150;[58] other ex-Austrian Centre members transferred their allegiance to the London Hungarian Club or to the Heinrich-Heine Bund, for a while a successor organisation to the Free German League of Culture.[59] Clearly, however, with the return home of the activists, political activity of any significance had ceased and with it the keen MI5 interest which the Austrian Centre had previously provoked.

Notes

1 On the Austrian Centre, see Marietta Bearman, Charmian Brinson, Richard Dove, Anthony Grenville and Jennifer Taylor, *Out of Austria: The Austrian Centre in London in World War II*, London: Tauris Academic Studies 2008.

2 'Generalversammlung des Klubs Austrian Centre, London, 26. Juni 1939', Friedrich Otto Hertz Papers, Archiv für die Geschichte der Soziologie in Österreich [AGSÖ], p. 4, 26/5.15.

3 Cross-reference from Special Branch Report on the Austrian Centre, 14 February 1940, The National Archives [TNA], KV2/2982/1a.

4 See TNA, KV2/2982 and KV2/2983, and in particular MI5 reports, 'Weintraub, Franz Carl @ Franz West', n.d. (*c*. January 1941), TNA, KV2/2982/21a; and 'Weintraub, Franz Carl', n.d. (*c*. mid-1945), TNA, KV2/2983/100b.

5 Weintraub, Franz Carl @ Franz West', n.d. (*c*. January 1941), TNA, KV2/2982/21a.

6 'Scholz, Wilhelm (@ Perner)', *c*. early 1941, TNA, KV2/3068/19a.

7 MI5 internal memorandum, 2 July 1941, TNA, KV2/3068/29a.

8 Bagot to Special Branch, 11 July 1941, TNA, KV2/3068/30a.

9 Special Branch to MI5, 9 August 1941, TNA, KV2/3068/32a.

10 'Jenö Kostmann', MI5 internal memorandum, 26 October 1942, TNA, KV6/99/35a.

11 'Secretariat of the Austrian Communist Party', 8 August 1942, TNA, KV6/99/27b.

12 'Jewish Organisation for War Work (Austrian Centre)', 2 September 1942, TNA, KV6/99/33a.

13 Chief Constable Lancashire Constabulary to Brigadier Sir David Petrie, MI5, 18 January 1943, TNA, KV6/99/39a.
14 Originally numbered PF 49563.
15 'Report on the Austrian Centre', 15 December 1940, TNA, KV5/138/18a.
16 On Kolmer, see Charmian Brinson, 'Eva Kolmer and the Austrian Emigration in Britain, 1938–1946', in Anthony Grenville, ed., *German-Speaking Exiles in Great Britain: Yearbook of the Research Centre for German and Austrian Exile Studies*, vol. 3, 2003, pp. 143–69.
17 See Eva Kolmer, *Das Austrian Centre: 7 Jahre österreichische Gemeinschaftsarbeit*, London: Austrian Centre [1946].
18 Cooper to Vansittart, 20 October 1939, TNA, KV5/138/1a.
19 See, for example, Friedrich Hertz, 'Rundschreiben an die Mitglieder des Ausschusses der Österreicher in England', 14 October 1939, Friedrich Otto Hertz Papers, AGSÖ, 28/5.15.
20 Friedrich Hertz to Martin Fuchs, 3 February 1940, Friedrich Otto Hertz Papers, AGSÖ, 28/1.1.
21 Untitled memorandum enclosed in Hertz to Franckenstein, 13 February 1940, Friedrich Otto Hertz Papers, AGSÖ, 28/1.1.
22 Cooper to Vansittart, 20 October 1939, TNA, KV5/138/1a.
23 TNA, KV2/2516/67a.
24 Source 'Ariel', 'Notes on the present situation in the Austrian Centre', 31 January 1940, TNA, KV5/138/4.
25 Penguin Books to Kolmer, 20 November 1940, TNA, KV2/2518/111a.
26 For example, Sir Richard Acland MP to Kolmer, 21 November 1940, TNA, KV2/2518/111ax.
27 Corbett Ashby to Kolmer, 25 December 1940, TNA, KV2/2518/120a.
28 White to Kolmer, 21 August 1940, TNA, KV2/2517/98b.
29 Lytton to Kolmer, 16 December 1940, TNA, KV2/2518/118B.
30 Minute (Roger Makins), 21 February 1942, TNA, FO371/30910.
31 Robson-Scott to Milicent Bagot, 21 March 1941, TNA, KV2/2519/147e.
32 Robson-Scott to Bagot, 4 February 1942, TNA, KV2/2521/193b.
33 TNA, KV2/2517/98d.
34 TNA, KV2/2517/102a.
35 However, a report from the following year, 'Eva Kolmer', records that on 31 July 1940 MI5 did succeed in minuting Kolmer's Home Office (HO) file to record that her internment had been recommended several times (n.d. [*c.* January 1941]), TNA, KV2/2518/126a, p. 6.
36 Cmd. 6223, 'Civilian Internees of Enemy Nationality'.
37 9 October 1940, TNA, KV2/2517/107a.
38 Report of 9 November 1940, TNA, KV2/2517/109k.
39 Extract from SIS report on the Austrian Centre, 23 November 1940, TNA, KV2/2518/111z.
40 See, for example, 'Intelligence Report by Captain S.E. Kraul' on Kolmer's visit to Onchan, 9 December 1940, TNA, KV2/2518/116x.
41 Lord Lytton to Kolmer, 16 December 1940, TNA, KV2/2518/118b.

42 MI5 to Sir Cecil Hurst, 18 January 1941, TNA, KV2/2518/129a.
43 See TNA, KV2/2518/136b and TNA, KV2/2519/143a.
44 Hurst to MI5, 30 April 1942, TNA, KV2/2520/155a.
45 Part of 'Report on the Refugee Communist Organisations', 14 March 1941, TNA, KV2/2519/147c, p. 11.
46 TNA, KV2/2520/165a.
47 Cooper minute, 12 July 1941, in 'Extract from HO file W6176 re Eva [Kolmer] and Jacob Wolloch', TNA, KV2/2520/165a.
48 Minute no. 168 (Turner), 5 September 1941, at front of TNA, KV2/2520.
49 *Ibid.*
50 *Ibid.*
51 Hollis memorandum, n.d. [March 1941], TNA, KV2/2519/143a.
52 Minute no. 172 (Hollis), 9 September 1941, at front of TNA, KV2/2520.
53 For example, source Miller, 'Free Austrian Movement', 18 January 1942, TNA, KV2/2521/191yx.
54 See, for example, extract from report (source Hiller) on the Austrian Communist Party in British exile, 15 April 1944, TNA, KV2/2522/281d.
55 See, for example, 'Extract from a Source Miller Report re a Meeting between Czechoslovaks and Austrians', 29 April 1943, TNA, KV2/2522/229a.
56 See source Kaspar report on 'Hans Kahle', 29 June 1944, TNA, KV2/2522/292.
57 Source 'Hi' report, 'Austrian Centre', 16 December 1946, TNA, KV5/137/208a.
58 Special Branch report, 17 December 1946, TNA, KV5/137/208a.
59 Source Kaspar (Lamb) report, 'Austrian Centre', 2 February 1947, TNA, KV5/137/211b.

14

'About the most dangerous of all these organisations': the Czech Refugee Trust Fund

The Czech Refugee Trust Fund (CRTF) was a matter of particular concern to MI5, with Dick White referring to it in March 1940 in some despair as 'this appalling organisation'.[1] Its predecessor organisation, the British Committee for Refugees from Czechoslovakia (BCRC), had been founded in October 1938 in the wake of the Munich Agreement – under which the Sudetenland had been ceded to Nazi Germany – to assist racial and political refugees from Czechoslovakia who were threatened by Nazism. The committee extended its help not only to Czech nationals but also to refugees of German and Austrian origin who were taking refuge in Czechoslovakia when the Nazis occupied it. The BCRC's successor organisation, the CRTF, was created by the British government in July 1939.[2]

Funding for the BCRC/CRTF came from both official and unofficial sources. The British government provided the substantial sum of £4,000,000; and appeals were also set up, *inter alia*, by the *News Chronicle*, *The Manchester Guardian*, the Lord Mayor of London and Lord (Stanley) Baldwin. Between October 1938 and March 1939, the BCRC brought around 3,500 refugees from Czechoslovakia to Britain of whom perhaps 2,500 were Sudeten Germans and the remainder Reich Germans and Austrians.[3] Moreover, after the Germans had invaded the rest of Czechoslovakia in March 1939, the numbers of refugees spiralled: by September 1939 there were 8,000 refugees in the care of the CRTF, and by December 12,000.[4]

The CRTF was overseen by three trustees and a director who ran the organisation on a day-to-day basis, initially the retired civil servant Sir Henry Bunbury. He had a sizeable staff, mostly British but supplemented by refugees employed on an honorary basis. Refugees registered for assistance with the Trust were divided for administrative purposes into groups along political, national and occupational lines, each group having a leader whose name frequently denoted the whole group. Thus the 'Schmidt Group', one of the most active, was the 'German Salda Committee' of German Communists that was led by Heinz Schmidt. The Austrian

Communists were led by Hans Winterberg and the Sudeten Communists by Gustav Beuer. There were similar groups of Social Democrats, Liberals and Trade Unionists, a German Democratic Committee led by Otto Wollenberg, a (Jewish) Hicem Group under Paul Rehfeldt and a 'Thomas Mann Group' of writers and intellectuals under Bernhard Menne – twelve groups in all.[5]

Initially, the BCRC/CRTF headquarters were situated in Bloomsbury (briefly in Gordon Square and then in nearby Mecklenburgh Square). Following the outbreak of war, the CRTF moved its headquarters firstly to Redbourn, near St Albans, and finally to New Lodge, Windsor Forest, where it remained until the end of the war. As for the CRTF members themselves, many of them were accommodated in the organisation's own hostels throughout Britain.

The basic difference between the CRTF and such organisations as the Austrian Centre and the Free German League of Culture – though all of these were established for the benefit of the refugees in Britain – was as follows: whereas the latter two were refugee-run enterprises with some British supporters, the CRTF was a British-run organisation with some refugee assistants. In the case of the CRTF, MI5 surveillance focused not only on the refugees but also on the British staff. It was, so an internal MI5 document concluded in February 1940, 'about the most dangerous of all these organisations'.[6]

From the start, there were refugee and British concerns regarding the possible Nazi penetration of the CRTF, as exemplified by the first case outlined in the MI5 files on the Trust Fund. Irmgard Sattler had aroused suspicion among fellow Czech domestic employees at New Lodge for using a staff typewriter and for allegedly typing a letter containing words like 'frontier', 'coast' and 'sea'. She had also been observed not to be using the letterbox provided but to be cycling some distance to post letters to Norway and Sweden. The information compiled on Sattler by the Berkshire Constabulary at Ascot included the fact that she had recently joined the Wollenberg Group. It was also recorded that this group was regarded with suspicion by the CRTF leadership and that Wollenberg himself was suspected of political intrigue and – a grave indictment – of having been in touch with the Gestapo while he was in Prague.[7] It was characteristic of this kind of case that the suspicions against Sattler originated in refugee circles before being passed on to the British authorities.

The authorities took such allegations seriously. They were, it was stated in an MI5 memorandum of March 1940,[8] certainly interested in Sir Henry Bunbury's material on the three groups of which he was most suspicious (i.e. the Wollenberg Group and the Menne Group as well as a group not officially affiliated to the CRTF, Rudolf Moeller-Dostali's group of Catholic refugees from Prague) and indeed some Gestapo connections had been uncovered.[9] The memorandum continued:

> MI5 regard the task of eliminating the agents of the Gestapo and of the German Intelligence Service, whom [*sic*] we have reason to believe are frequently given the cover of refugees, as a first claim on their investigating staff [...] In this connection we would welcome closer collaboration between our own investigating officers and those officials of [the] Czech Refugee Trust Fund who bring the cases to the notice of the Home Office, with a view to influencing the decisions of the Aliens Tribunals.

MI5 was not in agreement with Bunbury, however, concerning refugees condemned by the CRTF because of former connections with the Czech Intelligence Service (at least one of whom, Josef Lampersberger, had passed on useful information to MI5 concerning Gestapo agents), nor did they concur with material provided by Bunbury to the effect that the Social Democrats and Catholics posed a greater danger to British security than did the Communists.[10]

On the contrary, of still greater concern to MI5, particularly but not only during the Nazi–Soviet Pact, was their fear of Communist penetration of the CRTF. Nor was this an unfounded fear: a large number of Communists, who were of course particularly threatened by National Socialism, had featured among the political refugees rescued from Czechoslovakia in 1938 and 1939. In January 1940, Sir Vernon Kell of MI5 wrote to Alexander Maxwell at the Home Office that since he had recently received information on collaboration 'for a long time past' between the German and Soviet Intelligence Services, the presence of many foreign Communists in Britain was inevitably a source of anxiety.[11] Two months later, an internal MI5 letter wrote of there being a 'serious Communist problem': for, despite MI5 opposition to large numbers of foreign Communists being admitted as refugees, there were now in Britain 'at least 100 Communists with long records of political activity in Central Europe in fully organised groups, and still under the direct instructions of Moscow'.[12] (There is a certain irony in the fact that those refugees to whom the British authorities were least keen to play host were brought to Britain on the strength of British government money.)

However, it was not just the refugees whom MI5 suspected of Communist infiltration but also the CRTF's British staff. As early as December 1939, a Special Branch report filed by MI5 reported that three of the CRTF officials were Communists: the solicitor Bruce Binford Hole, an unnamed treasurer, and Margaret Meinhardt or Mander [i.e. Mynatt] of the Tribunals Department (which prepared the documentation on behalf of CRTF members about to appear before one of the Aliens Tribunals). In fact, as mentioned above, the journalist Margaret Mynatt presented the British security services with an unusual problem of categorisation in that, although she had fled Germany as a political refugee, she held a British passport. After several years of scratching a living from part-time jobs, she was taken on by the CRTF on the strength of her wide knowledge of refugee problems; she was soon put in charge of the Tribunals Department, giving her unparalleled access to refugee records as well as what her critics considered to be an undue degree of influence. The Special Branch report even went on to claim that the Party members serving in the CRTF, like Mynatt, were taking advantage of their key position vis-à-vis the Tribunals 'by alleging that anti-Communist refugees are Gestapo agents'.[13]

Another – crucial – member of the CRTF administration, who was not mentioned in this particular report, was Yvonne Kapp. Kapp, who was Secretary and Personal Assistant to Sir Henry Bunbury, was sometimes referred to as the Assistant Director of the CRTF. Professionally, she was exceptionally effective and had a great deal of influence over Sir Henry. She, too, was soon revealed to be a Communist. A Berkshire Constabulary report from November 1939, which was based on information provided by Kapp, clearly demonstrates the inbuilt bias towards the Communists and against the Social Democratic refugees that was the subject of so many Social Democratic complaints: 'There is [...] a great deal of disquiet and enmity amongst the refugees, but this is undoubtedly the work of the Social Democrats and not the Communists.'[14]

Some of the bitter disagreements between Social Democrats and Communists experienced within the CRTF can be regarded as par for the course. Similar ideological infighting could be observed in and between a number of refugee organisations at this time and was indeed a continuation of the intense factional arguments in Germany and Austria from before the National Socialist era. In the case of the CRTF, these arguments and, in particular, the many denunciations also derived from the refugees' prior experiences in Prague which, with the Nazis literally at the door, had become a hotbed of suspicion and political agitation. A Special Branch report on the CRTF, dated 11 January 1940, recorded there being 'a great deal of political terrorising among the refugees';[15] and although such actions were by no means unique to the Communists, many of the non-Communists in the CRTF complained that they had been denounced by the Communists, with the denunciations often taking the form of allegations of prior Nazi contacts. The complaints of Kurt Hiller and Eugen Brehm, who later both wrote about the discrimination they allegedly experienced in Czech and British exile,[16] were recorded in MI5 files as were those of Rudolf Moeller-Dostali, Walter Schultz and numerous others. Allegations ranged from the relatively minor (such as having been allocated less central accommodation) to the major, including allegations of political denunciations leading to internment.

Hiller and Brehm were probably denounced for their connections with the controversial Otto Strasser, a former Nazi turned anti-Nazi, during their time in Prague. Kurt Hiller, a celebrated literary and political figure in Weimar Germany, was an equally controversial figure, a pacifist who had become both passionately antifascist and anti-Communist. Having made his way to Britain with the help of the BCRC, he became one of its most vociferous critics. Still concerning himself after the war with what he had perceived as Communist abuses, Hiller claimed in his 1951 book *Rote Ritter* that in Prague the Communist refugees had been prioritised for evacuation, thus giving them a head start in Britain not only in acquiring accommodation but also in securing key positions within the CRTF administration.[17] He and his friend the journalist Eugen Brehm, a former SAP member, who had a similar complaint to make,[18] were critical not only of the Communist refugees who had scrambled to gain positions of influence, but also of members of the CRTF's British staff, like Elizabeth Allen and Beatrice Wellington, and Sir Henry Bunbury himself, whom they saw as knowingly or unknowingly complicit in Communist misdeeds. Brehm, Moeller-Dostali, Schultz and, in particular, Hiller were among those refugees prepared to inform on their fellow-refugees (as discussed in chapter 15).

The journalist Rudolf Moeller-Dostali became a particular object of both refugee and British distrust as a former Communist Party member, Moscow trained, who had allegedly re-embraced Catholicism whilst in exile in Prague. As SIS wrote to MI5 in January 1939, Moeller-Dostali was suspected of 'endeavouring to double-cross us in a very secret matter'.[19] Sir Henry Bunbury, in a 'very confidential' memorandum filed by MI5, reported just over a year later that Moeller-Dostali was generally regarded by the political refugees in Britain as someone with whom it was unwise to associate; moreover, most of the refugees he had brought with him from Prague under the auspices of the Czech Catholic Committee had 'something doubtful or unsatisfactory about them'.[20] Moeller-Dostali himself was so disenchanted with the CRTF that he compiled an 'Exposé about the incidents in Czech Refugee Trust Fund', which he sent to the Foreign Secretary Lord Halifax (who in the event did not get to see it).[21] His complaints ranged from the particular – the repeated refusal of the CRTF to include his Catholic group within its group framework – to the general: the issuing of denunciations of non-Communist refugees for the benefit of the Tribunals, moreover on official CRTF notepaper.[22]

The journalist Walter Schultz, a close friend of Kurt Hiller's, had found himself in precisely this situation when going before his Tribunal. He had received a letter of recommendation from the CRTF but simultaneously a second letter had reached the Tribunal denouncing him as a Nazi agent. Both of these had been signed by Sir Henry (who claimed, however, to have no recollection of signing the second one). Schultz attributed the incident to the fact that since he had previously been a Communist but had left the Party, 'the Communists were out for revenge on him'.[23]

Sir Henry Bunbury was by all accounts unequal to his task of CRTF Director, with the Socialist politician Willi Eichler, for instance, contending that he was a 'benevolent old gentleman [...] but [...] too ready to take people and things on trust'.[24] On 3 January 1940, in a 'Strictly Confidential' memorandum, Bunbury attempted to answer the charge that the CRTF was 'dominated by Communists, British and foreign, who use their position to protect or advance the interests of Communists and to injure those of refugees who are opposed to Communism'. He was, he conceded, aware of the animosity existing between the different political factions (though he considered the Social Democrats to be largely to blame for it). However, when Sir Henry had sought advice on this from the CRTF's Advisory Council, the Trustees and the Home Office, it had been agreed that the proper line for the Trust Fund to adopt would be equal treatment of all refugees, regardless of party (since, after all, any actions harmful to Britain's prosecution of the war would remain the province of the police). According to Bunbury (though contrary to the information already in MI5's possession), there were no known British Communists employed by the CRTF, and while there were some Communists among the refugee voluntary workers, the numbers were not disproportionate; moreover, they 'are among the best of the refugee workers in the office'. He was not, he added, aware of a single incident in which Communist refugees had attempted to abuse their position, endorsing them as follows:

> In general, the disciplined and restrained attitude of the Communist Group members with whom the officers of the Trust come in personal contact is in rather striking contrast with the irresponsible violence of some members of anti-Communist convictions.[25]

MI5 was not impressed by Bunbury's statement, dismissing it as 'insubstantial' and indeed factually incorrect.[26] That same day, 15 January 1940, MI5 compiled a memorandum on the Communist infiltration of the CRTF: there were allegedly six Communists in the Card Room at Windsor Forest where files – and sensitive information – on individual members were kept, there were Communists in the all-important Tribunals Department and the Hospitality Department was now in effect Communist-run (with Social Democrats claiming that the Communists would punish a political opponent by dispatching him to a place he disliked).[27] In a further MI5 document, it was recorded that Yvonne Kapp, Bunbury's right-hand woman, had been known as a Party member since 1937, as had her contacts with a large number of leading Communists.[28] The following day, Roger Hollis and Dick

White of MI5 had an interview with E.N. Cooper at the Home Office on the CRTF at which Cooper professed himself 'appalled' at the effect it would have on Sir Henry Bunbury to learn that his chief assistant was a Communist, a fact of which he was sure Bunbury was unaware.[29]

A fortnight later, MI5 submitted a nine-page report to the Home Office on, firstly, the British aspect of the case, that is, what was described as the 'CPGB cell' in the Trust Fund; secondly on foreign Communists associated with the CRTF; thirdly, on Communist influence within the Trust Fund; and fourthly on 'Recommendations as to action for curtailment of Communist activities inside the Czech Refugee Trust Fund'. The last of these included the dismissal of the 'Cell of the CPGB from executive positions in the Czech Refugee Trust Fund'.[30] The matter came to a head at a meeting that same day, 30 January 1940, between MI5, Cooper and Bunbury at which Bunbury was reportedly 'shocked and rather grieved to hear that Mrs Yvonne Kapp was a Communist as he had only the previous evening tackled her on this point and she had denied that she was one'.[31]

However, it would still take several months for MI5's views to prevail and for at least some of the British Communist officials in the CRTF to be dismissed. In April 1940, Bunbury was still maintaining that 'a general campaign [was] now being organised against the CRTF', possibly emanating from Berlin; that there was no evidence that the Communist refugees were abusing their position; and that the idea of a Communist cell within the Trust Fund was far-fetched. Even though Yvonne Kapp's continued denial of her Party membership 'does not quite convince me', he had no criticisms to make whatsoever 'as to her loyalty or standards of conduct in official matters'.[32] Two weeks later, Kell wrote to Maxwell at the Home Office that since Bunbury was clearly not disposed to accept MI5's case, 'immediate action' was called for. It was, Kell maintained, 'a highly unsatisfactory situation' that members of the CPGB should occupy executive positions in a public trust fund, and while the situation persisted, 'I cannot feel that the claims of security have been met'.[33] But nothing was done for a further month during which Sir Henry suffered a nervous breakdown while Kapp largely replaced him in running the Czech Trust Fund. Only on 24 May did E.R. Haylor of MI5 note a conversation with E.N. Cooper at the Home Office to the effect that Bunbury – his resistance no doubt lowered by his illness – had now been instructed that the three Communists Yvonne Kapp, Margaret Mynatt and George Musgrove were to be dismissed.[34]

The dismissals took place at the beginning of June 1940. Yvonne Kapp has described the procedure in her autobiography and, while adopting an ironic narrative stance, leaves the reader in no doubt that she took her 'victimisation' badly: 'I thought it sinister and unjust in the same way that I deplored the hounding of the refugees as a disgrace.'[35] She and Margaret

Mynatt, by now close friends, retreated to the Lake District where they immediately began work on their book, *British Policy and the Refugees*, a damning critique of the government policy of the day, with many insights gleaned from their work with the CRTF.[36]

At almost exactly the same time as Kapp, Mynatt and Musgrove were dismissed, the government replaced its policy of selective alien internment with one of mass alien internment. Regarding the members of the CRTF, the British authorities found themselves in something of a quandary. Czech nationals were 'friendly aliens', and as such not subject to internment. Among them, however, were numerous men and women of Sudeten German origin who might well carry Czech papers but about whose 'Czechness' the British authorities remained unconvinced. Moreover, a proportion of the Czech refugees, both German and Czech-speaking, were Communists and of course under particular suspicion during the Nazi–Soviet Pact. Even worse, as far as the British were concerned, was the presence of the hundreds of former Reich Germans and Austrians, many of them highly political, who had been brought to Britain by the CRTF yet had an even more tenuous claim to be Czech (possessing merely Czech interim passports).[37]

In the conversation of 24 May 1940 between Haylor (MI5) and Cooper (Home Office), Cooper had appeared to accept that Communists on an MI5-compiled list 'ought to be interned immediately as being subversive' and had even asked 'if there was any reason why the majority of Czechs should not be interned'.[38] This was a question raised repeatedly by different branches of British officialdom and within MI5 papers. On 24 May 1940, a month after his previous letter on the Czech refugees – and at a time when category 'B' refugees had already been interned, but not yet the many in category 'C' – Kell wrote to Maxwell again, once more urging 'stricter control [...] in the interests of public security'. Specifically, 'Czech suspects' ought to be interned at once, as ought 'all Czechs of Austrian or German origin who acquired nationality since 1933'. Czechs who had lived in the Sudeten area should be 'specially vetted', while Communist leaders should be removed from executive positions in the CRTF.[39] In reply, Alexander Maxwell set out the official Home Office policy: the Home Secretary would be willing 'to intern any Czech about whom there are grounds for suspicion'. This would include any CRTF member refusing to undertake war work, for instance in the Czech Legion. However, as the Home Secretary had reiterated on several occasions, 'the policy ought to be not to intern thousands of people because amongst them there may be a few suspicious characters'. In a handwritten marginal note, MI5, although overruled by the Home Office on the matter, had registered its fundamental disagreement: 'This is the only policy at a time like this.'[40]

MI5 was, predictably, particularly anxious to intern CRTF members belonging to the three Communist groups headed by Schmidt, Winterberg and Beuer. But the Communists were not its sole concern: for within the CRTF, additionally, there 'remains the problem of possible German agents and sympathisers who may have filtered into this country as part of the emigration'. In a memorandum entitled 'Recommendations for dealing with the Czech Problem in the UK' of 16 June 1940, it was reported that MI5 was drawing up 'White Lists' of persons whose reliability could be guaranteed by the Czech authorities and 'Black Lists' of Czech suspects. Furthermore, MI5 recommended that men and women with Czech papers but of German or Austrian origin should be interned 'at the moment it is decided to take action against Germans and enemy aliens in category C'.[41]

However, MI5's work was impeded by the CRTF's evident reluctance to pass on information on its members; and indeed the Security Service had to resort to various stratagems to obtain the intelligence it required. In June 1940, for example, it succeeded in obtaining thirteen bundles of CRTF index cards with the assistance of E.N. Cooper at the Home Office, and when asked to return them, managed to postpone doing so.[42] A sardonic internal MI5 note on the subject from Haylor to Bagot, although in the event not acted upon, speaks volumes about the tensions between MI5 and the altogether more liberal Home Office:

> I enclose a letter which I have received from your bosom friend Cooper. No doubt you have sent the bundles of index cards down to the Registry, where they have been duly lost. Would you, however, be good enough to convey the sad news to Cooper with your usual literary felicity?[43]

Beatrice Wellington of the CRTF had herself drawn up a confidential Black List of refugees which was passed on to MI5 officer Claud Sykes by Bernhard Menne, one of Sykes's numerous informants from the refugee community. Menne had obtained the list from an unnamed person who had reportedly found it in Miss Wellington's drawer. In terms reminiscent of the attacks on Yvonne Kapp and Margaret Mynatt, though possibly with rather less justification, Sykes had dismissed Wellington as 'one of the Communist or near Communist officials of the Czech Trust Fund' and her list as 'no doubt [...] a list of persons drawn up by Miss W. for denunciation to the authorities as Gestapo agents'.[44] In a report entitled 'Miss Wellington's Black List', Sykes had added information from 'my outside contacts' Menne and his fellow CRTF group leader Otto Wollenberg,[45] while in an accompanying document also acknowledging receipt of information from Willi Eichler and journalist Hans Jaeger.[46] It is interesting that these particular informants, Menne, Wollenberg, Eichler and Jaeger, had been amongst those refugees most mistrusted by the original officials of the CRTF.

Sykes had, he noted, gleaned further information in relation to the Wellington Black List 'during my trip up north', that is, his visit to the internment camps. Here he had apparently had useful conversations with the Socialists Wilhelm Sander and Gustav Tille, the ever informative Kurt Hiller and, once again, Hans Jaeger whom he described as 'a sympathetic personality who may be of use to us later'. Indeed, Sykes was considering recommending the transfer of Gotthard Schild, whom the CRTF had suspected of involvement with the Gestapo while in Prague,[47] to Central Promenade Camp, where Jaeger was interned, 'so that Jaeger can make contact with him, as he thinks he might be able to get something out of him'.[48]

Mass internment of enemy aliens had been introduced on 22 June 1940. Meanwhile the debate about who was or was not Czech – and therefore exempt from internment – had continued, with Prestige at the Home Office sending White at MI5:

> lists [...] of refugees from Czechoslovakia who claim to be Czech nationals. Most of them have been content all this time to be registered as German or Austrian, but now have discovered documents on the strength of which they hope to escape internment.[49]

MI5 files contain, *inter alia*, a letter from the CRTF to the Camp Commandant, Race Course York, concerning seven 'Sudeten Czech' refugees 'who we believe were interned in error' – since 'we understand that the authorities do not intend to intern Czech citizens' – and whose situation was all the more urgent in light of their imminent deportation.[50] In reply to this, however, the CRTF was rebuked for communicating directly with the Camp Commandant who in any case judged the Sudeten Czechs to have been quite rightly interned 'owing to their admitted Communist views'.[51]

The anomalous character of the British internment policy was nowhere illustrated more clearly than in the contrasting treatments of two of the CRTF Communist group leaders Heinz Schmidt and Gustav Beuer. Schmidt, a Reich German who was known to be especially influential among the refugee community, was exempted from internment – contrary to the recommendations of both Special Branch and MI5[52] – because he held a leading position in a refugee organisation. Beuer, on the other hand, a Sudeten German of Czech nationality, *was* interned, despite his holding a directly comparable position.

In July 1940, MI5 had, in fact, advocated the imprisonment of nine leading Czech Communists connected with the CRTF and the Home Office had agreed in the case of six of them: Gustav and Otto Beuer, Otto Fantl, Karl Kreibich, Ludwig Freund and Anton Rubal (a seventh, Alfred Kahler, was released on medical grounds).[53] As Czechs, that is, as 'friendly aliens', they were detained under Article 12 (5a) of the Aliens Order. The CRTF protested, maintaining that Gustav Beuer's internment 'would disorganise the fund immeasurably',[54] while the Czech Provisional Government also requested Beuer's release.[55] A campaign was mounted for the release of the Beuer group in which sections of the British press played their part: the *News Chronicle*, for instance, pointedly compared the harsh treatment meted out to the anti-Nazi Gustav Beuer with the reportedly luxurious conditions enjoyed by the imprisoned Nazi Rudolf Hess.[56] The London-based National Council for Democratic Aid published the pamphlet, *Morrison's Prisoners: The Story of the Czechoslovakian Anti-Fascist Fighters Interned in Britain* (1941) to highlight the case. Following the entry of the Soviet Union into the war in June 1941, Eleanor Rathbone MP, always a faithful supporter of the refugees, asked the Home Secretary in the House of Commons whether:

> In view of the changed political situation he will review the cases of those aliens whose release from [...] detention under Regulation 12A has been refused only on the ground that they were suspected of Communist activities or propaganda injurious to the war effort.[57]

MI5 took an unsympathetic view of Rathbone's proposal, however. On 7 August 1941, Bagot noted that 'although we might have to give way about the weakest case, Anton Rubal, we should, in the interests of security, oppose the release of the other five'. There had, she continued, also been discussion about reopening the cases of enemy alien Communist internees during which she had indicated the difficulty of preventing the release of such internees under Category 19 'now that a supporter of the USSR only may be described as "actively friendly to the Allied cause"'.[58]

The cases of the Beuer group Czechs were reviewed by the Home Office Advisory Committee just a few days later, on 12 August 1941, which in turn reported that the entry of Russia into the war and the Anglo-Russian Alliance had 'completely revolutionised the attitude of the Czech Communist refugees towards the British war effort and converted them into willing and even enthusiastic supporters of our war effort'. Consequently, it was recommended that the two Beuers, Fantl, Kreibich, Rubal and, with some reservations, Freund be released from internment.[59]

In fact, the entry of the Soviet Union into the war proved a source of confusion for the refugees themselves. The refugee informant 'Miller' revealed on 24 June 1941, two days after the German invasion, in his fifteenth report on the CRTF hostel in Bloomsbury, Canterbury Hall, that:

> The news of Germany's invasion of Russia came as a great surprise to the communists in Canterbury Hall. They do not yet appear to have received any instructions as to the policy they are to adopt in the face of this new development. Some of the communists were very distressed, others, particularly the Czechoslovak Youth, are confident that the Russians will get the better of the Nazis.[60]

'Kaspar', another of MI5's most diligent refugee informers (i.e. the Austrian Josef Otto von Laemmel), reported to W.D. Robson-Scott in August 1941 that:

> there have been various meetings in the Fortis Green Hostel [in North London] and other communist resorts in the last few weeks in order to give party members information about the new line to be adopted as a result of the invasion of Russia.

Two CRTF members from as far away as Cumberland had been trying to attend, so 'Kaspar' reported further, in order to be able to take back with them the 'new instructions'.[61]

Although, once the Soviet Union had become Britain's ally, much of the perceived urgency evaporated, MI5 continued its surveillance of CRTF refugees throughout the war. Reports continued to be compiled on where Communist influence was suspected, for instance among the residents of Canterbury Hall, where, *inter alia*, a branch of the Communist-inspired Czechoslovak–British Friendship Club had been established.[62] A Communist preponderance was likewise noted at the Fortis Green Hostel[63] whose British warden, Hetty Bower, had been marked down by MI5 as early as July 1940 as 'not being entirely suitable'.[64]

Planning for the post-war period by Communists in the CRTF was also a matter of interest to MI5. 'Kaspar' reported, for example, on 18 November 1944 that Heinz Schmidt had advised the CRTF trustees that a Prague office should be established after the liberation of Czechoslovakia. According to Schmidt's plan, the office was to be staffed by leading officials of the CRTF groups who would facilitate the return of individual members. In 'Kaspar's' opinion, there was more to this proposal than met the eye, however:

> As Communist circles admit in confidence, the motive behind this plan is the anxiety lest German and Austrian Communists will be prevented from returning to the continent as soon as they wish. They are therefore trying to ensure their return at the most opportune moment through other organisations.[65]

After the war, MI5's informants still remained watchful, with 'Kaspar' noting, for instance, the proposal of the Communist CRTF refugees that all CRTF members should initially be repatriated to Prague before being dispatched to their ultimate destinations, evidently 'to provide the Communists with an early opportunity of leaving this country outside the general repatriation scheme'.[66] After that, however, the number of reports on the CRTF that were filed by MI5 decreased to a trickle, and indeed, between September 1946 and the beginning of 1949, MI5 apparently received no such papers at all. By 1949, a new wave of refugees had begun arriving from Czechoslovakia who, like their predecessors, would call on the CRTF to support them; but these were refugees from Communism rather than from Fascism, a different set of circumstances altogether.

Notes

1 White to Vivian, 13 March 1940, The National Archives [TNA], KV2/2715/34.
2 On the BCRC/CRTF, see, for example, Peter Heumos, *Die Emigration aus der Tschechoslowakei nach Westeuropa und dem Nahen Osten, 1938–1945*, Munich: R. Oldenbourg Verlag 1989, pp. 209ff.; Jana Buresova, 'The Czech Refugee Trust Fund in Britain 1939–1950', in Charmian Brinson and Marian Malet, eds, *Exile in and from Czechoslovakia during the 1930s and 1940s: Yearbook of the Research Centre for German and Austrian Exile Studies*, vol. 11, 2009, pp. 133–45.
3 'Czech Refugee Trust Fund: Annual Report to 31 March 1955', [p. 1], Introduction, TNA, HO294/5.
4 'Czech Refugee Trust Fund: Consideration of Future Activities', n.d., [p. 1], TNA, HO294/7.
5 Sometimes given as thirteen, to include a separate group of Czech Communists.
6 Source M/S report, 20 February 1940, TNA, KV2/2715/26ax.
7 Berkshire Constabulary Report on Irmgard Sattler, 11 November 1939, TNA, KV2/2714/1a.
8 'Czech Refugee Trust Fund: In continuation of MI5 Memorandum of 30.1.40', 11 March 1940, TNA, KV2/2715/33a.
9 The names Wilhelm Senger and Gotthard Schild were cited in this connection.
10 'Czech Refugee Trust Fund: In continuation of MI5 Memorandum of 30.1.40', 11 March 1940, TNA, KV2/2715/33a.
11 Kell to Maxwell, 30 January 1940, TNA, KV2/2714/17a.
12 White to Vivian, 13 March 1940, TNA, KV2/2715/34.
13 'Czech Refugee Trust Fund', 14 December 1939, TNA, KV2/2714/3a.
14 'Alien Communists', Report from Berkshire Constabulary, 23 November 1939, TNA, KV2/2714/4a.
15 'British Committee for Refugees from Czechoslovakia', Special Branch Report, 11 January 1940, TNA, KV2/2714, n.no.
16 See Kurt Hiller, *Rote Ritter: Erlebnissen mit deutschen Kommunisten*, Gelsenkirchen: Ruhr-Verlag 1951; Eugen M. Brehm, 'Zu Kurt Hillers *Roten Rittern*', appendix to 1980 reprint of *Rote Ritter*, published Berlin: A.W. Mytze.
17 *Rote Ritter*, pp. 92ff.
18 'Zu Kurt Hillers *Roten Rittern*'.
19 SIS to Liddell, 3 January 1939, TNA, KV2/2686/1a.
20 Bunbury, Memorandum, 22 January 1940, pp. 4–5, TNA, KV2/2715/25B.
21 Note appended to Moeller-Dostali to Halifax, stamped as received 13 December 1939, TNA, FO371/24106.

22 Moeller-Dostali, 'Exposé about the incidents in Czech Refugee Trust Fund', n.d., TNA, FO371/24106.
23 *Ibid.* In Hiller's *Rote Ritter*, however, which reproduces an account of this incident by Schultz (or 'D') himself, it was recalled that the signatures had been those of 'Miss A.', i.e. Elizabeth Allen (pp. 100–1).
24 MI5 Report, source M/S, 28 December 1939, TNA, KV2/2714/6a.
25 Bunbury, Memorandum, 3 January 1940, TNA, KV2/2714/8a.
26 MI5 Memorandum, 15 January 1940, TNA, KV2/2714/10a.
27 Source 'H' Memorandum, 15 January 1940, TNA, KV2/2714/9a.
28 Untitled MI5 document, 15 January1940, p. 3, TNA, KV2/2714/10a.
29 White, Memorandum, 16 January 1940, TNA, KV2/2714/11a.
30 MI5 Memorandum, 'Czech Refugee Trust Fund', 30 January 1940, TNA, KV2/2714/16a.
31 White, Memorandum, 31 January 1940, TNA, KV2/2715/18a.
32 Bunbury, Memorandum, 10 April 1940, TNA, KV2/2716/42B.
33 Kell to Maxwell, 22 April 1940, TNA, KV2/2716/44a.
34 Haylor, Memorandum, 25 May 1940, TNA, KV2/2716/50a.
35 Yvonne Kapp, *Time Will Tell: Memoirs*, London/New York: Verso 2003, p. 219.
36 Yvonne Kapp and Margaret Mynatt, *British Policy and the Refugees, 1933–1941*, London/Portland: Frank Cass, 1997 (i.e. published nearly 50 years after completion).
37 On this, see, for example, source Sloane report, 'Memorandum on Czechoslovakian Passports', 19 May 1940, TNA, KV2/2716/47b.
38 Haylor Memorandum, 25 May 1940, TNA, KV2/2716/50a.
39 Kell to Maxwell, 24 May 1940, TNA, KV2/2716/49a.
40 Maxwell to Kell, 27 May 1940,TNA, KV2/2716/51b.
41 'Recommendations for dealing with the Czech Problem in the UK', 16 June 1940, TNA, KV2/2716/51c.
42 White to Cooper, 20 August 1940, TNA, KV2/2718/101c.
43 Haylor to Bagot, 18 August 1940, TNA, KV2/2718/99a.
44 M/S Report, 'Miss Wellington's Black List', hand dated 17 August 1940, TNA, KV2/2718/99b.
45 *Ibid.*
46 *Ibid.*
47 See note 9, above.
48 TNA, KV2/2718/99b.
49 Prestige to White, 16 July 1940, TNA, KV2/2718/89x. The documents were largely Czech interim passports and certificates of right of domicile in Czechoslovakia.
50 10 July 1940, TNA, KV2/2718/88c.
51 Commandant, Racecourse Aliens' Camp, York to War Office, 11 July 1940, TNA, KV2/2718/88e.
52 See, for example, Special Branch Report, 'Czech Refugee Trust Fund Officials, Internment', 9 July 1940, TNA, KV2/2718, 86a; MI5 Memorandum forwarded to New Scotland Yard, 22 July 1940, TNA, KV2/2718/89a.

53 Bagot Memorandum, 4 December 1940, TNA, KV2/2719/135a.
54 Internal MI5 Memorandum, 25 July 1940, TNA, KV2/2910/380a.
55 See Report of Home Office Advisory Committee, n.d. [1941], TNA, KV2/2911/293a.
56 *News Chronicle*, 24 May 1941.
57 On 3 July 1941, *Hansard*, 5th Series, *Parliamentary Debates*, House of Commons, vol. 372, col. 1473.
58 Bagot Memorandum, 7 August 1941, TNA, KV4/326/17a. The reference is to the August 1940 White Paper, *Civilian Internees of Enemy Nationality* (Cmd. 6223), and its nineteenth category for release from internment which applied to exiles engaged in anti-Nazi activity.
59 'Report of the Home Office Advisory Committee on the Czech Communist Cases Referred to them for Consideration', 13 August 1941, TNA, KV4/326/21b.
60 Source Miller Report, 'Canterbury Hall: 15th Report', 24 June 1941, TNA, KV2/2725/276k.
61 Robson-Scott Memorandum, 14 August 1941, TNA, KV2/2725/293x.
62 Source Kaspar Report, 'Communist Agitation in Canterbury Hall', 20 February 1942, TNA, KV2/2726/329zy.
63 'Extract from Source Miller Report dated 5.6.43 re the Czechoslovak Hostel at Fortis Green', 12 June 1943, TNA, KV2/2728/392a.
64 In 'The Czech Refugee Trust Fund', 29 July 1940, TNA, KV2/2718/94b. It was noted that Hetty Bower's husband was a member of the CPGB and that she herself had 'Communist contacts'.
65 TNA, KV2/2728/40r.
66 Source Kaspar, 'The Czech Refugee Trust Fund', 28 May 1945, TNA, KV2/2728/408a.

15

Whispers and lies: the informers

Central to MI5's business of information gathering was the intelligence obtained through informers. Compiling information on the German-speaking refugee population was frequently achieved by enlisting members of that same community: refugees spying on other refugees. Since Security Service files generally set out to obscure the identity of their individual refugee informers, it is sometimes not easy to state with any certainty who they were, though much can be gleaned through careful detective work.

Firstly the motives: why would refugees who themselves had suffered hardship, displacement and loss choose to inform on their fellows? Financial gain scarcely seems to have been a factor, as outlined below, nor was preferential treatment – such as exemption from internment – on offer to any great extent. In some cases, it is possible that gratitude to Britain, the country that had offered them asylum, may have acted as an inducement – informing being viewed as a contribution to the war effort? – and there is some evidence to support such a supposition. However, in many cases, deeply felt personal grudges seem to have been the driving incentive, combined with political enmities often dating back to the ideological battles in Germany and Austria in the years leading up to emigration.

Above all, the period that some of the German and Austrian political exiles had spent in Prague between 1933 and 1938–39 appears to have exerted a powerful influence on refugee relationships in Britain thereafter. Non-Communists were convinced that the Communists had gained the upper hand within the refugee organisations in Prague (thereby giving them priority for evacuation) and within the Czech Refugee Trust Fund after arrival in Britain. The motivation of some of the refugee informers can certainly be traced back to hostile relations in Prague as well as to alleged denunciations in Britain of non-Communist refugees, and in particular of ex-Communists who had broken with the Party, by the Communists of the Trust Fund.

Other refugee informers were apparently motivated by more recent ideological battles on British soil: in particular, the skilful gaining of control by the Communists of the large-scale refugee organisations, the Free German League of Culture and the Austrian Centre. These organisations, which started life as ostensibly non-political and directed their appeal at a wide spectrum of the refugee community in Britain, soon came under strong Communist influence, even if this was not always apparent to outsiders. The fact that this was achieved by the hard work and commitment of the Communist activists did not alter the fact that non-Communists felt themselves excluded and indeed personally wronged by these developments.

One of those ousted from the Free Austrian organisations in disagreeable circumstances, and consequently with a particular axe to grind, was the Austrian Christian Socialist Josef Otto von Laemmel[1] who, as well as being a member of the Council of Austrians, served as Austrian Centre librarian between April 1939 and May 1940. So embittered was he by the experience that he turned informer – the cover names 'Kaspar', and later 'Kaspar (Lamb)', frequently found in MI5 files, are his – and kept MI5 supplied until the end of the war and beyond with information on the 'abuses', as he saw them, of the Communist functionaries. 'Kaspar' was assisted in this by his wife Renate, particularly during the period that he himself was interned. Renate von Laemmel, sometimes identified by name in MI5 papers, was another ex-employee of the Centre, who at the end of 1940 was quoted as stating that 'almost all the members of staff [at the Centre] are Communists. If anybody said he was a Social Democrat he became an object of ridicule'.[2]

Laemmel, like most other refugee informers, was not spared from internment in return for his information, although in his semi-autobiographical novel, *Das Unzerstörbare*, of 1981, his protagonist's 'special services' do receive recognition when he arrives in Mooragh Internment Camp. Indeed they earn him a number of exceptional privileges (a room to himself, fast access to his mail and the use of a typewriter). These services, which Laemmel's semi-fictional counterpart Andreas Lengbach undertakes before, during and after internment, consist of informing the British authorities 'about the political structure of Austria and the Austrian refugees living in London'.[3]

'Kaspar' was particularly active in informing on Austrian activities, organisations and personalities, for example, on the Austrian Centre, on the Austrian Communist Party in Great Britain, on the Circle of Friends of Austrians in H.M. Forces, on the National Union of Austrian Students, as well as on leading Austrian Communists like Eva Kolmer (repeatedly), Willi Scholz, Jenö Kostmann, Engelbert Broda and Paul Löw-Beer. Some of this information evidently came from his own previous knowledge and present observations, though it is clear that 'Kaspar' also had his personal sources within the chain of information, 'insiders' like himself within the ranks of the Austrian emigration. One of these was a certain Rudolf Peiker who on 4 January 1941 reported to 'Kaspar' on the current state of affairs at the Austrian Centre, which he defined as 'the political centre of the Austrian Communist Party'. Whereas formerly political discussions had been held on Centre premises, now they mostly took place externally in Westbourne Court (a nearby block of flats where Peiker himself and a number of the political exiles lived), at Windsor Court (to where the headquarters of the Czech Refugee Trust Fund had decamped) or in Oxford, 'a centre of Communist political activity'.[4]

However, 'Kaspar' did not confine himself to Austrian activities, but also began to report on comparable German events: on a FGLC meeting, for example, at Caxton Hall, on 28 March 1942.[5] The following month, he was reporting on strife among exiled German Communists Ernst Hermann Meyer and Heinz Schmidt, on the one hand, and Wilhelm Koenen, on the other.[6] It is not known who 'Kaspar's' informants within the German exile community were; but his MI5 handler, the Germanist William Robson-Scott, whose wartime role it was to gather information about the German-speaking political exiles, wrote that 'Kaspar' would now try to supply him with names of leading German Communists and moreover that he could name most of the Czech Communists.[7]

Nor is it certain who, by 1943, was supplying 'Kaspar' with information from the internment camps, yet on 6 August 1943, Kaspar delivered a damning report on Heinz-Alex Nathan, who was still being held in Camp 'P', the former Hutchinson Camp. Not only, according to 'Kaspar's' information, was Nathan generally regarded as homosexual but he also allegedly associated with interned Nazis.[8] It may be that this information derived from Horst Ifftner, described as MI5's camp informant in April 1943,[9] or alternatively from 'our reliable informant' Johannes Schmitt.[10] 'Kaspar' himself was described more than once by MI5 as 'normally considered reliable' or in similar terms.[11]

In addition to MI5, Special Branch carried out its own investigations into the Free Austrians, briefing MI5 on its findings. There was evidently an overlap between the sources employed by the intelligence agencies: on 27 February 1941, the indefatigable Laemmel reported to Special Branch, this time under his own name, on the pro-Communist stance adopted by the Council of Austrians, from which he had resigned for that reason, as well as by the Austrian Centre.[12]

'Kaspar' was only one of a number of insider informers on refugee activities. Indeed, reports from others also found their way to MI5 at this time on the Communist ascendancy in the Austrian Centre, for example, from one code-named 'Miller', who provided information throughout the war and indeed rivalled 'Kaspar' in the number of reports he submitted. Little is known about 'Miller' other than that, according to MI5 in July 1943, he was an 'ex-internee [...] for whom we have the highest regard'.[13]

Like 'Kaspar', 'Miller' reported to Robson-Scott, and the two informers were evidently considered practically interchangeable on some issues – an internal MI5 note from Wadeson to Robson-Scott, for example, regarding refugee soldiers serving in the Middle East and their suspected contacts with Communists in Britain, reads: 'Please ask Kaspar or Miller whether they have ever run across either of these two aliens on the continent.'[14] Like 'Kaspar' again, 'Miller' informed predominantly on Austrian affairs, reporting on 10 September 1940, for instance, that the Austrian Centre's strategy of courting Austrians of a range of political persuasions was just a cover for Communist activity, and moreover that Kolmer was in touch with the Soviet Embassy, which could well be funding the Centre.[15]

Like 'Kaspar', 'Miller' derived information from various refugee sources, among them Viktoria Johanna Katz, formerly personal assistant to Eva Kolmer and financial secretary to the Council of Austrians. Katz informed 'Miller' of the financial irregularities she had witnessed: records of the Austrian Centre's expenses or subscriptions were not kept, and when an accountant had come to check the books, Eva Kolmer had been 'so successful in sabotaging his efforts that the chartered accountant left without ever completing his work'.[16] In a further interview with Special Branch, Katz reported that she had been dismissed in December 1939, ostensibly 'on the plea of economy'; however, the fact that she was not a Communist had rendered her work 'unbearable'. In support of her statement, she submitted minutes from the Austrian Centre Finance Committee meetings of May and June 1940.[17]

In a 1943 report on the Austrian Centre, Miller passed on information he had obtained from writer and journalist Dr Walter Angel, formerly the Centre's housekeeper. Angel had in turn been speaking to Jan Schulz and Sidonie Hain, all three of them evidently still closely connected to the Centre.[18] Like Rudolf Peiker, Hain lived in Westbourne Court, in close proximity to many of the prominent Austrian Centre officials. Three years later, she was still reporting on these particular near neighbours to 'Miller'.[19] Dr Angel, too, featured again in an earlier 'Miller' report of 1943, this time by passing on information to 'Miller' from Adolf Faber, a member of the Austrian Centre committee and President of the Centre's Paddington branch, on the Centre's efforts to increase its influence over the FAM.[20] Interestingly, in a summary of intelligence reports on Franz West from 1945, MI5 noted the following chain of information: reports came from 'Miller' who had received information from Hans Hladnik whose source had been Dr Angel who himself was in contact with the Polish journalist Samuel Charendorf. Charendorf, so it was stated, was very well-informed about the affairs of the Austrian Centre.[21] Hans Hladnik was a member of the Austrian Socialist group who were bitterly hostile to the Austrian Centre.

In addition to his contacts in the Austrian Centre, 'Miller' evidently had a foothold in the centre-right Austria Office, reporting from there in the run-up to the formation of the FAM (of which the Austria Office was initially a constituent part) in December 1941 of the consultations between the Austria Office and the Austrian Centre. Within a matter of weeks, however, the Communists in the Centre had very obviously taken the upper hand in the new alliance. A meeting was held at the Austria Office in January 1942 between representatives of both groups which 'Miller' set out to observe by staying 'in the premises of the British Austrian Club which is in the same house'. The Austria Office representatives had appeared 'visibly depressed' at the increasing Communist control of the FAM. Eva Kolmer for the Austrian Centre was allegedly using her Austria Office equivalent Emil Müller-Sturmheim as nothing more than a 'cover', and the alliance was also proving unequal from a financial point of view, since the Austria Office had only limited resources whereas Kolmer 'positively threw money about'.[22]

Beyond inter-Austrian relations, 'Miller' reported on several occasions on relations between the exiled Austrians and exiled Czechs[23] and, in addition, evidently had his contacts within the German, as well as the Austrian, exile communities. 'Miller's' reports in the latter area often closely mirror 'Kaspar's': in June 1943, for example, 'Miller', like 'Kaspar', reported very unfavourably on the unfortunate Heinz-Alex Nathan in Camp 'P'. According to two of 'Miller's' informants, Nathan was allegedly very unpopular in the internment camp, where he had attempted to curry favour with fellow-internee Prince Friedrich of Prussia and gained himself a reputation for insincerity. Nathan 'is not a Nazi', so it was reported in an anti-Semitic aside, 'but a typical Jew'.[24] However, when it came to the German Communists grouped around Wilhelm Koenen, neither 'Kaspar' nor 'Miller' appear to have had the necessary contacts, as is clear from a reply of June 1942 from Robson-Scott to Bagot (who had requested details of an appointment of Koenen's with a certain 'Betty'):

> I am afraid this is beyond the powers of any of my flock. It seems to me that it would only be possible for someone who was in very intimate touch with Koenen to be able to answer your question, and none of my agents are in direct contact with him.[25]

Koenen, as leader of the German Communists in exile, played a key role in setting up the Free German Movement (FGM) the following year as an overtly political counterpart to the FGLC. From the outset, MI5 was successful in having informers at the very heart of the FGM. Firstly there was

'Fred', almost certainly Fritz Wolff, the former editor of the *Pariser Tageszeitung*. Wolff, like the journalist Victor Schiff, was one of the non-Communists who joined the FGM when it was founded in September 1943 in the hope of achieving the unity of the anti-fascist German exiles. Indeed Wolff became a member of the FGM's initial working committee and later of its press committee. 'Fred's' reports on the FGM all emanate from the period around April 1944 at the time he was elected chairman of the press committee. The chairmanship, so he reported a few days later in a long account of the FGM, would entitle him to attend meetings of the FGM's inner executive committee, though he doubted he would do so because of his political opposition to the FGM leadership. This was at exactly the time that the FGM was split from top to bottom concerning the plans for Germany's borders (at the Tehran conference of late 1943, Allied intentions to cede Germany's Eastern territories to Poland had become apparent). 'The activities of the Free German Movement [...] are practically paralysed by differences within the committee', 'Fred' claimed.[26] The resignations of Wolff, Schiff and others followed soon after, due to the 'complete organisatory and political domination of the FGM through the Communists',[27] and with them, insider reports from 'Fred' ceased.

Nevertheless information from inside the FGM continued unabated, notably through source 'H.B.', whom one can identify with some certainty as Hans Beermann, a Jewish refugee and former salesman by profession. Beermann had risen to a position of prominence among his fellow-refugees by serving as Deputy Camp Supervisor of Onchan internment camp, an elected role that he evidently carried out rather successfully. An extract from an intercepted letter to Eva Kolmer, dated 10 September 1940, from an internee with the pseudonym 'Onchianus', informed her that Beermann and another refugee, Otto Wantoch, had just been released from internment and that Beermann would shortly be contacting her (presumably in his official capacity with news from Austrians in the camp). This document also bore an appended handwritten note: 'Mr Sykes: Please contact these two released internees.'[28] It is likely that this was Beermann's introduction to British intelligence.

Like Wolff, Beermann rose to a position of some importance in the FGM (becoming chairman of its Organisation Committee and speaking in that capacity at all the FGM conferences). Whilst the Communists within the Movement were eager to foreground the non-Communists in their midst, whom they considered to offer their activities a degree of 'cover', it is evident that the non-Communists in general, and MI5 in particular, thoroughly exploited that fact for their own intelligence purposes. 'H.B.', certainly, was in a prime position to deliver insider reports on the FGM's meetings and events, including on an intensely agitated meeting of the

Organisation Committee in January 1944 on the recently announced Soviet–Polish plans for Germany's post-war borders. According to 'H.B.'s' account, Victor Schiff called the publication of these statements 'a present to Goebbels', which would help prolong the war while Professor R.R. Kuczynski, the first Chairman of the FGM, maintained that:

> the Russian plans for the future of Eastern Germany represented the same kind of barbarism that the Nazis practised. If Germans were to be put under the Poles he could only advise them to stick to the Nazis, for their lot would be far worse with the Poles than with the Nazis.[29]

First-hand information on disagreements of this magnitude within the highly suspect FGM would have been greatly welcomed by the British Security Service. Interestingly, 'H.B.'s' information does not appear to have been delivered to MI5 directly but was passed through the ardent anti-Communist Kurt Hiller, whom Beermann would undoubtedly have met in internment in Onchan.

The third of the insider informers on the FGM apart from 'Fred' and 'H.B.' was source 'Ri' whose detailed reports suggest that he too was well positioned within the organisation. 'Ri' was very probably the lawyer Karl Rawitzki who, despite being a Social Democrat, remained with the FGM from beginning to end, starting as a member of its 'Preparatory Committee for the Unity of the German Emigration' and latterly even becoming the Movement's chairman. Certainly, in his report of 18 April 1944, 'Fred' referred to Rawitzki by his full name as a source of information, Rawitzki having told him 'in strict confidence' of the large donation from Eleanor Rathbone MP to the leading Communist Heinz Schmidt, editor of the FGM's *Freie Tribüne*, which 'Fred' then relayed to MI5.[30] After 'Fred's' departure, 'Ri' reported regularly on FGM meetings, for example, on Koenen and the Movement on 27 June 1944[31] and, in his 1,016th (!) report on 12 October 1944, on the growing rift between Jürgen Kuczynski and other German Communists.[32]

However, 'Ri's' activities on behalf of MI5 started well before the advent of the FGM. A 'Ri' report of 8 January 1941 recorded a meeting between him and 'L.-R.' at which they 'renewed their friendship of former days in Berlin' and at which 'Ri' handed over a letter of introduction, presumably one vouching for him from British intelligence. 'L.-R.', sometimes referred to in MI5 files as 'O.L-R.', was the pacifist Otto Lehmann-Russbueldt who has already appeared in our narrative and who himself often provided the Security Service with information. On this occasion Lehmann-Russbueldt reportedly claimed to possess 'strictly confidential information' concerning the political goals of groups of refugees in Britain, including the FGLC, the German Social Democrats and the Notgemeinschaft deutscher Wissenschaftler im Ausland (a body which assisted exiled academics). 'I should like to know', 'Ri' wrote to MI5, 'which of these organisations you would like me to investigate.'[33]

Thereafter, 'Ri' informed on various refugee organisations, sometimes passing on information from Lehmann-Russbueldt,[34] sometimes writing reports himself on groups in which Lehmann-Russbueldt was himself involved, such as the 'Klub Konstruktivisten' (or Constructivist Club) founded by the former Communist Hans Jaeger in order to discuss current problems, especially the reconstruction of post-war Germany, on a non-party basis. The Club's inaugural meeting had taken place on 27 September 1942, with Lehmann-Russbueldt in the Chair.[35] It was clearly of interest to British intelligence since, apart from the watchful 'Ri', 'a number of British officers were present', so a Ministry of Information report recorded.[36]

Otto Lehmann-Russbueldt was unusually well connected, both among the German political émigrés and in British pacifist circles, and his information gathering was undoubtedly facilitated by his reputation within the German exile community. The British Security Service, too, had a generally high opinion of him, writing of him and his services on 7 April 1941:

> I am for the time being making use of an enemy alien named Otto Lehmann of 48 Melbourne Road, Leicester to make certain confidential enquiries for me among the German community in this country. [...] We have reason to think Mr Lehmann is entirely reliable from a political point of view.[37]

Upon his own and MI5's request, Lehmann-Russbueldt was, in fact, exempted from some of the movement restrictions to which aliens were then subject in order to carry out this work more easily.[38]

However, even though MI5 clearly viewed Lehmann-Russbueldt as reliable, his post, first intercepted as early as 1934, continued to be intercepted even after the end of the war.[39] Nor was he spared the attentions of other MI5 informers, one of whom reported as late as July 1946 that O.L.-R. had left London to give lectures to German prisoners of war, particularly on 'the problem of defence'.[40] Presumably, it was feared that his well-known pacifist views might pose a problem from the standpoint of prisoner reeducation. The report, marked 'confidential', came from source 'Hi', who can be confidently identified as the writer and pacifist Kurt Hiller.

Hiller was a prolific informer on his fellow-refugees: this report, for example, was headed 'Hi' Report no. 1001. As already noted, many informers were motivated by the urge to settle old political scores; Hiller was driven by the desire to pay back the German Communists for their ruthless treatment of him in Czech exile. Shortly after Hiller's arrival in Prague, they had falsely denounced him as a Nazi collaborator on the basis of a document that he, like others, had been obliged to sign in order to gain release from a concentration camp. Hiller also claimed that Communists in Prague had tried to remove his name from the lists of those granted visas to Britain in favour of fellow-Communists; his bitter resentment at these manoeuvres was still apparent in his memoir published over a decade later.[41]

Like most other informers, Hiller was eager to ingratiate himself with the British authorities, particularly to secure release from internment. As early as August 1940, he wrote from Onchan internment camp to the International PEN Secretary Hermon Ould, declaring his enthusiasm 'to fight for freedom' and his readiness 'to help Great Britain in its most decisive hour', grandly requesting Ould to forward the statement to the newspapers and to influential religious and political leaders.[42]

Hiller was recruited as an informer by Claud Sykes who became his MI5 controller. Sykes had met Hiller even before his internment, finding him 'an amiable but over-talkative person with great political aspirations but little political insight'. However, he also noted that Hiller was 'a fervent opponent of Communism and very loyally disposed towards this country'.[43] It is also evident that Sykes interrogated Hiller during a visit to the Isle of Man in December 1940; Hiller's 'personal file' contains a letter addressed to 'my dear Mr. Sykes', in which he raged against Communist subterfuge and malpractice.[44] Sykes almost certainly recommended Hiller's release from internment. He was freed in January 1941 and his earliest reports followed days later.

Few, if any, of those who turned informer were paid for their services. Shortly after his early reports, Hiller wrote to Claud Sykes, asking for re-imbursement of his expenses:

> writing paper, stamps all cost a great deal. I would like at the same time – however painful to me – to say that I would be very grateful if you could pay my expenses incurred in our joint work. Such as visits to places mentioned in your letters etc., whether monthly or in a lump sum to cover a year's expenses [...] It is and remains for me quite understood that the services I render to Churchill's England are out of a conviction of comradeship, and not for money, as a matter of honour.[45]

The outcome of Hiller's 'painful' request is not known. However, Sykes was obviously impressed by his fervent anti-Communism, describing him more than once as 'a reliable source'. Hiller reported relentlessly on the FGLC, which he denounced as a Communist front organisation, and later on its political offshoot, the FGM, attending various Free German events, and supplementing his own observations with those of FGM insider Hans Beermann ('H.B.').

While refugees informed on fellow-refugees, these same informers also spied on each other. Hiller's MI5 file contains reports on him and his activities from political associates. One fellow-refugee reported shrewdly, if acerbically:

> He is a somewhat fantastic [*sic*] person who considers himself the most important living writer. His political reliability is undoubted but his judgement of other emigrants is unsound. He is fanatically devoted to a few friends and violently opposed to his enemies, especially the Communists.[46]

Hiller was very much a political maverick, a keen founder of political groups – particularly those in which he was the leading light. In March 1939, shortly after his arrival in London, Hiller set up the Group of Independent German Authors (GUDA), with himself as Chairman. Although GUDA met regularly for political and literary discussion meetings, it never amounted to more than fifteen members, one of whom, 'Ri', reported regularly on its activities.

In November 1939, Hiller also founded the Freiheitsbund deutscher Sozialisten or German Socialist Freedom League (FDS) – with himself again as Chairman. The FDS was conceived as a loose federation of unaligned Socialists in exile, though it never possessed more than thirty members, many of whom were overseas. One MI5 officer, who claimed 'we know all about Kurt Hiller', described the FDS as 'a minute Socialist organisation'.[47] MI5 nonetheless continued to keep Hiller and his political projects under observation. Much of his 'personal file' after 1941 consists of reports from informers on the proceedings of various lectures and meetings: records of the small change of political discourse in exile.

Others, like Hiller, who felt that they had been compromised or endangered in Prague by the actions of the KPD, and who subsequently turned informer in Britain, included the journalist and ex-Communist Walter D. Schultz (who had befriended Hiller in Oranienburg concentration camp).[48] Schultz is named in an M/S (i.e. Sykes) report as a source on Communists in leading positions in the Czech Refugee Trust Fund in Windsor and London.[49] They also included a source known as 'Mansfield', whose identity is uncertain. Like Hiller, 'Mansfield' claimed to have been treated shabbily by the Communists in Prague and indeed to have had to visit the CRTF office there in the company of Sir Walter Layton's secretary. 'Mansfield's' 'Report No 14', which contains these personal details, is almost entirely concerned with the 'Communist terror' he experienced in Prague.[50] It is possible that 'Mansfield' was the journalist Eugen M. Brehm, a former SAP member who had grown close to Hiller and Schultz, though this cannot be verified.

Brehm certainly acted as a long-term informer for MI5. Unusually, a collection of wartime letters from Claud Sykes to Brehm, who was by then working for the BBC Monitoring Service at Evesham, have survived, confirming that Brehm was reporting regularly to Sykes on fellow-refugees. On 29 May 1941, for instance, Sykes wrote: 'I have heard that a certain communist clique is trying to get possession of the German dept of the BBC. What have you to say about this?' In classic spymaster mode, Sykes warned Brehm in the same letter to be careful of what he said in any Lyons Corner House, but especially the one at the corner of Tottenham Court Road and Oxford Street, because 'a large number of Austrian Centre communists are now employed as waiters in such establishments'. By April 1942, Brehm was reporting on the erstwhile leader of the German Youth Movement, the influential 'Tusk' (i.e. Eberhard Koebel) who, like Brehm, was employed by the BBC at Evesham, and whom Sykes deemed 'dangerous'. Brehm evidently succeeded in eliciting information from 'Tusk' 'by sharing a certain sympathy for Vansittartism'. 'Let him talk as much as he will', Sykes instructed Brehm, 'and then let me know what he says'.[51]

Among those whom Kurt Hiller encountered in Onchan camp was the political journalist Rudolf Moeller-Dostali, a man whose political past was so murky that he commanded almost universal mistrust. The politically agile M-D (to use his MI5 code name) had begun his political life as a member of the SPD, before switching to the KPD in 1920. For fourteen years, he had been a Communist journalist and party functionary. In 1931, he had joined the Soviet Trade mission in Berlin, giving rise to the accusation that he was working for the Soviet intelligence service OGPU (an accusation which pursued him even into his post-war political career in West Germany). In July 1934, M-D took refuge in Prague, then fell out with the KPD, left the Party and converted to Catholicism, a move earning him the hostility of his former comrades – which he reciprocated. Despite the alleged machinations of the Communists in Prague, he managed to escape to Britain under the auspices of the Jesuits.

Rumour and suspicion continued to dog M-D in London. Elizabeth Allen, of the CRTF, wrote of him that he was 'a German ex-Communist and an undesirable character [who] is regarded by political refugees as a person with whom it is unwise to associate'.[52] 'Mansfield', for example, called him 'a very bad egg indeed. Personally he is a crook and a mean swine.'[53] Another refugee commented that 'he is a very unreliable person whose sole object in life is to make money.'[54] Special Branch eventually interviewed him at some length, concluding that 'Dostali is undoubtedly an undesirable person and a very dangerous one'.[55] As a highly suspect figure, he was interned in May 1940.

M-D's activity as an MI5 informant began only during his internment in Onchan, where he was interviewed by Claud Sykes in December 1940. He was subsequently transferred to the Oratory Schools in London for more intensive questioning. His file contains a twenty-page transcript of his interrogation by Sykes, conducted over two days. Clearly the purpose of the interrogation was to elicit information from Moeller-Dostali on Comintern practices as well as KPD party structures, based on his own first-hand knowledge.[56] Sykes was evidently convinced of his reliability in such matters, emphasising that 'as an ex-Communist, Moeller-Dostali is a very valuable source'.[57] For his part, M-D clearly hoped that collaborating with British intelligence would help secure his release, as Sykes indeed recommended: 'I would urge that in view of the information he had given us, he may be fairly said to have earned his release'.[58] M-D was freed shortly after, though he was kept under regular surveillance.

Karl Otten, who has already figured in this narrative, was also an eager informer on his fellow-refugees. However, he differs from other informers in that he was actually employed – and paid – by British intelligence. Shortly before the war, he had been recruited to a secret department of the Foreign Office, known as Department EH, an acronym for Electra House, the building it occupied on London's Victoria Embankment. Department EH was responsible for planning and devising propaganda to the enemy, including, for example, leaflets dropped by the RAF over Germany or wireless broadcasts. In July 1940, Department EH was absorbed into the Special Operations Executive (SOE). Otten was attached to Department SO2, which considered him 'a trusted employee'.[59]

Hans Wolffsohn, with whom Otten had stayed when first in London, commented disparagingly, that 'all his life Otten had always managed to make money out of politics'.[60] However, although Otten was actually paid an 'allowance' by Department EH, his principal motive in collaborating with British intelligence was evidently a growing loyalty to Britain and commitment to the war against Nazism. He told his publisher Gottfried Berman Fischer: 'We must act now. There is no going back and the existence of every one of us, the existence of Europe, depends on the victory of the Allies.'[61]

Otten was also driven by a virulent anti-Communism, which led him to denounce the FGLC, sometimes on rather flimsy evidence. Nonetheless, MI5 appear to have accepted his judgements as authoritative and reliable. At Otten's prompting, an MI5 agent (easily identifiable as Claud Sykes) visited the League in the guise of a journalist interested in refugee matters. He found much to arouse suspicion, particularly the catering facilities:

> The KULTURBUND supplies its members with excellent meals at the price of one shilling – meals that would cost at least 2/6 in any London restaurant, so Otten told me, and what I saw bore it out. I can only agree with him that the KULTURBUND must be subsidised from some unknown source to be able to afford such luxuries.[62]

The implication was clear: such excellent catering must be subsidised by a source such as the Soviet Embassy, a suspicion long held by MI5, though never proven. Regarding the League's hidden sources of income, Otten also noted that Jürgen Kuczynski was surprisingly flush with money (unusual for any refugee), claiming to have learned from a fellow-refugee, and former banker, that the money came from the party funds of the KPD, held in an Amsterdam bank and invested on the stock market.[63]

By then, Otten had begun to filter information through Claud Sykes: 'Otten reports to me that Kuczynski has been very much on the warpath again, voicing his hatred of England and making remarks of a defeatist nature.'[64] Otten accused Kuczynski and his fellow-Communist Alfred Meusel of spreading defeatist propaganda, by asserting that Britain and Germany intended to make peace in order to make common cause against the Soviet Union. He denounced Meusel melodramatically as 'a very dangerous man, capable of committing every crime'.[65] Sykes and Otten later discussed a plan to ensnare Kuczynski into making incriminating statements to witnesses who would be prepared to repeat them to the authorities.[66] The plan never came to fruition but, in a parallel existence, Sykes the translator was just completing his English version of Otten's novel *The Trip to Germany*.

Despite his privileged position, Otten himself remained under surveillance – indeed early in 1940 Millicent Bagot requested 'two copies of all Otten's correspondence for the next few weeks', adding: 'This warrant is particularly important at the moment.'[67] Otten remained at SO2 until his intelligence career was cut short during the last winter of the war. He had virtually lost the use of his left eye in a childhood accident. During 1944, his other eye gradually deteriorated and, despite an operation to save his sight, he finally became completely blind in December 1944. Coincidentally, MI5 officer Claud Sykes left the Security Service in the same month, the internees who provided his raison d'être having been largely released.

It is striking that almost all the refugee informers, in so far as they can be identified, chose in the long run not to remain in the country that they had endeavoured to help in wartime. Rudolf Moeller-Dostali, who had rejoined the SPD in London, returned to Germany in 1946, working as a journalist and later as an SPD functionary in Essen. Most other refugee informers took time to consider their options. Otto Lehmann-Russbueldt returned to Berlin in 1951; he and his wife kept on their London flat, however, as a precautionary measure. His fellow-member of the 'Primrose League', Karl Otten, became a British citizen in 1947; he did not return to Germany but in 1958 moved to Switzerland, his creative work requiring greater proximity to a German-speaking readership. Josef Otto (von) Laemmel or 'Kaspar' remained in Britain for some fifteen years after the war, but finally returned to Graz in 1962, making a late career for himself as a writer and speaker.

The lawyer Karl Rawitzki returned to Bochum in 1952 where he went on to play an important role in local government. He had been excluded from the SPD in 1944 on account of his position within the FGM, but was accepted back into the party after the war, suggesting that he was able to offer a convincing explanation for his apparent disloyalty. Only Hans Beermann or 'H.B.', that other non-Communist functionary at the heart of the FGM, remained in Britain, dying there in 1987. Although his surviving relations had not been aware of his colourful wartime career, indeed they were surprised to learn of it, family legend has it that every year for the rest of his life Beermann would receive a Christmas card from an official British source whose provenance he would not disclose.

Notes

1 Laemmel's entitlement to the aristocratic 'von' and the title of Baron, which he used to some effect in British emigration, has been disputed (see 'Josef Otto Laemmel', http://geneal.lemmel.at/JosefOttoLaemmel.html, consulted 14 August 2011).

2 Robson-Scott, 'Further Report on the Austrian Centre', 6 December 1940, source 'Miller', information from Renate Laemmel, The National Archives [TNA], KV2/2518/115x.

3 See Josef Otto Laemmel, *Das Unzerstörbare: Eine Art biographischer Roman*, Vienna: Heimatland-Verlag 1981.

4 Source 'Kaspar' report, 'Extract from Information from Rudolf Peiker on Austrian Centre, etc', 4 January 1941, TNA, KV2/2982/20b.

5 Extract source 'Kaspar' report on Kulturbund meeting, 28 March 1942, TNA, KV2/2521/196b.

6 Source 'Kaspar' report, 17 April 1942, TNA, KV2/2799/167a.

7 Robson-Scott to Bagot, 24 September 1941, TNA, KV2/2982/32b.

8 Source 'Kaspar' report, 'Heinz Alexander Nathan', 6 August 1943, TNA, KV2/1743/79a.

9 'Appeal Case: Report', 1 April 1943, TNA, KV2/1743/53a. Interestingly, a Home Office (HO) file on the alleged camp informant Ifftner, HO 405/24273, is closed until 2048 on the grounds that it contains 'sensitive personal information which would substantially distress or endanger a living person or his or her descendants'.

10 Report on 'Heinz Alexander Nathan' from P Camp, 15 May 1943, TNA, KV2/1743/60c.

11 Internal MI5 note signed B.H. Smith, 14 March 1946, TNA, KV2/2353/324b.

12 Laemmel statement to Special Branch, 27 February 1941, TNA, KV2/2520/165a.

13 H.I. Lee (MI5) to Aliens Department, HO, 25 July 1943, TNA, KV2/1743/73a.

14 Wadeson to Robson-Scott, 25 June 1944, TNA, KV2/2800/239b.

15 Source 'Miller' report, 'The Austrian Centre', 10 September 1940, TNA, KV2/2517/105b.
16 Robson-Scott report, source 'Miller', 'Further Report on the Austrian Centre', 6 December 1940, TNA, KV2/2518/115x.
17 Katz, Special Branch Statement, 3 March 1941, TNA, KV2/2520/165a.
18 Source 'Miller' report 'The Austrian Centre', 2 January 1943, TNA, KV2/3068/62z.
19 Source 'Miller' report, 'Members of the Austrian Centre and Service with H.M. Forces', 6 July 1943, TNA, KV2/3068/73b.
20 Source 'Miller' report, 'The Austrian Centre and the Free Austrian Movement', 2 January 1943, TNA, KV2/3068/62a.
21 Summary of intelligence reports on Weintraub [i.e. West], n.d. [1945], TNA, KV2/2983/100b.
22 Source 'Miller' report, 'Free Austrian Movement', 18 January 1942, TNA, KV2/2521/191yx.
23 See, for example, 'Extract from a Source Miller Report re a meeting between Czechoslovaks and Austrians', 29 April 1943, TNA, KV2/2522/229a.
24 Source 'Miller' report, 'Heinz Alexander Nathan', 6 June 1943, TNA, KV2/1743/67a.
25 D. Fuller for Robson-Scott to Bagot, 19 June 1942, TNA, KV2/2799/179a.
26 Source 'Fred' report, 18 April 1944, TNA, KV2/1876/351b.
27 See 'V. Schiff's and F. Wolff's letter to Prof. Kuczynski, May 7th', in Bundesarchiv Berlin-Lichterfelde [SAPMO-BArch], SgY13/V239/9/32.
28 MI5 handwritten note, appended to 'Onchianus' to Kolmer, 10 September 1940, TNA, KV2/ 2517/105ax.
29 See TNA, KV2/1876/335b.
30 Source 'Fred' report, 18 April 1944, TNA, KV2/1876/351b.
31 Extract source 'Ri' report on FGM meeting of 27 June 1944, 29 June 1944, TNA, KV2/2800/240a.
32 Source 'Ri' report, no 1016, sent from Robson-Scott to Bagot, 12 October 1944, TNA, KV2/1876/380a.
33 Source 'Ri' report, 'Otto Lehmann-Russbueldt', 8 January 1941, TNA, KV2/2005/253a.
34 For example, 'Free German Committee', information from 'L-R', source 'Ri', 15 August 1941, TNA, KV2/2799/143y.
35 Source 'Ri' report, 28 September 1942, TNA, KV2/2005/270a.
36 W.F. Henson, Ministry of Information, to Geoffrey Harrison, Foreign Office, 19 November 1942, TNA, FO371/30911.
37 T.F. Turner for Col. Sir David Petrie to Chief Constable Leicester Police, 7 April 1941, TNA, KV2/2005/255a.
38 See Chief Constable Leicester Police to Petrie, 15 April 1941, TNA, KV2/2005/256a.
39 See for example, 'Cross-reference to Censor's Comment', 25 April 1947, TNA, KV2/200/312a for post-war interception of mail.
40 Source 'Hi' report no. 1001, 1 July 1946, TNA, KV2/2006/306a.

41 Kurt Hiller, *Rote Ritter: Erlebnisse mit deutschen Kommunisten*, Gelsenkirchen: Ruhr Verlag 1951.
42 Hiller to Hermon Ould, 11 August 1940, cited in Michael Seyfert, *Im Niemandsland: Deutsche Exilliteratur in britischer Internierung*, Berlin: Das Arsenal 1984, p. 130.
43 M/S report, 21 June 1940, TNA, KV2/2811/21a.
44 Hiller to Sykes, 12 January 1941, TNA, KV2/2799/128b.
45 Report from Kurt Hiller re. Allen and Co., 28 March 1941, TNA, KV2/1872/137c. This extract from Hiller's report occurs in Jürgen Kuczynski's file, but is not to be found in Hiller's own file.
46 Report, source 'Mansfield', 25 February 1941, TNA, KV2/2811/32a.
47 Report 20 July 1942, TNA, KV2/2811/52a.
48 See Eugen Brehm, 'Zu Kurt Hillers *Roten Rittern*', given as appendix in 1980 reprint of Kurt Hiller's, *Rote Ritter*, Berlin: A.W. Mytze, [p. 132].
49 M/S report, 'Distribution of Communists in the Czech Trust Fund', 24 May 1940, TNA, KV2/2716/50x.
50 Source 'Mansfield', 'Report no. 14', 11 October 1941, TNA, KV2/2799/146a.
51 Letters from Sykes to Brehm held at Institut für Zeitgeschichte, Munich, ED228/49.
52 Cross-reference report Miss Allen, secretary CRTF, TNA, KV2/2686/36ax.
53 Report C.W. Sykes, B8c (source 'Ma') 21 January 1941, TNA, KV2/2686/68a.
54 M/S report, 27 August 1940, quoting Martin Christian Sander, TNA, KV2/2686/40a.
55 Special Branch report to MI5, 5 April 1940, TNA, KV2/2686/42a.
56 Report of interrogation of Rudolf Moeller-Dostali, 17 February 1941, TNA, KV2/2687/74b. The report, signed by Sykes, contains references to M-D's 'Onchan statement'.
57 Report C.W. Sykes, B.8.c, 18 June 1941,TNA, KV2/3502/46a.
58 Report C.W. Sykes, B.8.c, 17 February 1941, TNA, KV2/2687/74b.
59 SIS to MI5, 29 August 1947, TNA, KV2/1123/339.
60 TNA, KV2/1120/89b.
61 Otten to Gottfried Bermann Fischer, 16 November 1939, S.Fischer Verlag Papers, Lily Library, Indiana University.
62 Report re Kulturbund', 21 June 1940, original in OF 42/9, a file on the FGLC, not released, copy in John Heartfield's file (PF 47198), TNA, KV2/1010/25b.
63 Report SIS (Vivian) to MI5 (Bagot), 8 May 1940, TNA, KV2/1872/87a.
64 M/S report, 15 July 1940, TNA, KV2/1872/95b.
65 SIS (Vivian) to MI5 (Cpt. Derbyshire), 22 April 1940, TNA, KV2/1872/81a.
66 M/S report, 2 August 1940, TNA, KV2/1872/101a.
67 Bagot to B4b, 16 March 1940 TNA, KV2/1122/243a.

16

Friends in need: British supporters of the refugees

One of the characteristics of the German-speaking refugees was the surprisingly high level of support they received from some, at least, of their British hosts. Fundraising and relief work were carried out on a fairly large scale by philanthropic individuals and organisations of various kinds. The refugees not infrequently received help from British religious bodies such as the Religious Society of Friends or from prominent Englishmen and women, moving predominantly in liberal or intellectual circles, who were prepared to offer them financial and/or moral support or even intercede with British officialdom on their behalf.

In addition, specific groups of refugees were often able to find sponsors among their British counterparts: writers, for instance, were assisted by the English and International PEN groups led by such figures as Hermon Ould and Storm Jameson, artists by the British-based Artists International Association. Refugee Socialists or trade unionists might well receive assistance from Britons with similar political affiliations. Jewish refugees were in many cases helped by their British co-religionists – via the Jewish Refugees Committee, for example – as were Christians by such bodies as the Church of England Committee for Non-Aryan Christians.

When the refugees began to establish their own organisations in Britain, these frequently enjoyed the backing of British patrons from a variety of walks of life whose support was vital in legitimising their existence, not least in the eyes of the general British public. When, for example, the first of the Austrian refugee groups, Austrian Self-Aid, was founded in London in 1938, it was under the variegated patronage of the Liberal feminist, Margery Corbett Ashby, the influential if eccentric Duchess of Atholl, the Cardinal Archbishop of Westminster and the Chief Rabbi, amongst others. Successor organisations, the Council of Austrians and the large-scale Austrian Centre could boast among their British patrons such prominent champions of the refugees as Lord Hailey, the Chairman of the Coordinating Committee for Refugees; the radical Labour MP, D.N. Pritt; the Conservative MP Captain Victor Cazalet; and the Archbishop of

York. Similarly, when in December 1938 the FGLC was founded, its numerous British patrons included the journalist Wickham Steed; the Labour MP David Grenfell; and representatives of British cultural life such as the writer J.B. Priestley, the actors Walter Hudd and Sybil Thorndike and the composers Ralph Vaughan Williams and Alan Bush. George Bell, Bishop of Chichester, who was a particularly good friend to the refugees as has already been noted, was to be found as a patron both of the Austrian Centre and of the FGLC.

These two large refugee organisations, set up as broad-based and non-political but subject to increasing Communist influence – as well as the CRTF which included in its remit the responsibility for a sizeable number of Communist refugees – were of particular concern to the British Security Service, as has been seen, as were, not infrequently, the British friends and supporters of these particular associations. Moreover, as time went by, entire British support groups were established such as the Friends of Austria and the Allies Inside Germany Council (later called the British Council for German Democracy), which increased the refugee organisations' level of influence in Britain as well as the vigilance of the Security Service.

It is known, for example, that MI5 kept files on a number of the MPs who supported the refugees – on the Liberal Geoffrey Mander, for one, who was a keen supporter of the exiled Austrians and who intervened regularly in Parliament on their behalf (though Mander's MI5 file has not been released). Communists or suspected Communists were, of course, of particular interest to the Security Service (especially, though not only, between August 1939 and June 1941, when the Nazi–Soviet Pact was in force). D.N. Pritt's file, which has been released, reports on his radical political activities from 1932 onwards: his Chairmanship of the Commission of Inquiry into the Reichstag Fire in September 1933, his support for the Nobel Peace Prize candidature of the imprisoned German journalist Carl von Ossietzky in 1936 and, as the 1930s proceeded, his assistance to individual political refugees attempting to come to or already in Britain.

An intercepted letter from the Labour MP Ellen Wilkinson, of November 1938, recorded that Wilkinson had obtained a British permit for the Communist parliamentarian Wilhelm Koenen, 'providing he is guaranteed a living and Pritt is doing that'.[1] A few weeks later, Pritt's MI5 file noted that 'it seemed probable that Koenen had gone to stay at [...] the address of D.N. Pritt with whom he had been in contact and who had guaranteed him a living in England'.[2] The following year, so this same MI5 file reveals, Pritt was also writing to Osbert Peake at the Home Office on behalf of another of his refugee protégés, this time the interned Communist Jürgen Kuczynski, a 'personal friend of his' whose internment he failed to understand. Indeed, in his view 'a great mistake had been made'.[3] Pritt, who was an ardent supporter of Soviet policy and a faithful supporter of the Communist refugees, was in fact expelled from the Labour Party in March 1940 for defending the Soviet invasion of Finland (though he did not resign his parliamentary seat).

Kuczynski's internment, as is discussed in greater detail elsewhere in this study, was the subject of a great deal of correspondence between his British supporters, like Pritt, and the British authorities. His MI5 file even contains an intercepted letter, dated 26 January 1940, to his wife Marguerite, from the maverick Lilian Bowes Lyon, first cousin to the Queen, sympathising with Marguerite Kuczynski on her husband's plight.[4] Kuczynski was indeed released on 19 April 1940 as a direct result of the pressure his influential British friends had brought to bear on his behalf. An MI5 report, stamped 'SECRET' and entitled 'Tactics of the German Communist Refugees', concluded ruefully: 'Everyone of these emigrés has, of course, an English Professor or MP, who testifies to their good character and anti-fascist conviction, so that it is really very difficult to bring them down or get them locked up.'[5]

Eva Kolmer, too, the Secretary of the Austrian Centre and later also the moving force behind the FAM, succeeded in assembling a large number of British friends and supporters which stood both her and the Austrian organisations she represented in good stead. From the time of Kolmer's first visit to Britain, in 1936, she had come under MI5 surveillance as a 'fanatical Communist',[6] yet her early contacts in Britain included men and women of the widest range of political opinion, who themselves were regarded as being among British opinion formers: Wickham Steed; Margery Corbett Ashby; the editor of *The Spectator* Wilson Harris; Lady Layton (wife of the then editor of *The Economist* and editorial director of the *News Chronicle*); the feminist, Socialist and pacifist Catherine Marshall; Hilda Browning, the Secretary for the Society for Relations with Soviet Russia; and the distinguished historian R.W. Seton-Watson, among others. Once Kolmer had been compelled to flee Austria in 1938, it was evidently Wilson Harris, Lady Layton and Seton-Watson who vouched for her with the Home Office, indicating their preparedness to maintain her while in Britain.[7]

All these links and more were brought into play in the course of Kolmer's work for Austrian refugees in wartime Britain. Intercepted mail in her MI5 file records that, at the time of alien internment, she was canvassing multi-party support in Parliament on behalf of the interned refugees from D.N. Pritt and Ellen Wilkinson of the Labour Party, the Conservative Oliver Locker-Lampson and the Liberals Richard Acland and Graham White, among others.[8] On 30 November 1940, prior to a parliamentary debate on aliens, she was invited to attend a meeting with the Labour politician Josiah Wedgwood, well known as one of the most committed and active champions of the refugees, and to bring with her a memorandum regarding the position of the internees.[9] And Wedgwood's support was put to good use for Kolmer's own personal purposes as well: on 20 February 1941, for example, Wedgwood asked the Home Secretary to explain the reason for the delay in releasing Kolmer's then husband, Jakob Wolloch, from internment.[10]

Kolmer herself, as an official of a refugee organisation, was not interned,[11] despite repeated requests for this on the part of MI5 (as discussed in chapter 11). On the contrary, she was permitted in her official capacity to visit Austrian internees in the camps, bearing letters of introduction from Lord Lytton, Chairman of the Advisory Committee on Aliens, and the Bishop of Chichester. This, so it was reported in Kolmer's MI5 file, caused 'general indignation' at the Internment Camps headquarters such that it was recommended that Lytton and Chichester should be 'given a discreet hint'.[12] A plan was even concocted to influence the Bishop against Kolmer, as MI5 officer Claud Sykes outlined to Milicent Bagot in March 1941:

> Can you make me up a sketch of Eva Kolmer? [Paul] Bondy is arranging for me to meet the Bishop of Chichester next time he is in London, but wants to be able to retail him some tidings of her mischievous activities before the meeting takes place. Then I corroborate and in this way we put the wind up the good bishop about her. Just a résumé of what can be told without giving anything away we shouldn't.[13]

This was by no means the only occasion on which George Bell, the Bishop of Chichester, would find himself at odds with the British authorities, and with British public opinion generally, for his support of the refugees. On 16 October 1940, a report had appeared in the *News Chronicle* criticising the conditions in the Rushen Women's Internment Camp on the Isle of Man,[14] its source being the FGLC. The local newspaper, the *Isle of Man Examiner*, soon deduced that, since George Bell was the only one of the FGLC's list of British patrons to have visited the camp, the blame for these allegations must rest with him. In a blistering attack, the *Examiner* accused Bell of being 'the self-appointed champion of Nazis and Fascists in our midst', moreover as one who 'deliberately feeds the enemy propaganda machine with the same blatant falsehoods which Dr Goebbels turns out with such facility'.[15] In reply, Bell had put up a spirited defence of himself and the FGLC which, *inter alia*, revealed something of his motivation in supporting the (not infrequently uncomfortable) refugee causes:

> So far am I from being a 'self-appointed champion of captive Nazis and Fascists' that I became a patron of the Free German League for the very reason that it is a League of those who are utterly opposed to the Nazi regime [...] Its members have suffered, in many cases terribly, at the hands of Hitler and the Gestapo. They, and I, and the refugees now interned desire nothing so much as the overthrow of Hitler and the ending of Hitlerism.[16]

George Bell's support for the refugees was a broad one, extending to groups whose political outlook was by no means his own. As indicated earlier, however, help from British sponsors was just as likely to be politically or professionally specific, as was the case with the British Marxist composer Alan Bush. Bush was exceptionally generous with his time and energies when it came to helping his fellow Communist musicians, such as Georg Knepler of the Austrian Centre and, in particular, Ernst Hermann Meyer of the FGLC as well as their respective organisations. Bush's MI5 file records, among other things, his visits to and performances at refugee musical events: for example, he visited the FGLC, of which he was of course a patron, speaking at an afternoon devoted to the composer Hanns Eisler in March 1941[17] and he conducted a choral concert at the Austrian Centre on 9 December 1941.[18] Other contemporary sources confirm that Bush regularly offered moral support and performed at such events, introducing and conducting the very successful Young Austria Choir, for example, at the Conway Hall in 1943 and participating the following year in a widely publicised FGLC concert at the Adolph Tuck Hall, Woburn Place, that focused on his friend Ernst Hermann Meyer's compositions. Yet, while Alan Bush clearly went out of his way to assist his beleaguered exiled comrades, it is evident that he was also going through some difficult times himself in these wartime years. As a signatory to the Communist-backed People's Convention, Bush's own compositions were banned by the BBC (though the ban was later lifted);[19] moreover Bush's progress in the British Army was seriously curtailed and his applications to join ENSA and later the Army Education Corps rejected on account of his political affiliations, despite repeated reports of his exemplary conduct.[20]

MI5 was particularly nervous about the possibility of collaboration and collusion between British and foreign Communists. At the beginning of the war, the information had been received and noted that the FGLC was in close touch with the Communist Party of Great Britain.[21] For that reason, Alan Bush's friendship with Ernst Hermann Meyer came under particularly close official scrutiny. The informer code-named 'Conquest', evidently a member of the William Morris Musical Society of which Bush was Chairman, informed occasionally on the links between the two musicians. Meyer, so it was reported, was a great friend of Bush and indeed totally dominated by him; he was a secret member of the radical William Morris Society, which Bush had personally invited him to join; and Meyer was not to be contacted by the Secretary of the Society but rather only by Bush himself.[22]

In other cases, however, even where it is known that there were close political links between British men and women and members of the refugee population, MI5 files on these individuals do not always prove especially informative. As can be deduced from numerous other sources, the

Independent Labour Party (ILP) politician Fenner Brockway, for one, identified himself closely with a great many anti-fascist causes, including with the plight of the exiled Socialists from 1933 onwards: he was, for instance, very involved in the case of Dora Fabian and Mathilde Wurm and supported some of their fellow refugees who were anxious to carry out an enquiry into their unexplained death.[23] He was particularly helpful towards members of the exiled Sozialistische Arbeiterpartei or SAP, of which Dora Fabian had been a member, since this party was closely aligned with his own ILP. An intercepted letter referred to in his MI5 file also pointed to the assistance he was offering to Helmut Goldschmidt, an SAP member who had been expelled from Britain for political activity.[24] Apart from this, however, there is little in his MI5 file up until 1940 to indicate his work for refugees – possibly because Brockway's stance on other issues such as pacifism or the independence of India was of greater concern to the authorities. Certainly official suspicion of Brockway had been made explicit in May 1933 in MI5's request for a Home Office Warrant to intercept his mail on the grounds that although he was not a 'member of the Communist party of Great Britain, nor, as far as we know, of any other communist organisation', he was considered 'a communist by conviction if not by profession'.[25]

The situation is rather similar in the cases of both Storm Jameson and Hyman Levy. Although PEN President Jameson was a patron of the FGLC, there is little in her MI5 file to indicate the Security Service's concern at or awareness of her consistent support for the refugees other than a record of her acting as a referee to the Austrian writer Alexander Roda-Roda, who had applied for entry to Britain, together with a blanket statement concerning her association 'with a great variety of anti-fascist and pacifist activities'.[26] These activities were evidently deemed sufficient to put paid to her recruitment by the Civil Service Commission in 1939 for employment in the Ministry of Information, to which the Security Service objected, as it did to her writing a book the following year on the women's war effort, which would have involved her in visiting factories.[27] Her position in the English PEN-Club enabled her to offer help to numerous German and Austrian refugees, like Roda-Roda, for example in raising money to rescue endangered refugee writers from Prague in 1938–39.[28] She was also of great personal assistance to the Secretary of German PEN in Exile, the writer and journalist Rudolf Olden and his wife Ika, as well as to Olden's Austrian counterpart, the writer Robert Neumann.

In the case of the Marxist mathematician Professor Hyman Levy, while much was noted in his MI5 file about his Left Book Club activities and similar, the only indication of his links with German-speaking refugees was a note from as early as 1934 recording his prominence in the (Communist-backed) Relief Committee for the Victims of German Fascism.[29] What was not recorded there was that, through his membership of the left-wing British professional organisation the Association of Scientific Workers (AScW), and his strong support of the AScW's Foreign Scientists' Committee (which was chaired by Jürgen Kuczynski), Levy helped campaign for the integration of refugee scientists into the British war effort, from which 'enemy aliens' had previously been barred.[30] Furthermore, Levy was a committed patron of the Free German Institute which, as an adjunct to the FGLC, put on a wide range of high-level courses for adults. Levy was one of a number of British supporters of the Institute, others including Levy's fellow mathematician from Imperial College London, Professor Sydney Chapman, the journalist and author H.N. Brailsford, Corder Catchpool from the Religious Society of Friends, the Germanists Professor L.A. Willoughby from University College London and Professor Roy Pascal from Birmingham University, and the historian Dr G.P. Gooch, all of whom offered their services as lecturers free of charge.

Yet although there are certainly gaps in the files, there are still extensive – if fragmented – records indicating MI5's surveillance of prominent Britons who were acting as friends and sponsors to individual exiles or refugee groups. Even where the relevant personal file has not been released or has been destroyed, such information is not infrequently obtainable from cross-posting in other related files. There is, for example, no file available on the writer J.B. Priestley, although the fact that his hugely popular Sunday night wireless programme *Postscripts* was taken off the air in 1940 after a few months for allegedly being too left-wing confirms that an official record was kept of his activities. He was, of course, also an FGLC patron who permitted the League's Little Theatre to perform his play *They Came to a City* free of royalties. In addition it is noted in the MI5 file on John Heartfield that Priestley was one of a committee of prominent British sponsors, others including D.N. Pritt and Vernon Bartlett MP, who were negotiating for an empty shop in Regent St (where there were premises available to rent as a result of the Blitz). At a cost of £25 per week, the shop was to be used to house an exhibition being prepared by the FGLC.[31] This was the very successful *Allies Inside Germany* exhibition, featuring material devised by John Heartfield and others in support of anti-Nazi resistance inside Germany, that opened in Regent Street in July 1942 before touring the provinces.

References to numerous other British friends who devoted time and effort to assisting the refugees emerge from the MI5 files, if only in this rather roundabout way. Margaret Lloyd, for example, who was an employee of the CRTF and therefore professionally involved with the refugees, also became Vice-Chairman of the Executive Committee of the Allies Inside Germany Council, an organisation in which British friends and sponsors of the FGLC played a leading role, and later remained active in its successor organisation, the British Council for German Democracy. An intercepted letter of 12 October 1944 has Margaret Lloyd writing to the politicians and luminaries in the Free German Movement (FGM), Wilhelm Koenen and his later wife Emmy Damerius, with arrangements for the use of her house including the whereabouts of the key, the peculiarities of the Aga and hot water system, feeding arrangements for her chickens and rabbits, and instructions to make themselves at home there.[32] The radical British journalist Gordon Schaffer of *Reynolds News* was another leading light in the Allies Inside Germany Council, later also becoming editor of its journal, *Searchlight on Germany*. Schaffer was reported on by 'Kaspar' when attending a large-scale meeting organised by the FGLC in Caxton Hall on 28 March 1942. Schaffer had addressed this meeting of around 400, eighty per cent of whom reportedly consisted of Communist officials and Party members, as 'Comrades' – unsurprisingly, perhaps – before tasking them with 'calling on the German people to revolt against Fascism'.[33]

Moreover there were also British friends prepared to give money as well as moral support in aid of refugee causes in Britain and in other countries of emigration. The novelist Virginia Woolf, for example, donated the proceeds from the sale of the manuscript of *Three Guineas* to the American League for German Cultural Freedom, an organisation set up to assist exiled German writers and intellectuals.[34] The refugee organisations were in general very far from well off, with the FGLC and its associated organisations living a particularly hand-to-mouth existence.[35] Since Jürgen Kuczynski's mail was consistently intercepted, his files make a good source for details of this kind. On 10 June 1941, for example, the British Marxist novelist Leo Myers offered his friend Kuczynski a little more money 'out of the fund', adding: 'But, if the League is bound to die, for lack of money sooner or later, is it *still worth* struggling on? I might in all let you have a £100, of which I enclose £50 now.'[36] It is not clear whether the 'fund' referred to by Myers bore some connection to the reportedly rescued German Communist Party funds, to which it was rumoured that Kuczynski had access, or to Myers' own money. (Interestingly, it is reported elsewhere that Myers, who was a wealthy man, had previously made an anonymous donation to enable George Orwell to travel to Morocco to convalesce from tuberculosis.)[37] Ben Tobert, a former pupil of one of the founding presidents of the FGLC, Oskar Kokoschka, was persuaded to lend the League some money in 1944[38] (at the same time becoming a patron), as was a contact of Ernst Hermann Meyer's, the British organist and conductor Arnold Goldsbrough, who later declared himself willing to forego repayment.[39] It was also reported in April 1944 that Eleanor Rathbone MP, known widely if unofficially as 'the Member for Refugees' because of her exceptional commitment towards the refugees from National Socialism, had donated a 'large sum' to the Communist functionary Heinz Schmidt towards the running of his anti-Nazi journal *Freie Tribüne*, Schmidt having asked her for a donation of 'several hundred pounds' some weeks previously.[40]

In fact, donations to refugee causes from British friends, as recorded in contemporary documents, were wide-ranging and often somewhat unexpected in origin. A further intercepted letter in the MI5 file on Jürgen Kuczynski, dated 26 January 1943, was from Posy (Rosemary) Croft, enclosing £20 towards the cost of ING (i.e. Inside Nazi Germany) Publications, a series of pamphlets that were closely associated with the FGLC and the FGM.[41] The Hon Rosemary Croft was the daughter of the Conservative politician Brigadier-General Sir Henry Page Croft (from 1940, Lord Croft) who was known for his extreme right-wing views and lack of sympathy for the refugees. More to the point here, Rosemary Croft was the sister-in-law of the German refugee Fred Uhlman, one of the founders of the FGLC, who – to his father-in-law's chagrin – had married Rosemary's sister Diana, thereby gaining a foothold in the British aristocracy (and a larger number of useful contacts in Britain than was customary in the refugee population). It is interesting to note that Milicent Bagot's reaction to this particular letter was to ask William Robson-Scott, who ran a number of informers within the refugee organisations, to look more closely into the financial support received by ING Publications.[42]

There were similar surprises in store for the British authorities with regard to the broad-based British support attracted by the (likewise strongly Communist-influenced) FAM. The Anglo-Irish politician Sir Patrick Hannon, MP, an enthusiastic supporter of the Austrians, attended several Free Austrian events, including the first public reception of the Friends of Austria in November 1944, while on 22 October 1945 he raised the question in Parliament as to when exiled Austrians who were awaiting repatriation would finally be permitted to return home.[43] There is no MI5 file available on Sir Patrick, but a brief comment from Con O'Neill at the Foreign Office is sufficient to indicate the British official reaction: 'Odd that Sir P. Hannon, an extreme right-wing Catholic, should champion the Communist FAM!'[44]

It is possible, of course, that Hannon was not fully aware of the political background to the FAM since the FAM's public stance always made much of its broad-based composition and support base. A similar confusion was apparent in the case of the liberal political scientist Professor Sir Ernest Barker, of the University of Cambridge, whose patronage was sought by rival Austrian political groups, with an initial approach being made by the nascent Anglo-Austrian Democratic Society (AADS). This was an organisation established by Social Democrats together with other groups of a more centre-right orientation. An intercepted note in the MI5 file on the refugee scientist Engelbert Broda, who was working in Cambridge, to Eva

Kolmer in London in 1944, enclosed an English-language statement drafted for Barker condemning the AADS as pan-German in sentiment. In contrast, the rival FAM was presented as striving for Austrian independence, as was its support group, the Friends of Austria, which was not, so it was emphasised, 'to be confused with the proposed Anglo-Austrian Democratic Society [...] dominated by the more or less camouflaged Greater Germans'.[45] By the following day, this statement had evidently had its effect since Broda was able to report that Barker had decided against taking up his proposed function in the AADS.[46] The following year, however, Ernest Barker had a conversation with Otto Harpner, a leading light in the Anglo-Austrian Democratic Society, who had informed him, so Barker wrote to Broda in a further intercepted letter, that the FAM and the Friends of Austria were actually Communist in affiliation. 'I don't know where I am', Professor Sir Ernest Barker lamented.[47]

As has been seen, British attitudes to the German-speaking refugees and their organisations, during a war that was being fought against Germany, thus ranged from keen support to intense suspicion. MI5 was consistently mistrustful of the refugees and often of the Britons who went out of their way to assist them, their support being viewed as naive at best and at worst unpatriotic. It says much, however, about the calibre of many members of the refugee population in Britain and the force of their convictions that they attracted the backing of many distinguished British friends from all walks of life who were prepared to commit themselves to an essentially unpopular cause, whether the British Security Service approved of this or not.

Notes

1 Extract Ellen Wilkinson to Otto Katz, 18 November 1938, The National Archives [TNA], KV2/1062/160a.

2 Extract information sent to SIS on 21 February 1939, TNA, KV2/1062/165a.

3 Cross reference Pritt to Peake, 22 January 1940, TNA, KV2/1062/177c. See also, TNA, KV2/1871/68a.

4 Lilian Bowes Lyon to Marguerite Kuczynski, 26 January 1940, TNA, KV2/1871/63a.

5 'The German Communist Refugees', n.d., TNA, KV2/1872/81a.

6 See MI5 minute (Cumming) for V. Vivian, 30 October 1936, TNA, KV2/2516/10a.

7 Extract Home Office (HO) file K6773, 19 March 1938, in TNA, KV2/2516/52A.

8 TNA, KV2/2517/95c, 98b, 107z; KV2/2518/111ax.

9 S. Simmons (Wedgwood's private secretary) to Kolmer, 30 November 1940, TNA, KV2/2518/112x. The debate was presumably that on Alien Internees on 3 December 1940 (see *Hansard*, 5th Series, *Parliamentary Debates*, House of Commons (HC), vol. 367, col. 437ff.).

10 *Hansard*, 5th Series, *Parliamentary Debates*, HC, vol. 369, col. 271.

11 Relatively few women, i.e. only those categorised 'A' or 'B', were interned, leaving the overwhelming majority of female refugees at liberty. Nevertheless, since MI5 were of the firm opinion that Kolmer posed a danger to British security, her re-categorisation and internment would have come as no surprise.
12 MI5 Report, 'Eva Kolmer', n.d. [December 1940], TNA, KV2/2518/128a.
13 From B8c b (F.D. Lambert) for C.W. Sykes to Bagot, 21 March 1941, TNA, KV2/2519/147b.
14 'Women Aliens Underfed (says German Culture League)', *News Chronicle*, 15 October 1940, p. 6.
15 'A Busy Bishop', *Isle of Man Examiner*, 25 October 1940, p. 4.
16 Bell to *Isle of Man Examiner*, 31 October 1940, Bell Papers, Lambeth Palace Library, London, vol. 30, fol. 393.
17 Extract B8 report, source Hi, 15 March 1941, TNA, KV2/3515/n.no.
18 Extract Special Branch report, 31 March 1942, held in TNA, KV2/3515/n.no.
19 MI5 memorandum, 12 February 1942, TNA, KV2/3515/46b.
20 See, for example, TNA, KV2/3515/64a for the MI5 comment, 13 August 1942, that it was deemed wiser to leave Bush where he was for surveillance purposes. See also Pritt's Parliamentary Question of 8 May 1945 on the decision not to transfer Bush to the Army Education Corps (*Hansard*, 5th Series, *Parliamentary Debates*, HC, vol. 410, col. 1864).
21 Draft MI5 minute for HO, 25 September 1939, TNA, KV2/1010/19a (file on John Heartfield).
22 Reports dating between April and June 1941, in TNA, KV2/3515.
23 See Charmian Brinson, *The Strange Case of Dora Fabian and Mathilde Wurm: A Study of German Political Exiles in London during the 1930's*, Berne: Lang 1997, pp. 295ff. and *passim*.
24 Cross-reference on 'Brockway, A. Fenner', 21 June 1934, TNA, KV2/1919/119a. Goldschmidt, to whom Brockway was writing to appoint him Paris correspondent of the ILP's *New Leader*, was deported from Britain in February 1934, having been the leader of the tiny British branch of the exiled Sozialistische Arbeiterpartei.
25 Minute at front of TNA, KV2/1919, 2 May 1933.
26 'Application by Alexander Roda-Roda to enter UK: Extract from HO file R11749', 18 April 1939, TNA, KV2/2415/14x.
27 Documented in TNA, KV2/2415.
28 See Werner Berthold and Brita Eckert, eds, *Der deutsche PEN-Club im Exil 1933–1938: Eine Ausstellung der Deutschen Bibliothek Frankfurt am Main*, Frankfurt a.M.: Buchhändler-Vereinigung 1980, p. 310f.
29 Note dated 19 March 1934, TNA, KV2/3211/9b.
30 See Charmian Brinson, 'Science in Exile: Imperial College and the Refugees from Nazism – A Case Study', in *Leo Baeck Institute Year Book*, 51 (2006), p. 149.
31 Extract Intelligence Report, 28 May 1942, TNA, KV2/1010/45b.
32 Lloyd to Koenen on Allies Inside Germany notepaper, 12 October 1944, TNA, KV2/2800/243a.
33 'Kulturbund meeting in Caxton Hall on 28.3.42', 1 April 1942, TNA, KV2/2364/39b (file on Gerhard Hinze).

34 Hermione Lee, *Virginia Woolf*, London: Vintage 1997, p. 687.
35 On this, see Charmian Brinson and Richard Dove, *Politics by Other Means: The Free German League of Culture in London, 1939–1946*, London: Vallentine Mitchell 2010, pp. 176ff.
36 Myers to Kuczynski, 10 June 1941, TNA, KV2/1872/150b.
37 See Jeffrey Meyers, *George Orwell, The Critical Heritage*, London: Routledge and Kegan Paul 1997, p. 16.
38 See Siegfried Zimmering to Kokoschka, 2 August 1944, Siegfried Zimmering Papers, Stiftung Archiv der Parteien und Massenorganisationen der DDR im Bundesarchiv, Berlin-Lichterfelde (SAPMO-BArch), NY4953, Box 2, File 12, Letters 1940–58.
39 'Protokoll des Treuhänderausschusses vom 1.3.1946', SAPMO-BArch, SgY13/V239/1/3.
40 MI5 Report, source 'Fred', 18 April 1944, TNA, KV2/2800/106b.
41 P. Croft to Marguerite Kuczynski, 26 January 1943, TNA, KV2/1875/265.
42 Bagot to Robson-Scott, 7 February 1943, TNA, KV2/1875/267a.
43 See *Hansard*, 5th Series, *Parliamentary Debates*, HC, vol. 414, col. 1815.
44 18 October 1945, TNA, FO371/46659.
45 Statement enclosed in Kolmer to Broda, 21 July 1944, TNA, KV2/2351/ n.no.
46 Broda to Kolmer, 22 July 1944, TNA, KV2/2351/234b.
47 Barker to Broda, 17 March 1945, TNA, KV2/2351/274b.

Part III

Preparing for the Cold War

17

Red alert: keeping watch on the Communists

The German invasion of the Soviet Union in June 1941 transformed that country overnight into a war ally. In an evening radio broadcast on the day of the German attack, Winston Churchill declared: 'The cause of any Russian fighting for his hearth and home is the cause of free men and free peoples in every quarter of the globe.' Shortly after, on 12 July 1941, an Anglo-Soviet Pact of Mutual Assistance was signed, with Britain promising to deliver weapons and other war materials to the Soviet Union.

Churchill was not alone in his political volte-face. Following the German attack, the Communist critique of an 'imperialist war' simply melted away. The CPGB declared total support for the Allied war effort, soon followed by the German and Austrian Communist parties. Refugee organisations such as the FGLC joined the chorus, exhorting their members to join 'the war against Hitler Fascism'.[1]

MI5 had no such Damascene conversion. If its suspicions of alien Communists had been reinforced by the Nazi–Soviet Pact, they were only partially dispelled by the realignment of forces after June 1941. On the one hand, there was a shift of policy in counter-intelligence, notably in relation to political vetting.[2] Before June 1941, MI5 had advised that alien Communists released from internment should be refused industrial employment on the grounds that they were opposed to the war effort, although they could be released for work in agriculture or forestry where, it was calculated, they would be living in more remote and isolated parts of country.[3] After June 1941, this policy was relaxed. MI5 agreed to the employment of 'enemy aliens' in war industries provided that they had no access to confidential material. This was particularly vital in the case of secret government designs, such as the Tube Alloys project – the code name for the British plan to produce an atomic bomb, started with the utmost secrecy in July 1940. However, precisely here, MI5 often found itself overruled, as one (post-war) MI5 report tacitly acknowledged: 'This policy had to be waived in a few cases, such as that of Dr. Engelbert Broda, whose employers at the

Cavendish Laboratory, DSIR [Department of Scientific and Industrial Research], felt that his immediate value as a scientist outweighed his potential danger as a Communist.'[4] Broda's value and potential danger are the subject of chapter 20.

The government had initially refused to allow 'enemy aliens' to enlist in British forces, with the notable exception of the non-combatant Pioneer Corps; for their part, Communists had strongly opposed young men joining the Pioneer Corps, but now they waived their objections. After 1942, 'enemy aliens' were even allowed to apply for active service in British forces or were recruited by the SOE for field operations abroad. In some cases, MI5 was asked to vet alien Communist applicants for enlistment in the armed forces and, where consulted, was still concerned to ensure that recruits had only limited access to confidential material.[5]

While MI5 adopted a more liberal attitude to the question of political vetting, it continued the surveillance of leading Communists, including Jürgen Kuczynski, Ernst Hermann Meyer and Wilhelm Koenen, their information frequently coming, as already noted, from informers within the refugee community. Early in 1942, MI5 had been passed a list of members of the Central Committee of the KPD in Britain, acquired when one of its refugee 'agents', named Martin Bieber, broke into the room of Communist Siegbert Kahn at the Canterbury Hall hostel of the CRTF.[6] While certainly genuine, the list was probably out of date, naming E.H. Meyer as KPD leader in Britain at a time when he had been superseded by Wilhelm Koenen, after the latter's return from internment in Canada. MI5 had in fact tried to keep Koenen under lock and key but had been frustrated by the more liberal views of the Internment Tribunal.

Above all, MI5 had continued to log the activities of Jürgen Kuczynski, whom it suspected of espionage. When Claud Sykes (by then an MI5 officer) had visited internment camps in December 1940, his main purpose had been to establish a functioning intelligence network inside each camp and to recruit informants who would supply information after their release. Reporting from Huyton Camp, Sykes detailed an interview with the trade union official (and SPD member) Hans Gottfurcht.

> Turning to the Communists still at large, Gottfurcht (reliable) told me that he considered J. Kuczynski to be a GPU agent. He met him several times in London prior to his internment, but did not know then that he was a member of the Communist Party. He only knew that he had many friends in the Party. Kuczynski was then declaring that he was not a Communist and was trying to make contact with the Trade Unions.[7]

This appears to be the first reference in Kuczynski's security file to suspicions that he was engaged in espionage.

After June 1941, MI5 intensified its surveillance of Kuczynski. Throughout 1942, his post was intercepted, copies being added to his file. There were frequent reports of lectures he gave and meetings he attended (often supplied by the indefatigable Kurt Hiller) as well as copies of articles he published. Kuczynski was indeed a great asset to Soviet intelligence, having a good network of contacts, which included the publisher Victor Gollancz, left-wing Labour figures like Ellen Wilkinson and John Strachey and the poet Cecil Day-Lewis. He also had strong links to the Soviet Embassy, not least to the Ambassador, Ivan Maisky, whom he met frequently and considered to be a close friend.[8]

At the same time, MI5 had turned its attention to other members of his family. Robert Kuczynski, the patriarch of this Communist clan, was an eminent statistician and demographer, whose work gave him access to senior British civil servants and Labour politicians, including Sir Stafford Cripps, newly returned from his post as ambassador to the Soviet Union. Also under surveillance was Jürgen's younger sister Brigitte, now Bridget Lewis, who had married the British journalist Anthony Gordon Lewis, known to MI5 as a Communist. The couple lived at 4 Lawn Road Flats, near her parents who lived at no. 12 and next door to Jürgen who lived at no. 6.

In early 1941, there was also a significant new arrival – Jürgen's younger sister Ursula, now known as Ursula Beurton following her marriage to fellow-Communist Leon (Len) Beurton. By the time of her arrival in Britain, Ursula Beurton had already spent a decade as an agent of Soviet military intelligence (GRU), under the code name 'Sonya', a decade she described over thirty years later in the memoir *Sonya's Report*.[9] Initially recruited during a visit to Moscow with her first husband Rudolf Hamburger, 'Sonya' had been inducted into the ways of Soviet intelligence at the Lenin School in Moscow, a training ground reserved for elite party cadres. She was also trained as a wireless operator, a skill she used regularly to transmit messages to her controllers, known as Moscow Centre.

'Sonya' had initially been sent to Shanghai, an international port, in which countries like Britain and France had established foreign concessions and enjoyed substantial trading privileges. Among those she encountered in Shanghai's close-knit expatriate community was Roger Hollis, a young journalist working for British American Tobacco, who was to join MI5 in 1938, becoming its Director-General in 1956. This early contact in Shanghai later gave rise to persistent rumours that he was in fact a Soviet deep penetration agent who used his post to shield, among others, the atom spy Klaus Fuchs.[10] 'Sonya' had subsequently worked as a GRU agent in Manchuria, then under Japanese occupation, later being ordered to Poland and finally to Switzerland.

'Sonya's' marriage to Len Beurton in 1940 had given her not only his name but the right to a British passport. This enabled her to enter Britain but also ensured that she came to the attention of the security services. Len Beurton was already known to Special Branch, having fought in Spain with the British Battalion of the International Brigade; the name drew their attention to Ursula Beurton when she landed in Britain in February 1941. MI5's rapporteur in Liverpool described her with a hint of anti-Semitism: 'Her height is about 5' 8", thin build, dark hair and eyes, Jewish appearance'.[11] Sonya landed in Liverpool shortly after the arrival there of the young atomic scientist Klaus Fuchs, following his release from internment in Canada. They were as yet unaware of each other's existence, but the long arm of Soviet Military Intelligence was soon to bring them together.

MI5's interest was not confined to the Kuczynski family, or even to the KPD. It maintained surveillance on the Austrian Centre, including its leading activists, such as Willi Scholz and Franz West. And it began to take a renewed interest in the affairs of Edith Tudor-Hart. As a naturalised British subject, Tudor-Hart escaped internment or even the need to appear before a tribunal, but the outbreak of war brought increasing difficulties in her life. The political somersault of the Nazi–Soviet Pact must have been a source of unease and confusion. There were also declining professional opportunities, not least because of her known Communist associations. Furthermore, she lost her studio during the Blitz and was forced to find a job with a photographic printer. In May 1942, an MI5 watcher reported that 'from her dress and habits, she does not seem to be in affluent circumstances'.[12]

Professional hardship was compounded by personal misfortune. She and Alexander Tudor-Hart had divorced after his return from Spain in 1939, and her private life was increasingly marked by the anxiety of coping with a young child who was showing signs of what was later diagnosed as severe schizophrenia. Despite these setbacks in her professional and personal life, she was not deflected from her activity as a Soviet spy. MI5 had long suspected her involvement in espionage, but lacked the evidence to prove it, as Vernon Kell himself (shortly before his removal as Director of MI5) implicitly acknowledged in a letter to the Chief Constable of Birmingham concerning Alexander Tudor-Hart:

> My impression is that he is not a very effective person and is of much less importance in the Party than his first wife [who] is associated with underground activities and she was almost certainly involved in the Glading organisation.[13]

Edith's importance to the Soviet spy network in Britain at this time was primarily as a go-between, a role to which she was ideally suited: she was unobtrusive, self-effacing and discreet (though she later became much less so). Soviet records disclose that she had been used as a courier by the British spy, Guy Burgess, to take information to the Comintern HQ in Paris. During the war years, she was a vital channel of communication between the Austrian Communist Party in exile and the CPGB. Even more crucially, when the Cambridge spy ring had been out of contact with the Soviet *rezidentura* in 1940, communications had been maintained through Edith, who had passed the ring's information to Bob Stewart, the British party's clandestine link with the Soviet Embassy.[14] As a pivotal figure in the CPGB, Stewart had long since been under MI5 surveillance and at least one of his phone conversations with Tudor-Hart was tapped in 1944.[15]

In April 1942, MI5 placed Tudor-Hart's movements under special observation, including a request to look into her bank account, although this proved 'very unproductive of results'.[16] Watchers noted that she lunched regularly at Café Possibile in Blandford Street and followed her every evening to the London Clinic of Psychoanalysis to collect her son Tommy, 'who bore a striking resemblance' to her.[17] Observation later extended to breaking into her flat, though this too yielded nothing except proof of her straitened circumstances: 'This flat is poorly furnished and in an untidy state, probably owing to the nerves of the boy.'[18]

She remained a member of the CPGB throughout the war, but discretion dictated that she seldom appeared at Party meetings or functions; 'well-informed people maintain that she still carries on a liaison function between the Austrian and the English CP'.[19] She did indeed. In this way, she was also to be a covert link in the transmission of information from the Austrian physicist Engelbert Broda regarding Anglo-American research on the atomic bomb.

Notes

1 See the FGLC's 'Statement to Members' in *Freie Deutsche Kultur*, September 1941.

2 See the post-war report 'The Work of F2b (formerly B4b) in Wartime', The National Archives [TNA], KV4/57.

3 *Ibid.*, p. 9.

4 *Ibid.*, pp. 9–10.

5 *Ibid.*

6 Internal memorandum dated 18 February 1942, TNA, KV2/1873/182a.

7 Extract M/S report no. 3, Huyton Camp, December 1940, to B8c, 29 January 1941, TNA, KV2/1872/121k.

8 See Jürgen Kuczynski, *Memoiren: Die Erziehung des J.K. zum Kommunisten und Wissenschaftler*, Berlin/Weimar: Auflage, 2nd edition 1975, pp. 373f.

9 Ruth Werner, *Sonya's Report*, translated by Renate Simpson, London: Chatto and Windus 1991, particularly pp. 250–3. Ruth Werner was Ursula Beurton's pen name; Renate Simpson (née Kuczynski) was her younger sister.

10 See Peter Wright, *Spycatcher: The Candid Autobiography of a Senior Intelligence Officer*, New York: Viking 1987; Chapman Pincher, *Treachery: Betrayals, Blunders and Cover-ups: Six Decades of Espionage*, Edinburgh: Mainstream 2011.

11 See TNA, KV6/41/34.
12 Special Branch report, 7 May 1942, TNA, KV2/1013/58a.
13 Kell to Cecil Moriarty, 9 May 1940, TNA, KV2/1013/40a. Percy Glading had directed the Woolwich Arsenal spy-ring in the 1930s. MI5 had been aware of Tudor-Hart's involvement in the case, but had taken no action. See chapter 8.
14 Nigel West and Oleg Tsarev, *The Crown Jewels: The British Secrets at the Heart of the KGB Archives*, London: Harper Collins 1998, p. 182.
15 Report, 12 September 1944, TNA, KV2/1013/69a. Stewart's MI5 files have been released, see TNA, KV2/1180–3.
16 TNA, KV2/1013/52a.
17 O/B2 to F2b (Bagot), notes on observation, 30 April1942, TNA, KV2/1013/54b.
18 E7 to F2b (Bagot), 11 May 1942, TNA, KV2/1013/58a.
19 E7 to F2B (Bagot), 3 May 1942, TNA, KV2/1013/56a.

18

'Tube Alloys': the British atomic bomb project

While British plans to produce an atomic bomb first flourished as part of Britain's war effort, the feasibility of creating such a weapon had been discussed in scientific circles from the early 1930s. The discovery of uranium fission was made by two German scientists, Otto Hahn and Fritz Strassmann, in Berlin; its announcement in December 1938 rocked the world of physics; its significance was not lost on the politicians. In both Britain and America, work was begun to discover whether a nuclear bomb was not only theoretically possible but technically feasible.

A British government review on 'The Possibility of Producing an Atomic Bomb', submitted a few months before the outbreak of war, had expressed doubt whether such a weapon could be built, but had concluded:

> The issues at stake are too enormous to permit of a complacent attitude and even if there is only a remote chance of bringing it off, the situation ought to be most closely watched and the present experiments given every encouragement [...] this country must keep in the forefront of the work and give it high priority.[1]

An early breakthrough in nuclear research came in March 1940 when a team at Birmingham University, led by Otto Robert Frisch and Rudolf Peierls, issued a short memorandum for the British government, entitled 'On the construction of a "Super Bomb" based on a Nuclear Chain Reaction in uranium'.[2] It is worthy of note at this point that both the authors of this memorandum were Jewish refugees who had, with the outbreak of war, become 'enemy aliens'. Frisch was an Austrian physicist who had left Germany for London after Hitler's accession to power. He had subsequently spent five years working with the Nobel Prize-winning physicist Niels Bohr in Copenhagen, before settling in Birmingham. Rudolf Peierls was a German physicist who had actually been conducting research in Cambridge when Hitler became Reich Chancellor. Assessing the situation, he had prudently decided to stay in Britain. Their pioneering report, submitted to Churchill's scientific adviser Henry Tizard, set out the possibility of building an atomic bomb from a small amount of fissionable uranium 235. Both men were to be part of the British team working on the Manhattan Project (the American code name for the atomic bomb project) from 1942 onwards.

Peierls's perceived importance to British atomic research can be measured by his successful application for British naturalisation. His work was considered so valuable to the war effort that he was granted British citizenship as early as March 1940: a rare distinction, since naturalisation had been formally suspended for the duration of the war and was permitted only in exceptional circumstances.

In response to the Frisch–Peierls memorandum, the government set up the secret MAUD Committee, chaired by Professor G.P. Thompson of Imperial College, to explore further the possibility of producing an atomic bomb. The committee's draft report in July 1941, marked 'Most Secret', included the proposal 'to make bombs to be dropped from the air which will produce explosions by the release of nuclear energy'. The committee was making this proposal 'in the light of the fact that it is known that the enemy are working on similar lines'.[3]

The decision to embark on the atomic bomb project was taken by the British government on 2 July 1941, ten days after the Nazi invasion of the Soviet Union, an event which had transformed the strategic situation, turning Russia into an ally in the war on Germany. In a radio broadcast on the evening after the German attack, Churchill declared that 'the Russian danger is our danger' promising that Britain would 'give whatever help we can to Russia and the Russian people'.[4] However, such help did not extend to scientific research and least of all to the atomic bomb project. On the contrary, the decision to begin the British programme to construct an atomic bomb coincided with a strengthening of counter-espionage. On 4 July, as part of an internal reorganisation of MI5, B division became F division and, more significantly, also broadened the scope of its surveillance to include Soviet intelligence activity in Britain.[5]

Otto Frisch and Rudolf Peierls were now part of a secret British project to design and build an atomic bomb. Scientists working on the scheme, including Peierls and Frisch, were officially working under contract to the 'Directorate of Tube Alloys', a cover name for the atomic bomb project, operating under the auspices of the Department of Scientific and Industrial Research (DSIR). In May 1941, Rudolf Peierls invited the young German physicist Klaus Fuchs to join his team in Birmingham in order to carry out research on the gaseous diffusion process used in separating uranium isotopes.[6]

In view of the secrecy surrounding Tube Alloys, those recruited to the project needed security clearance, a job still assigned to MI5. Prior to June 1941, MI5 had routinely advised that 'enemy alien' Communists should be refused industrial employment on the grounds that they were opposed to the war and therefore might commit industrial sabotage. However, it is important to note that this rationale conflicted with the prevailing view among scientists, which held that scientific expertise should be the main, if not the only criterion in recruiting staff to a project of such importance to the war effort. It was feared that Germany was also developing an atomic bomb, and it was vital to develop an Allied bomb first, an aim that therefore transcended all other considerations. These attitudes were only reinforced when the Soviet Union was transformed into a war ally in June 1941. It was at this point that the divergence of opinion between the Security Service and the scientific community came to a head, when MI5 was called upon to give security clearance to Klaus Fuchs to work on the highly secret Tube Alloys project: a project so secret that not even MI5 was informed of the precise nature of the work he was to be involved in.

Notes

1 'The Possibility of Producing an Atomic Bomb. A review of the Position', 3 May 1939, The National Archives [TNA], AB1/9.

2 TNA, AB1/9.

3 MAUD Summary, TNA, AB1/10.

4 *The Times*, 23 June 1941.

5 TNA, KV4/56.

6 Robert Chadwell Williams, *Klaus Fuchs: Atom Spy*, Cambridge/London: Harvard University Press 1987, p. 42.

19

The spy who was caught: the case of Klaus Fuchs

When the twenty-one-year-old student of mathematics and physics, Klaus Fuchs, first arrived in Britain as a refugee from Nazi Germany, he was already known as a Communist. Emil Julius Klaus Fuchs was the son of the Lutheran pastor Emil Fuchs, who during the 1920s had become a Quaker and had joined the SPD – one of the first protestant pastors to do so. In 1931, he became Professor of Theology at the University of Kiel, a post he held only briefly. His pacifist activism had made him well known – and when the Nazis came to power, notorious.

Klaus later recalled that his childhood had been a happy one. Like Emil Fuchs's other children, he had become radicalised in the political and economic turmoil of the early 1930s, rejecting his father's pacifism. As a student in Kiel, he had joined the SPD, before switching to the KPD, which in his perception was the only political party effectively opposing the Nazis. Early in 1933, Klaus Fuchs had been earmarked for arrest by the police, which conducted a search at the family home, finding 'different leaflets and books of the Communist Party'.[1] Fuchs managed to flee to Berlin, then to Paris and finally, with the help of the Religious Society of Friends, to Britain. He arrived at the port of Folkestone on 24 September 1933.[2]

Fuchs was a promising physicist, who had already gained degrees in mathematics and science from the universities of Leipzig and Kiel. From 1934, he became a graduate student at Bristol University, where he completed a doctorate in theoretical physics in December 1936. MI5 became aware of Fuchs no later than November 1934, when the Chief Constable for Bristol wrote to Vernon Kell informing him that Fuchs was living locally and that the German consul had refused a request to renew Fuchs's passport, informing the police that he was 'a notorious communist'. At the same time, the Chief Constable observed that Fuchs was not known to have taken part in Communist activities in Bristol.[3]

Fuchs's supervisor in Bristol, the young Professor of Physics, Nevill Mott, warmly recommended him for a postgraduate position in Edinburgh under Professor Max Born, who was himself a German refugee physicist.

Max Born's presence in Edinburgh exemplifies how the British scientific community had been embellished by a number of refugee scientists from Germany, many of whom owed their positions to the support of the Academic Assistance Council, later known as the Society for the Protection of Science and Learning (SPSL). The Council was founded in April 1933 to help academic refugees find suitable posts in universities and research institutions in Britain. The British security services were well aware of the presence of the refugees within the scientific community and the potential security risk they represented, but had concluded (or been persuaded) that their value to scientific research far outweighed any possible threat to security.

During the summer of 1938, having been resident in Britain for five years, Fuchs approached the Home Office for an unlimited residence permit – and the request was granted without delay. Meanwhile, Fuchs's scientific career was progressing steadily: he was appointed to a research fellowship in Edinburgh with the enthusiastic support of Max Born. In July 1939, he applied for British naturalisation, but war broke out before his application could be considered.

By then Fuchs had been recognised as a theoretical physicist of great potential; he had also become an 'enemy alien'. Appearing before an internment tribunal on 2 November 1939, Fuchs was placed in category 'C' and exempted from internment. However, on 12 May 1940 he was arrested as part of the internment of aliens in protected areas (a prelude to mass internment) and held on the Isle of Man before being deported to Canada, where he was interned in Camp L, a Canadian army camp outside Quebec City. Internment inevitably brought Fuchs into contact with a number of fellow-Communists, one of whom was the influential Hans Kahle, a First World War officer who had been a senior military commander of the International Brigades in the Spanish Civil War and reputedly an OGPU agent in Madrid.[4]

Meanwhile, Max Born had contacted the Royal Society, asking it to intervene on behalf of Fuchs who, he said, 'was in the small top group of theoretical physicists in this country'.[5] The Society did so, urging Fuchs's release on the grounds that his research was important to the war effort. As MI5 later noted: 'This was an exceptional case [...] Fuchs was, in fact, one of the very first to be sent back.'[6] He was shipped back to Britain, landing in Liverpool on 11 January 1941. He later maintained that he felt no bitterness at his internment, 'because I could understand that it was necessary'.[7]

Once back in Britain, Fuchs returned to Edinburgh, but his second stay in the city was brief. In May 1941, Rudolf Peierls invited Fuchs, whom he had first met at scientific conferences before the war, to join his research team in Birmingham working on the secret British atomic bomb project. Fuchs later stated that when he joined Peierls's laboratory, he was not aware of the true nature of the work he would be involved in. There was indeed some delay before Fuchs could be fully briefed about the project because of MI5's reluctance to give him security clearance.

MI5 made somewhat routine inquiries, noting that 'Peierls, whose bona-fides have never been questioned, has vouched for the trustworthiness of Fuchs'. (At this point Fuchs was indeed lodging with the Peierls at 38 Calthorpe Road, Edgbaston.) An inquiry to the Chief Constable of Birmingham in August elicited the response that Fuchs had been resident there since 28 May 'and during this time he has not come adversely under notice'. MI5 eventually conceded, somewhat reluctantly, that 'if the work could not be done properly without Fuchs, we should have to accept such risk as there might be.'[8]

In fact, Fuchs represented a considerable risk. In June 1941, he signed the Official Secrets Act. Shortly after, however, the German invasion of the Soviet Union forced him to consider where his ultimate loyalty lay. As Fuchs would later testify, after the Nazi invasion he had come to the conclusion that the Soviet Union, having become a war ally, had the right to know what Britain was secretly working on. In his own words: 'I decided to inform Russia and I established contact through another member of the Communist Party.'[9] That person was none other than Jürgen Kuczynski. (Although it remains unproven, it may have been Hans Kahle who put Fuchs in touch with Kuczynski.[10])

Kuczynski directed Fuchs to the Soviet Embassy where he was well connected, being also a close friend of the Ambassador Ivan Maisky – himself no stranger to espionage. Towards the end of 1941, Fuchs visited the Embassy in Kensington Palace Gardens, London W8, meeting a man whom he knew only as 'Alexander', who became his intelligence controller. 'Alexander' was in fact Simon Davidovich Kremer, secretary to the Soviet military attaché, a post providing cover for his work as an officer of Soviet Military Intelligence (GRU). Exactly eighteen months earlier, the Soviet defector Walter Krivitsky had named Kremer as the centre of Soviet intelligence operations in London.[11] Although his role was therefore known to MI5, it had taken no action against him. Now it was Kremer to whom Fuchs began to pass secret scientific information.

They met regularly. Meetings were arranged to suit Fuchs's convenience, mainly at weekends; some were in quiet residential streets, others at busy bus stops, but always at a different location.[12] In his later 'confession' to MI5 officer William Skardon, Fuchs claimed that at that stage he had intended to give only information on work in which he was directly engaged.[13] Whatever he imparted, Moscow Centre thought it invaluable, and considered Fuchs a crucial contact. At this time, he was known by the code name 'Rest'; later he became 'Charles'.

Over the next two years, MI5 had two further opportunities to investigate Fuchs. On 30 April 1942, Fuchs applied for British naturalisation, an application the Home Office referred to MI5 to assess his suitability. Despite the obvious importance of the case, MI5 (in the person of Roger Hollis) made only desultory checks, eventually reporting that 'Security Service records have been consulted and no objection is seen to this application being granted'.[14] Fuchs became a British subject on 31 July 1942, swearing to 'bear true allegiance to His Majesty King George VI, his heirs and successors, according to law'.

By then, Fuchs had been passing information to Soviet intelligence for almost a year. In the summer of 1942, he was assigned to a new controller, Ursula Beurton, alias Ursula Kuczynski. In the course of a decade working as an agent of Soviet military intelligence, Ursula Beurton, code-named 'Sonya', had assumed several different aliases, but she had become Ursula Beurton through her marriage to fellow-Communist Leon (Len) Beurton, whom she had married in Switzerland on 23 February 1940, the anniversary of the founding of the Red Army. When Moscow Centre ordered her to leave Switzerland and go to Britain, she was therefore able to travel on a British passport. She had to follow a hazardous route through Vichy France and Franco's Spain to Lisbon, before finally arriving at Liverpool in February 1941 and travelling on to Oxford, where she initially stayed with her father, Robert Kuczynski, who had moved there from London during the Blitz.

After arriving in Britain, 'Sonya' waited several months before making contact with her Soviet controllers. The following year she was instructed to meet 'a young comrade' who had important information to disclose. She first met Klaus Fuchs, whose intelligence controller she became, in the early summer of 1942. At the time, he was still working in Rudolf Peierls's laboratory in Birmingham. She continued to live in Oxford, though by then she was living with her husband in a cottage in the Summertown district which she had rented from the barrister Neville Laski, a brother of Labour Party luminary Harold Laski. As she notes prosaically in her memoirs, she strung her radio aerial between their cottage and the Laskis' and began transmitting intelligence information to the Soviet Union[15] – though amateur radio transmission was strictly forbidden during the war years.

Sonya's Report, written long after the events it portrays, has the pace and mystery of a John le Carré thriller, if little of its literary style.[16] It tells the remarkable story of a dedicated Soviet spy, often operating under the noses of the authorities. Her memoir is occasionally disingenuous. She claims, for example, that she was no more than an insignificant cog in the wheel; she was of course the pivot of the whole espionage chain. Her first meeting with Klaus Fuchs was probably arranged through her brother Jürgen – who then distanced himself from the whole affair. She and Fuchs met in Banbury, a small market town conveniently situated between Oxford and Birmingham. She recalled that when they met for the first time, they took a walk arm in arm 'according to the old-established principle of illicit meetings'. During that first meeting, she noticed 'how calm, thoughtful, tactful and cultured he was'. Thereafter, they met regularly in Banbury, or rather just outside it. According to 'Sonya', she arranged meetings on a country road outside the town, both to be less conspicuous and to make it more difficult for anyone to tail them. The meetings were usually in the afternoon at weekends, the times being arranged to suit the trains from Birmingham. Fuchs remembered that 'the woman also arrived and left by train'.[17] He never visited her home, nor did she visit his, indeed neither even knew the other's address. She was confident that Fuchs did not know her real identity: such were the rules of espionage which, as she insists in her memoir, she followed faithfully. In the course of his later interrogation by MI5, Fuchs claimed that he was unaware of her identity or even her name, referring to her only as 'the girl from Banbury'.[18]

Fuchs would give 'Sonya' his reports in writing, after which she would encipher them and (as a trained radio operator) transmit them to Moscow. Their meetings were always brief, never lasting more than half an hour. They could have concluded their business in a couple of minutes, but always walked and talked for a short time, so as not to arouse suspicion. On one occasion, Fuchs gave her a thick book of blueprints, asking her to forward it quickly. She passed the material to Kremer, who could forward it through the diplomatic bag. Although her brother Jürgen had initially arranged the contact, she never spoke to him about Fuchs: 'Though my brother and I got on so well, I kept strictly to the rules.' Fuchs and 'Sonya' met regularly at intervals of two to three months, their meetings coming to an end only when Fuchs was transferred to the United States as a member of the British team working on the joint Anglo-American project to build an atomic bomb.

In August 1943, Britain, the United States and Canada, meeting at Quebec, signed the secret Agreement Relating to Atomic Energy. The agreement effectively relocated British atomic research to the United States as part of the top secret Manhattan Project to construct an atomic bomb. Rudolf Peierls and Otto Frisch were both part of the British team chosen to work on the project 'for an indefinite period'. Peierls elected to take Fuchs, whose work he considered indispensable to the project.

To leave Britain, Fuchs needed an aliens' exit permit and MI5 was asked to give security clearance: its third wartime opportunity to investigate Fuchs. In view of the secret nature of Fuchs's work, MI5 requested a mail intercept, but a report reaching Miss Bagot stated: 'He did not receive a single letter and it seems highly unlikely that he is in close touch with anyone of interest.'[19] Moreover, it came as a surprise to the Security Service that Fuchs was now a British subject. Bagot complained: 'We knew his naturalisation was under consideration, but the report [...] did not state that it was a fait accompli.'[20] Having been cleared by British security, Fuchs, like other members of the British mission, was not further vetted by the Americans.

Fuchs sailed for the United States in December 1943 as a member of the British mission to the Manhattan Project. He initially worked together with Peierls at Columbia University in New York, conducting theoretical work for the gaseous diffusion plant which was to be built at Oak Ridge, Tennessee, to produce fissionable uranium. Before leaving Britain, he had received specific instructions from 'Sonya' for contacting his new controller in New York. For purposes of recognition at their first meeting, his contact would be holding a pair of gloves in one hand and a green-covered book in the other; Fuchs was to carry a tennis ball. This contact, whom Fuchs knew only as 'Raymond', would meet him regularly at intervals of two to three months and remained his contact throughout his time in America.[21] 'Raymond' was in fact an American Communist called Harry Gold (codenamed GUS). Although Gold was an industrial chemist with some understanding of the material Fuchs gave him, he was simply an intermediary who passed Fuchs's information to his controller Anatoli Yaklovev ('John') who acted as Soviet Vice Consul in New York, a diplomatic cover for his role as head of Soviet intelligence in the United States.

When the majority of the seventeen-member British mission returned to the United Kingdom during 1944, Fuchs and Peierls remained in America, a measure of their importance to the atomic bomb project. Fuchs was transferred to Los Alamos, New Mexico, in August 1944 where he worked in the theoretical physics division under Hans Bethe (another German émigré who had also worked with Max Born). In Los Alamos, Fuchs the physicist was at the epicentre of the Manhattan Project; Fuchs the spy had unparalleled access to secret scientific information. During his time in Los Alamos, Fuchs contributed to the development of 'Little Boy', code name for the atomic bomb which was eventually dropped on Hiroshima in August 1945. At this time, he also continued his meetings with 'Raymond', whom he met in the neighbouring town of Santa Fe – undetected by the FBI.

By 1945, the political situation was on the brink of radical change. With the defeat of Nazi Germany and the break-up of the wartime alliance, the Soviet Union had become the new enemy. Brigadier-General Leslie Groves, head of the Manhattan Project, had declared within two weeks of taking charge in September 1942 that he was quite clear 'that Russia was our enemy and that the project was conducted on that basis'.[22]

Fuchs remained in the United States until June 1946 when he returned to Britain. On the basis of his outstanding work in New York and Los Alamos, he was invited to continue his research at the Atomic Energy Research Establishment, Harwell, where he was appointed head of the theoretical physics division.

At his last meeting with 'Raymond', Fuchs had been instructed to re-establish contact in London outside Mornington Crescent tube station at eight o'clock on a Saturday evening, but no meeting ever took place and Fuchs was obliged to take the initiative. Once again the willing volunteer, his efforts to renew contact with Soviet intelligence were alarmingly gauche. Disregarding the ground rules of espionage, he approached figures in the KPD. His first contact was Marguerite Kuczynski, whose husband Jürgen had returned to Germany a year earlier and whom she was hoping to follow. She directed Fuchs to her fellow-Communist Johanna Klopstech, who in turn approached the educationalist Hans Siebert – like her a leading figure in the FGLC.[23] Fuchs was treading a dangerous path, for both Klopstech and Siebert had long since been on MI5's black list as active Communists, but his luck held.

Fuchs eventually received instructions to meet his Soviet contact. In a scenario plucked from a spy thriller, they met at a public house in Wood Green called the Nag's Head. There were elaborate measures of identification: Fuchs was to carry a copy of *Tribune* and sit on a particular bench in the saloon bar; his contact would be carrying a red book. No words were exchanged in the pub. When his contact left, Fuchs followed, their meeting taking place in a nearby street. He met the same contact, who he thought was Russian, regularly over the next three years. If any arrangement was broken, there were extraordinary precautions for renewing contact. In a measure which would seem implausible even in spy fiction, Fuchs was to re-establish contact by throwing a copy of the magazine *Men Only* over the wall of 166 Kew Road, Richmond (a house occupied by Party comrades) with a message on page 10 stipulating a new place and date. In fact, he never had to take this action.[24] According to Fuchs's later testimony, the information he transmitted during this period related mostly to the British atomic energy programme.

In 1946–47, at the very time Fuchs was establishing contact with Soviet intelligence in the Nag's Head, MI5 was running yet another security check on him. This time the check, lasting some five months in all, was prompted by Henry Arnold, a retired RAF Wing Commander, who was employed as the security officer at Harwell. Arnold had joined Harwell shortly before Fuchs's own arrival. Aware of the extreme sensitivity of atomic research at Harwell, Arnold was surprised that a former German national with an alleged Communist background should be assigned to research of such importance. He contacted MI5.[25] Arnold's concern was understandable. Atomic espionage was certainly in the air. In September 1945, while Fuchs was still at Los Alamos, Igor Gouzenko, a cipher clerk at the Soviet Embassy in Ottowa, had defected, taking with him a large number of files. As a result of disclosures in these files, Scotland Yard arrested the British physicist, Alan Nunn May, who had worked in Montreal on the Manhattan Project. Nunn May was charged in March 1946 under the Official Secrets Act with having passed information to Soviet intelligence contacts.

Prior to Arnold's intervention, MI5 was apparently unaware that Fuchs was back in Britain. In the light of his information at least one MI5 officer had reservations about Fuchs: Michael Serpell of section B1c recommended that the Fuchs case should be followed up. His reasons seemed compelling:

> In 1943 [...] this case was dealt with on the rather unsatisfactory basis that he would be of less danger to security on the other side of the Atlantic. I am afraid the Canadian case has shown this argument (which was applied in other cases) to be quite unsound.

Serpell argued that, while it might have been permissible to risk employing such people in wartime, the political situation had changed 'and that whatever the value of a refugee scientist's work may be to atomic research, his possible danger to security will be considered a prime issue'.[26] Serpell's concern extended also to Rudolf Peierls who, he noted, was a close friend of Fuchs. However, Peierls did not work at Harwell, although he did have contact there in a consultant capacity.

Roger Hollis, who was asked for his opinion, concluded after reading the file that if the authorities wished to exclude people with records like Fuchs and Peierls, 'it will lead to a very considerable purge which will presumably have to include a number of very highly placed British scientists'.[27] The case was finally reviewed by Guy Liddell who concluded that 'as it stands there is really nothing of a positive nature' against either Fuchs or Peierls, but suggested that both cases should be further investigated. Early in 1947, MI5 therefore conducted a postal intercept on Fuchs, but his correspondence revealed nothing of consequence. Faced with this lack of evidence, even Serpell was forced to agree that there were insufficient grounds to advise against placing Fuchs on the permanent staff at Harwell. However, in view of the secret nature of Fuchs's work, Liddell convened a meeting of four senior officers (Dick White, Roger Hollis, Martin Furnival Jones and J.A. Collard) on 8 December 1947. The four 'wise men' (who included no fewer than three future Directors General of MI5) concluded that 'these records indicate only that Fuchs held anti-Nazi views, and associated with Germans of similar views, and we think the security risk is very slight'.[28] Fuchs continued to lead a charmed life, passing information to the Soviet Union for another eighteen months, his last meeting with his Soviet contact being in January 1949.

Fuchs was finally identified as a spy in circumstances which strikingly exemplify the looking-glass world that MI5 inhabited. He had once more come under suspicion as a result of information furnished by the FBI. In 1945, American and British cryptographers had begun to decipher a mass of intercepted Soviet intelligence telegrams sent since 1940, and including messages to Moscow from the Soviet consulate in New York. The investigation, code-named VENONA, made rather slow progress, but gained momentum after the outbreak of the Cold War. By the summer of 1949, American cryptographers had finally managed to break the Soviet cipher system. One remarkable document emerging from this intelligence treasure trove was a report on the Manhattan Project, written by Klaus Fuchs in Los Alamos and sent to Moscow from New York. While this did not prove that Fuchs himself had furnished the report, other details had come to light which seemed to corroborate his guilt.

The FBI hastened to open a case file on Fuchs, directing their attention to his sister, Kristel Heinemann, who was still living in the United States. In September 1949, the FBI also passed information to MI5, which placed the British agency in a situation of some delicacy. Although the finger of suspicion pointed clearly at Fuchs, MI5 could not use this evidence against him without disclosing the source – thereby also alerting Soviet intelligence to the fact that its codes had been cracked.

During the next three months, MI5 went to great lengths to find proof of Fuchs's guilt. At various times his phone was tapped, his post intercepted, and he was placed under surveillance. The investigation posed unusual difficulty because Fuchs spent most of his time inside the self-contained community of Harwell 'where you will appreciate that the task of maintaining continuous observation without arousing his suspicion produces a series of awkward problems'.[29] Henry Arnold was enlisted to report on Fuchs's movements, as well as his character, habits and acquaintances but he reported merely that Fuchs was a rather solitary individual, who mostly spoke only when spoken to, whose contacts were confined to his own field of scientific research and who travelled little, his universe apparently bounded by the aluminium prefabs of Harwell.[30] Meanwhile, MI5 had established a team of watchers at a crossroads outside Harwell to report any car journey Fuchs might make to London where other watchers were ready to pick him up. However, the watchers found little of consequence to report, apart from a trip that Fuchs made to London and the suggestion that he had spent the evening and part of the night with the wife of a colleague. Such was the small change of surveillance. It was deemed impossible to prosecute Fuchs without further evidence, such as a confession.

In the end, it was Fuchs himself who precipitated the final act in the drama. In October 1949, he came to see Arnold to say that his father was considering a move from Frankfurt in the American Zone of Germany to Leipzig in the Soviet Zone where he had been offered a Chair. In November, Fuchs reported that his father had accepted the offer and asked Arnold whether he should resign from his post at Harwell as a potential security risk. Arnold reported the meeting to MI5, which used Fuchs's concerns as a pretext to interview him.

The job of interrogation was passed to William James Skardon, a Special Branch officer assigned to MI5, and running its surveillance section. An experienced interrogator, Jim Skardon was instructed to win Fuchs's confidence and obtain a voluntary confession. This, as he knew, would be no easy matter. Two years earlier, he had visited Ursula Beurton ('Sonya') to extract a confession of espionage from her – but had failed.

The security file recording Skardon's successive interviews with Fuchs, in which every page is stamped 'Top Secret', is the stuff of a detective thriller, full of suspense, of move and counter-move – all couched in the drab syntax of a police report. On 21 December 1949, Skardon travelled to Harwell to interview Fuchs in the office of W/Cdr Arnold. During this first meeting, Skardon allowed Fuchs to recount his life story for 'the first seventy-five minutes of our interview', before unexpectedly telling him that MI5 already had 'precise information' that he had passed atom secrets to the Soviet Union. Fuchs seemed surprised, but then smiled and said somewhat ambiguously, 'I don't think so'. During a conversation lasting over four hours, Skardon twice repeated his claim that MI5 had evidence of Fuchs's espionage, which Fuchs strongly denied. Skardon ended his report: 'I find it extremely difficult to give a conclusive view qua the guilt or innocence of Fuchs' but 'reviewing all the facts in the light of the interrogation, I feel sure that we have selected the right man.'[31] In the course of a second interview with Fuchs on 30 December, Skardon again asserted that MI5 had proof of his espionage – which Fuchs once more denied. Skardon reported that 'Fuchs was not in the least discomposed by the interview or my questions'.[32]

Early in January, Skardon conducted further interviews with Fuchs, mostly at the latter's house at 17 Hillside, Harwell, during which he attempted to establish a basis of trust between them. In fact, a somewhat disarming friendship began to develop. Skardon convinced Fuchs that he could not continue at Harwell because of his father's move to East Germany. On 13 January, Skardon paid a further visit to Harwell, at which Fuchs again denied having engaged in espionage. He was, Skardon noted, 'completely composed' and happy with the prospect of a university post outside Harwell.[33] Ten days later came the breakthrough.

On 23 January 1950, Arnold telephoned MI5 to report that Fuchs had asked to see him 'for a long quiet talk'.[34] The two men had lunch together, during which Fuchs expressed a wish to see Skardon again as 'he had something else to tell him about the matter under inquiry'. Fuchs, so Arnold reported, seemed to be under mental stress.[35] When Fuchs and Skardon met again – their fourth meeting – on 24 January, Fuchs once more spent almost two hours telling the story of his life – but made no mention, still less admission, of spying. It was clear, Skardon confirmed, that Fuchs 'was under considerable mental stress', which he was quick to exploit: 'I suggested that he should unburden his mind and clear his conscience by telling me the full story', to which Fuchs replied: 'I will never be persuaded by you to talk.' At this stage, they broke off for lunch; during the meal, Fuchs 'seemed to be considerably abstracted'. With exemplary patience, Skardon bided his time. After lunch, he put 'certain questions' to Fuchs whose resistance suddenly collapsed. He finally admitted 'that he was engaged in espionage from mid-1942 until about a year ago [...] This illegal association commenced on his own initiative, no approach having been made to him.'[36] Skardon had finally secured the confession he had so long sought – but not yet in a form that could be used in a court of law.

At the end of their conversation, Skardon commented that MI5 would require more detailed information on this association; it was agreed they should meet again on 26 January. When they did, Fuchs said that he was most anxious that his situation should be resolved as quickly as possible. Skardon seized the chance to ask him directly if would like to make a written statement, which Fuchs agreed to do at a meeting in London the following day. So it was that on 27 January 1950 Skardon met Fuchs off the train at Paddington station and took him by car to the War Office. There, in room 055, Fuchs dictated a long statement which Skardon took down and Fuchs, after reading it through and making any alterations he wished, then signed.

His statement was the main evidence against him in his subsequent trial. In it Fuchs claimed, perhaps disingenuously, that in the post-war period he had begun to have renewed doubts about Soviet policy, 'but I still believed that they would build a new world and that one day I would take part in it'. At the time these doubts began to emerge, he had failed to keep one rendezvous because he was ill and chose to miss the next one, arranged for February 1949 at a pub in Putney. In fact, he claimed he had passed nothing to the Soviets since late 1948. He insisted that he knew none of his contacts by name: 'There are people whom I know by sight whom I trusted with my life and who trusted me with theirs.' Only later, some time after his arrest, did he finally identify a photograph of Ursula Beurton as being 'the girl from Banbury'. By then, 'Sonya' was safely in Berlin.

Fuchs was arrested on 2 February 1950. He was tried under the Official Secrets Act, which was most frequently used in cases of espionage. When his case was heard on 1 March 1950, the full majesty of British justice was brought to bear. The case was heard at the Central Criminal Court, the Old Bailey, before the Lord Chief Justice, Lord Goddard; the prosecutor was the Attorney General, Hartley Shawcross, well known for his role at the Nuremberg Trials.

It was a brief trial. There was no jury, since a jury trial involving witnesses and their cross-examination might well have exposed political secrets that the British government was anxious to conceal, most notably that Fuchs was engaged in secret research to produce a British atomic bomb, a project the government had chosen not to make public. In fact, the case against Fuchs rested almost entirely on his own statement to Skardon, selected parts of which were read out by the trial judge. At the end of a trial lasting only an hour and a half, Fuchs was sentenced to fourteen years' imprisonment, the maximum sentence possible for the offence of which he was convicted. He was released after nine years.

The trial of Klaus Fuchs was a considerable embarrassment to MI5 – which felt obliged to mount a robust, if wholly unconvincing, defence. On the day after Fuchs's trial, B Division drafted a note sketching answers to three questions that would probably be raised: Why was Fuchs taken on for employment in atomic energy? Why was Fuchs's espionage activity not detected? And thirdly: Why did the Americans appear to know all about Fuchs's Communist history but not the British?[37] In fact, the reverberations of the Fuchs affair were much louder, confirming American suspicion of the laxity of the British security services and extinguishing any lingering hope that nuclear information-sharing would be resumed.

The only reputation at MI5 to be enhanced by the Fuchs case was that of Jim Skardon. Indeed, Skardon's fame as an interrogator rested largely on his success with Fuchs, but it was not repeated in subsequent assignments. He interrogated Britain's super-spy Kim Philby no fewer than ten times, with little or no result. Among others he interviewed – on no fewer than eleven separate occasions – was Anthony Blunt, whose upper-class bluster even convinced Skardon that he was innocent. Skardon also interviewed – and cleared – Soviet spy John Cairncross, who promptly left the country.

Klaus Fuchs, the spy who was (eventually) caught, was a spy by conviction. His ideological antagonist Dick White, who became Director General of MI5 in 1953, suggested that Fuchs's motives 'were relatively speaking pure', contrasting his altruism with the desire for money that had motivated some other spies.[38] The same can be said of Fuchs's Austrian counterpart, Engelbert Broda, the spy who got away.

Notes

1 The National Archives [TNA], KV2/1245/1a.
2 TNA, KV2/1245/3.
3 Chief Constable to Kell, 5 November 1934, TNA, KV2/1245/1. This information was also sent to the Home Office (HO).
4 Fuchs was 'a close friend of Kahle at Camp L, managing their Communist activities etc'. Source Nep letter, extracted 20 June 1942, TNA, KV2/1245/18.
5 Letter Max Born to Royal Society, 29 May 1940, TNA, KV2/1246/136z.
6 Memo B1a (G.R.Mitchell) to B1 (Mr Hollis), 3 December 1946, TNA, KV2/1245/54.
7 Statement of Emil Klaus Julius Fuchs to Mr Skardon, 27 January 1950, TNA, KV2/1263/2a, Appendix D.
8 Note D3 (J.O.Archer), 10 October 1941, TNA, KV2/1245/11.
9 Fuchs's statement to Skardon, TNA, KV2/1263/2a.
10 Robert Chadwell Williams, *Klaus Fuchs: Atom Spy*, Cambridge/London: Harvard University Press 1987, p. 33. Williams's scholarly study is somewhat impaired by his being unable to consult Fuchs's MI5 file which had not then been released. He did, however, have access to Harry Gold's confessions to the FBI, and also Fuchs's confessions to Jim Skardon and Michael Perrin, copies of which were sent to the FBI, all of which Williams published as appendices to his book.
11 'Contacts of Fuchs', TNA, KV2/1256/756a.
12 Note on 'Contacts and Meetings, TNA, KV2/1263/59a.
13 Statement of Emil Klaus Julius Fuchs to Mr Skardon, 27 January 1950, TNA, KV2/1263/2a, Appendix D.
14 MI5 (C3b) to HO, 2 June 1942, TNA, KV2/1245/16.
15 Ruth Werner, *Sonya's Report*, London: Chatto and Windus 1991, pp. 294–5.
16 Werner, *Sonya's Report*, pp. 250–3.
17 'Notes by Fuchs on Contacts and Meetings', TNA, KV2/1263/59a.
18 Fuchs's statement to Skardon, TNA, KV2/1263/2a.
19 TNA, KV2/2145/32.
20 Minute F2b (Bagot), 22 November 1943, TNA, KV2/1245/35.
21 Details from Harry Gold's statements to the FBI. printed in Williams, *Klaus Fuchs*, pp. 195–220.
22 Quoted in David Burke, *The Spy Who Came in from the Co-op: Melita Norwood and the Ending of Cold War Espionage*, Woodbridge: Boydell Press 2008, p. 131.
23 Nigel West and Oleg Tsarev, *The Crown Jewels: British Secrecy at the Heart of the KGB Archives*, London: Harper Collins 1998, pp. 239–40. This useful reference is marred by the misnaming of Klopstech as Klopstock, and Siebert as Zibert. Klopstech was Welfare Secretary within the FGLC's 'Sozialkommission' or welfare committee; Siebert played a leading part in the Free German Institute of Science and Learning.
24 TNA, KV2/1253/575a and TNA, KV2/1256/756a.
25 Minute, 10 October 1946, TNA, KV2/1245 and 'Statement of Henry Arnold', TNA, KV2/1263/2a, Appendix B.

26 M.F. Serpell, minute, 13 November 1946, TNA, KV2/1245/49.
27 B1 R.H. Hollis note, 4 December 1946, TNA, KV2/1245/55.
28 B1 R.H. Hollis note, 8 Dec 1947, TNA, KV2/1245/106.
29 Sir Percy Sillitoe to Sir Archibald Rowlands, 19 January 1950, marked 'top secret and personal', TNA, KV2/1250/422a.
30 B2a report on visit of W/Cdr Arnold, 26 September 1949, TNA, KV2/1246/175c.
31 MI5 report on Emil Julius Klaus Fuchs, Mr Skardon's first interview', TNA, KV2/1263/2a, Appendix A.
32 MI5 report on Fuchs, Mr Skardon's second interview, TNA, KV2/1263/2a, Appendix C.
33 MI5 report on Fuchs, Mr Skardon's third interview, TNA, KV2/1263/2a, Appendix C.
34 J.C. Robertson note, 23 January 1950, KV2/1250/426a.
35 MI5 report on Fuchs, statement of Henry Arnold, TNA, KV2/1263/2a, Appendix B.
36 MI5 report on Fuchs, Fourth, Fifth, Sixth and Seventh interviews, 31 January 1950, TNA, KV2/1263/2a/, Appendix G.
37 Note, J.C. Robertson, 2 March 1950, TNA, KV2/1253/568c.
38 Tom Bower, *The Perfect English Spy: Sir Dick White and the Secret War 1935–90*, London: Heinemann 1995, p. 96.

20

The spy who got away: the case of Engelbert Broda

The Austrian scientist Engelbert Broda – half-Jewish and a known Communist – arrived in Britain in 1938, having previously suffered imprisonment for his political activities both in Germany and in Austria. Born in 1910, he had originally been a Social Democrat and a student party functionary, but joined the Communist Party in the autumn of 1930. He was a highly intelligent, good-looking, well-connected man who sought refuge in Britain with his wife Hilde, a doctor of medicine. Both Special Branch and MI5 took an interest in him virtually from the start: in July 1938, for instance, Special Branch reported on the activities of a group of Austrian Communist refugees who had been meeting in London for some months and of whom Broda was the leader. The same report also mentioned the photographer Edith Tudor-Hart, with whom Broda would remain closely connected throughout his years in Britain, as being responsible for liaison between the Austrian group and the Central Committee of the Communist Party of Great Britain.[1]

British security continued to keep watch on Broda until his return to Vienna in 1947, and beyond. Indeed after Broda, a talented physical chemist, had been taken on to work at the Cambridge Cavendish Laboratory from 1941 and had become involved in the top secret Tube Alloys project, MI5 grew ever more watchful, advising caution with regard to his employment there and even giving vent to the suspicion that Broda, as a convinced Communist in possession of highly classified information, might well be inclined to pass on his atomic secrets to the Soviets. That he did just that during his years in Britain, and the manner in which he did it, will form the subject of this chapter. At the time, however, no conclusive proof against him was ever found, and he lived out the rest of his life as a respected scientist in Vienna, dying there in 1983.

MI5's original suspicions of Broda only became public knowledge when his Security Service file was released in 2006, more than twenty years after his death. A book had been published in 1999, *The Haunted Wood* by Allen Weinstein and Alexander Vassiliev, using material Vassiliev had gleaned from KGB records, which had named two previously unknown atomic spies by their code names, 'Persian' and 'Eric', though without disclosing their true identities ('Eric' is in fact referred to as 'an Englishman' which would have successfully deflected attention away from Broda).[2] The 'outing' of Broda as a Soviet spy and his identification as 'Eric' came about in 2009, in a second book co-authored by Vassiliev, *Spies: The Rise and Fall of the KGB in America*;[3] this book was reviewed in *The Times* under the startling heading 'The Spy Who Started the Cold War'.[4] Then in 2011, Engelbert's son Paul Broda published a memoir that combined personal and family recollections with material from his father's MI5 file, as well as those kept on his mother Hilde and the man who became his stepfather, the convicted atom spy, Alan Nunn May. The involvement of Engelbert Broda in scientific espionage at the highest level while in Britain appears to be beyond doubt; how did he, unlike the British scientist Nunn May, unlike the refugee Klaus Fuchs, succeed for so long in evading detection?

Broda's MI5 file indicates that the British authorities were well aware of his connections with 'suspect' Austrian organisations such as the Austrian Centre as well as with leading Austrian Communists like Eva Kolmer and of course Edith Tudor-Hart. Broda was in fact one of those exiles about whom the authorities felt sufficiently uneasy to intern them twice: once soon after the outbreak of war and again in mid-1940, although in Broda's case his detention did not last for more than a couple of months on either occasion. In a rather curious episode that accompanied his first arrest in October 1939, the police impounded his personal papers including much material relating to the Austrian Centre. Asked to explain his connection with the Centre, Broda had claimed to be the editor of its news sheet *Austrian News* as well as a member of the Centre's Executive Committee. Neither claim could be corroborated; he was unable, so it was reported, to explain the discrepancy satisfactorily.[5]

Broda was released from his first internment in December 1939; letters had been written to the authorities on his behalf by a variety of agencies, including the SPSL, and by individuals, like the former Austrian ambassador to Britain Sir Georg(e) Franckenstein and the eminent British scientist Sir William Bragg (who was very helpful to Broda and his wife and young son in exile, offering them accommodation when needed).[6] A few days after his release, the Home Office Warrant authorising the interception of his mail was cancelled, but Broda was nevertheless still termed 'a dangerous Austrian communist' in a Special Branch report of early February 1940[7] – an example of the disjointed security procedures characterising the British surveillance of the German-speaking refugee population in general and this case in particular.

Regular entries in his MI5 file, some of these being extracted from the usual reports by 'Kaspar' (Josef Otto von Laemmel) or 'Hi' (Kurt Hiller), indicate that Broda, even after his second release from internment in September 1940, continued to be of interest from a security point of view. In March 1941, for instance, in a 'Kaspar' report on the Austrian Communist Party in Great Britain, Broda was listed as the Party's 'Training Leader';[8] in April, according to 'Hi', a lecture Broda had delivered at the Austrian Centre on the 'War Budget of Great Britain' had included 'defeatist' discussion of whether Britain would be able to maintain its current 'enormous expenditure';[9] while in May Hiller condemned a further Austrian Centre lecture of Broda's, this time on 'Raw Material Production and the War Strength of the Great Powers' as 'faked and defeatist'.[10] In the meantime, MI5 had long since resumed interception of Broda's mail, 'suspicious' examples – such as a communication from Paolo Treves of Free Italy suggesting collaboration with the Free Austrians[11] – being retained in his file.

Before his second internment, Broda had been employed as a research scientist at University College London (on a project subsequently transferred to King's College London). After his release, having lost the Medical Research Council grant that had been funding his research, he found a job with a consultant metallurgist, later working as a scientist for a company in Barking. The possibility that Broda might be employed at the Cavendish Laboratory first arose in his MI5 file on 27 November 1941 (in an intercepted letter from the Cavendish),[12] followed soon after by an internal memorandum to Sir Thomas Bazley of MI5 to the effect that Broda now had the required AWS [Aliens War Service Department] permit for employment there. Moreover 'the D.S. & I.R. [Department of Industrial and Scientific Research, or DSIR, responsible for the Tube Alloys project] consider that the exigencies of their Department outweigh any security objection to such employment'.[13] Hence, MI5 found itself in the same position as in the case of Klaus Fuchs: unwilling party to a decision taken against their better judgement. In the case of Broda, at any rate, they were reassured to a degree by information from the DSIR that, although Broda would be employed on Government research in Cambridge, the work 'is divided into 2 parts, the more secret of which he would not be employed on'.[14]

The contact between Broda, who was keen to leave his job in Barking, and Hans Halban who, with Lew Kowarski, had fled from France carrying with them the world's supply of heavy water, was established, or re-established, through Broda's friend Esther (Tess) Simpson of the SPSL. Broda and Halban already knew one another from their younger days in Austria, and Halban was evidently keen to have Broda join his Atom Project team in Cambridge. By 1941, when the official decision was taken to promote research in the new area of nuclear fission, most British scientists were already employed in war-related activity of other kinds with the result that Halban's and Kowarski's team was largely made up of foreign scientists.[15] As for the division of the research into its more, and less, secret aspects, this apparently never took place, despite the assurances given to MI5 by the DSIR. Certainly the historian of science Andrew Brown contends that, in practice, at the Cavendish (unlike in the comparable American Manhattan Project) there was never any hint of compartmentalisation and that the Cambridge scientists discussed all aspects of their work freely.[16]

Of course, the fact that Broda was recruited to the Tube Alloys project at all provides yet another clear example of the degree to which the entry of the Soviet Union into the war, just a few months before, had transformed the situation for many Communists, including foreign Communists, in Britain. Yet it should still surely be seen as surprising that, as MI5 papers make clear, Sir Edward Appleton, the secretary of the DSIR, should have been so very firm that Broda's services were required. In any case MI5, though overruled, continued to keep watch on Broda while he was in Cambridge: in April 1942, for example, Milicent Bagot enquired of the Cambridge-based MI5 regional officer, Major Dixon, about Broda's activities. Given that the latter's scientific work was deemed to outweigh security considerations, it was, she told Dixon, a 'delicate case' – hence her approach to him on the subject rather than to the local police. She continued:

> In view of the nature of his work I am particularly anxious that Broda should not be aware that he is the subject of suspicion, but if you should obtain any information to show that he is taking part in any political activities I should be grateful if you could let me know immediately.[17]

Dixon replied that Bagot's news was 'rather disquieting', such that he had arranged through a contact of his for surveillance of Broda's spare time activities and, specifically, of whether he was playing a part in local Communist activities.[18] In the meantime, post delivered to Broda's Cambridge address was being intercepted.

The findings of Major Dixon's unnamed contact did not amount to very much, other than to record that Broda was a leading member of the committee of the Cambridge branch of the Austrian Centre. One report maintained that Broda's views pointed to his having been a Social Democrat [*sic*] back in Austria;[19] another contended that 'it seemed to be taken for granted by the people with whom I discussed Broda, that he was very much to the Left. Most of the people in the Free Austrian Movement are very much so themselves'.[20] In London, MI5 remained unconvinced by assurances of Broda's relative harmlessness, however, with Roger Hollis writing in some frustration in May 1943: 'As we cannot be told the nature of the work for which Broda is required we can only state what we know of Broda's connection with the Communists, and mention the definite risk that any information which he gets will be given to the Communists.'[21]

It is ironic that the work should be deemed so secret that even the Security Service should not be informed of its nature. When two months later Hollis enlarged on his previous statement, he gave the impression of washing his hands of the whole matter:

> Our very wide system of observation on the Communist Party and its contacts shows that there must be a very definite risk that Broda will give to the Communist Party details of the work on which he is engaged, in order that these particulars may be transmitted to the Soviet Union. It is however most unlikely that we shall be able to get actual proof that Broda has done this, and the ordinary methods of investigation are likely merely to put Broda on his guard. I am therefore opposed to employing them.[22]

It was, of course, such apparently laissez-faire statements as these that have since caused writers on intelligence matters like Peter Wright and Chapman Pincher to question Hollis's loyalties and indeed to suspect him of having been a Soviet agent (though their suspicions remain unconfirmed).[23]

From 1942 onwards, members of the Cavendish team were being transferred to Montreal to take part in the Anglo-Canadian atomic energy project. Broda, according to his son Paul, could have joined them in Canada but had chosen to remain in Britain, possibly because it would have meant leaving his young child behind (the Brodas had separated in September 1940 and the boy was largely in the care of his mother Hilde). Alternatively, his decision may have been Party-related or indeed might have been influenced by the close personal as well as political relationship that had developed between Broda and Edith Tudor-Hart.[24] By mid-1943, in any case, official concern was being expressed at the fact that, contrary to the original compartmentalisation plan, Broda 'now knows a considerable amount of the more secret aspect of the work';[25] and by June 1944, the DSIR had decided 'that at all costs they will not send Broda overseas. They have given the latter a sufficient excuse for not doing so'.[26]

Thanks to KGB records as divulged by Vassiliev in 2009, we now know not only that Broda was indeed in possession of a considerable amount of information about the most secret aspects of the atomic bomb project but that, as feared by MI5, he was passing this information on to the Soviet Union. Following the collapse of the Soviet Union, Vassiliev had been given access to KGB files in order to write an official history; however he had left for the West instead, his notebooks on the files being sent on after him. These notebooks revealed that the first materials from Britain on the atomic bomb project had been received by the Soviets at the end of 1941; these, because of the technical information exchange between Britain, the United States and Canada, had yielded intelligence on the progress of the atomic research in all three countries. The information had initially come through the Foreign Office official and SIS officer John Cairncross or 'Liszt' (now known to have been the 'Fifth Man' alongside Guy Burgess, Donald Maclean, Kim Philby and Anthony Blunt), while two further valuable sources in Britain had been 'Tina', that is, Melita Norwood,[27] and 'Quid', previously code-named 'Eric', identified by Vassiliev as Engelbert Broda.[28] Broda himself, so we learn from this source, began to pass on information to the Soviets from late 1942.

According to Vassiliev's account, the KGB's London station had informed Moscow that the contact had come about in the following way: Edith Tudor-Hart had received a report from Broda on the state of atomic research in Britain and the United States, which she had passed on via an intermediary to the station. The Soviets, impressed by the report, had instructed Tudor-Hart to press Broda for more and to persuade him to meet with a KGB officer. Initially reluctant to do so, Broda had first met the KGB officer 'Glan' in January 1943, subsequently agreeing to a meeting with him every two to three weeks.[29] At these meetings, involving him in regular journeys to London which he passed off as visits to the Austrian Centre or to see his son, he is thought to have provided the Soviets with thousands of pages of confidential documents on British atomic research. Additionally, because of the access he enjoyed to American bulletins on the work, he was able to report on American progress in the field – the Americans were significantly ahead, so Broda informed his Soviet contacts. By August 1943, the Soviets were regarding Broda as 'the main source of info. on work being done on E. [i.e. 'Enormous', code name for the Manhattan project] both in England and in the USA', while by the following year, thanks to a key to the laboratory library given to him by a colleague who had left to work in Canada, Broda was in a position to pass on a still greater range of information, consisting of 'all available Amer. reports of the second batch as well as oth. interesting mater-s on En-s'. More flexible contact procedures were then agreed that would enable him to meet his Soviet handlers without prior arrangement: whenever he wished to talk to them, he had merely to enter a designated telephone box and mark a page of a directory – the stuff of a classic spy story – thereby indicating his desire for a meeting.

In the meantime, official concern about the security of the atomic bomb project was growing. By the autumn of 1944, there were considerable doubts regarding the reliability of foreign scientists working on atomic research. It was feared, for example, that the exiled French scientists working in the Montreal laboratory who could now visit liberated Paris would pass on information to their former boss there, the Communist Frédéric Joliot-Curie, who in turn would pass it on to the Soviet Union.[30] Such official fears about atomic espionage were seen to be amply justified in September 1945, when Igor Gouzenko, a clerk in the office of the Soviet

Military Attaché in Ottawa, defected with one hundred official documents pointing to an extensive spy network in Canada.

Following this, British security stepped up the attention it paid to the atomic scientists, particularly those known to be Communists. In November 1945, the informer 'Kaspar' reported on Broda to MI5, basing his report on information from Broda's friend Edith Tudor-Hart:

> Although I have no definite proof, I have always suspected Broda of being engaged in scientific espionage and according to Edith Tudor-Hart he has for some time occupied himself with secret scientific research at Cambridge connected with atomic energy. She stressed Broda's importance to the Party in view of his qualifications and connections. In view of the intimate relations existing between Edith Tudor-Hart and Broda it must be presumed that she is well informed of her lover's activities.[31]

This was only one of a number of interviews between 'Kaspar' and Tudor-Hart at this time in which the latter appears to have been less than discreet: on 18 March 1946, for example, following a visit from an unknown caller that had alarmed her, Tudor-Hart suggested to 'Kaspar' that the incident was very probably connected with Broda who was 'too careless'. She continued: 'When a man is involved in such a business as he is [...] he ought to be careful and not endanger his friends by writing to or visiting them.'[32] And in September 1946, 'Kaspar' reported that Broda had had several confidential talks with Tudor-Hart concerning the current Soviet experiments on atomic bombs:

> According to Broda, the Russians have already solved the problem or are near the solution. Broda states that, contrary to the Anglo/American method, the Russian scientists have found a way of releasing atomic energy through the combination of [handwritten insertion '?'] 'four hydrogen atoms to helium' which proves to be much cheaper and more efficient.[33]

Brown records his astonishment at 'Kaspar's' report, on two counts: firstly that Broda was even aware of the Russian research into thermonuclear weapons, given the level of Soviet security; and secondly that he would share his information with Edith Tudor-Hart.[34] There is, however, a third and equally astonishing aspect to this report, namely that Edith Tudor-Hart, a Soviet agent herself, would have talked so freely to 'Kaspar', that is, Josef Otto von Laemmel. Certainly she would have known Laemmel from the earliest days of the Austrian Centre, when both held a position there, but she would also have known that Laemmel had been forced out of the Centre and was extremely disgruntled with the Austrian Communists as a result, and that he was a leading member of the tiny Austrian Christian Socialist group in exile and very far removed from her own political position. One should perhaps assume that Tudor-Hart was not aware that in talking to Laemmel she was also informing MI5[35] – though here too one may merely speculate – but it is of course also possible that Tudor-Hart, as an experienced political operator, was deliberately spreading disinformation. Unfortunately, those MI5 papers on her that have been released are too thin to enable one to come to any definite conclusion.

On 4 March 1946, Broda's fellow atomic scientist, Alan Nunn May, was arrested and charged under the Official Secrets Act, as a direct result of the information provided by the Gouzenko defection. Broda's name now began to be linked with that of Nunn May in MI5 documents: the two men had, so it was reported, been associated at the Cavendish Laboratory, and they had met after Nunn May's return from Canada both in Cambridge and in London.[36] The 'Kaspar' report of 18 March, based on a Tudor-Hart interview, noted: 'Any discussion about intelligence work or even the mention of anything of the sort is now strictly prohibited.'[37] Broda also began at this time to seek permission to return to Austria, applying for a permit for August 1946 (although he had in any case always planned to return to Austria in keeping with Free Austrian ideology). The Directorate of Atomic Energy, in discussing the case with MI5, were initially reluctant to let Broda go. It was true, they concluded (erroneously), that Broda had only had limited access to the research but 'on the other hand he will have picked up in the course of conversation quite a lot about other aspects of the work'.[38] Eventually, however, after exchanges between the official bodies involved in the case, and despite the continuing misgivings of the Security Service, the Directorate decided that there were no grounds on which to prevent Broda from returning home. Consequently, in April 1947 he arrived back in a war-torn Vienna to work for the Federal Ministry for Electrification and Energy, obtaining a post at Vienna University the following year. He was given a professorship in 1964 and continued to have a successful university career in physical chemistry until his retirement in 1980.

Broda's return to Vienna did not mean that MI5 lost interest in him. On the contrary, the statement made by Alan Nunn May in 1949 that the person who had recruited him as a spy was by then beyond the reach of British jurisdiction suggested to them that Broda might well have been the recruiter in question. And when in August 1953, a few months after his release from prison, Nunn May married Broda's former wife Hilde, British suspicions inevitably focused on Broda once again. A five-page report from 14 October 1953 summarised the information MI5 had collected on Broda over the years. Among its final points was the fact that in April 1950 a USAF [United States Air Force] report had linked him to the Soviet espionage service both before his arrival in England in 1938 and in wartime Britain. Since leaving Britain, moreover, 'for the Soviets, he has organised an information network with tentacles in every department of the Chemistry Institute [at Vienna University]'. It was noted in the MI5 summary's penultimate paragraph that in August 1950 the Director of Scientific Intelligence at the British Ministry of Defence had suggested that if Broda returned to Britain, a 'special watch' should be put on him as 'owing to his many friends at Harwell he would be in an ideal position for collecting intelligence'.[39] This was of course after Klaus Fuchs, who had returned from Los Alamos to work at Harwell, had been arrested. Interestingly, the 'special watch' was never required since Broda, who had made just one post-war visit to Britain in 1948, never visited the country again (the relationship with his son Paul was maintained by the boy's regular visits to Vienna). Presumably, post-Fuchs, Broda was aware of the consequences that re-entering Britain might bring.

An internal MI5 minute, written on the same date as the report, 14 October 1953, set out some of the British suspicions – still unproven – against Engelbert Broda:

> Your enquiry about the possibility that the Brodas played some part in the espionage of Nunn May came at a happy time, for we were already studying Engelbert Broda's case in another connection. As a result of that study we feel sure that Broda was engaged in espionage during the war, although we have no proof of it.[...]
>
> I think therefore that the answer to your question is that Engelbert Broda might well have been the person who recruited Nunn May for the R.I.S. [Russian Intelligence Service]. You will remember that one of Nunn May's few admissions [...] was that he was recruited for the R.I.S. only a very short while before he left this country for Canada and that the individual who recruited him was still no longer within reach [...] In March 1949 when Nunn May said this Broda was no longer in the country.[40]

Much of the rest of Broda's MI5 file, including the front of file minutes on documents 496 to 563, has been heavily redacted, although why can only be a matter for speculation. It is possible that it was done to suppress information about a person or persons unknown, inside or outside the Security Service. Or it may be that this case, which appears to reveal MI5 as particularly inept in its protection of atomic secrets, was an exceptionally sensitive one in terms of Anglo-American relations, though some later correspondence between the British and the Americans on the subject still remains in the file. One of the last documents left in the file, dated 31 March 1955, written in answer to an American enquiry about Broda, concluded that there was no evidence of Broda having been involved in espionage while in the United Kingdom.[41] This may perhaps be compared with a previous exchange in the file: eighteen months before, MI5's R.T. Reed had noted, in answer to an FBI request for information on Hilde Broda, that since the Scientific Section was 'reluctant to tell the Americans anything at all', it was agreed that the British answer should say as little as possible.[42] Certainly, so concerned did the Americans become at security leaks to the Soviets, that they abandoned the policy of technical information exchange with Britain.

How significant were Engelbert Broda's disclosures? Vassiliev reports that among the information Broda was credited with passing on were some plans for one of the Manhattan Project's early nuclear reactors. These were regarded by the Soviets as containing 'all the necessary information to build a plant, and [it] is exceptionally valuable'.[43] In fact, details of the Manhattan Project were apparently being passed on to the Soviet Union almost as soon as they arrived at the Cavendish Laboratory. In the estimation of Haynes, Klehr and Vassiliev, Engelbert Broda and his fellow scientist agents Klaus Fuchs and Alan Nunn May, among others, 'offered [the Soviet Union] technological and scientific information that saved untold billions of roubles and years of scientific experiments and blind alleys'.[44] Russia was thereby enabled to test its first nuclear bomb as early as 1949. Although the epithet 'the spy who started the Cold War' is clearly facile, it can be argued that 'intelligence from Broda and others laid the groundwork for Soviet nuclear scientists, paving the way for the nuclear confrontation of the Cold War'.[45] Conversely, as Paul Broda points out, the 'balance of terror' resulting from the Soviet Union's development of the atomic bomb may well have prevented war between the United States and the Soviet Union.[46]

And a further question: why did Engelbert Broda, a refugee offered asylum in Britain because it was too dangerous for him to remain in Austria, turn spy? Certainly his espionage activities brought him no financial gain, indeed he consistently refused payment for his services, as KGB files make clear:

> 'Eric' continues to work willingly with us, but he still balks at even the slightest hint about mater. assistance. We once gave him more than he asked to cover his expenses. He was displeased by this and said that he suspects we want to give him a certain kind of help. He asked us to give up any such thoughts once and for all. In such circumstances, we fear that any gift from us as a token of appreciation for his work will make a negative impression. 'Eric' is completely selfless in his work with us and extremely scrupulous when it comes to anything that could be seen as 'payment' for his work.[47]

The answer is that, like Fuchs, Nunn May and others, Broda's motivation was entirely political. As a convinced Communist, moreover at a time when the Soviet Union was a military ally in the struggle against Hitler but was not being made party to Anglo-American nuclear developments, he would have felt it his duty to pass on whatever information he could. The fact that his activities remained undetected, or at any rate unproven, within his own lifetime, was partly a matter of luck on his part – had he been apprehended he would almost certainly have served a lengthy prison sentence. But it was also to a large extent the result of serious misjudgement and inaction on the part of the British Security Service.

Notes

1 Special Branch report, 'Austrian Communist Party Group in London', 23 July 1938, The National Archives [TNA], KV2/2349/2a.
2 Allen Weinstein and Alexander Vassiliev, *The Haunted Wood: Soviet Espionage in America – The Stalin Era*, New York: Modern Library, paperback edition 2000, p. 181.
3 John Earl Haynes, Harvey Klehr and Alexander Vassiliev, *Spies: The Rise and Fall of the KGB in America*, New Haven/London: Yale University Press, 2009.
4 *The Times*, 10 June 2009.
5 'Engelbert Broda', Extract from Home Office (HO) file B14618, n.d. [October 1939], TNA, KV2/2349/85A. In fact, a report of a General Meeting held at the Austrian Centre on 26 June 1939 cites Broda and Dr Franz Klein as representing *Austrian News* ('Generalversammlung des Klubs Austrian Centre London, 26. June 1939', Friedrich Otto Hertz Papers, Archiv für die Geschichte der Soziologie in Österreich, Graz, 28/5.15).
6 Extract from HO file, B14618, 're Engelbert Broda', n.d. [February/March 1940], TNA, KV2/2349/103A.
7 Special Branch report, 'Edward and Gerda Newmark', 3 February 1940, TNA, KV2/2349/88a.
8 Source 'Kaspar' report, 'The Austrian Communist Party in Great Britain', 14 March 1941, TNA, KV2/2350/124z.
9 Source 'Hi' report, 'Austrian Centre' 19 April 1941, TNA, KV2/2350/125a.
10 Source 'Hi' report, 'The Austrian Centre Lecture on the Raw Material Production and the War Strength of the Great Powers', 7 May 1941, TNA, KV2/2350/126a.
11 Treves to Broda, n.d. [*c*. 30 October 1941], TNA, KV2/2350/n.no.
12 Hans Halban, Cavendish Laboratory, Cambridge, to Broda, 27 November 1941, TNA, KV2/2350/139a.
13 21 December 1941, TNA, KV2/2350/140a.
14 'Engelbert Broda – Austrian', 26 December 1941, TNA, KV2/2350/142a.
15 Paul Broda, *Scientist Spies: A Memoir of My Three Parents and the Atom Bomb*, Kibworth Beauchamp: Matador 2011, pp. 95–6.
16 Andrew Brown, 'The Viennese Connection: Engelbert Broda, Alan Nunn May and Atomic Espionage', *Intelligence and National Security*, 24, 2 (April 2009), p. 179.
17 Bagot to Dixon, 26 April 1942, TNA, KV2/2350/148a.
18 Dixon to Bagot, 1 May 1942, TNA, KV2/2350/149a.
19 Dixon report, 23 June 1942, TNA, KV2/2350/154a. In fact Broda had ceased to be a Social Democrat by 1930.
20 Further Dixon report, 23 July 1942, TNA, KV2/2350/157a.
21 Hollis to Bagot, front of file minute 188, 20 May 1943, TNA, KV2/2350.
22 Hollis front of file minute 197, 7 July 1943, TNA, KV2/2350.

23 On this, see Peter Wright, *Spycatcher: The Candid Autobiography of a Senior Intelligence Officer*, New York: Viking 1987; Chapman Pincher, *Treachery: Betrayals, Blunders and Cover-ups: Six Decades of Espionage*, Edinburgh: Mainstream, 2011.
24 Broda, *Scientist Spies*, p. 149.
25 A.C.M. Bennett front of file minute 196, 3 July 1943, TNA, KV2/2350.
26 'Extract from report of conversation at DSIR, 16 Old Queen St, SW1 on 1st June 1944', hand dated 11 June 1944, TNA, KV2/2351/231b.
27 On Norwood, see David Burke, *The Spy Who Came in from the Co-op: Melita Norwood and the Ending of Cold War Espionage*, Woodbridge: Boydell Press, 2008.
28 Haynes, Klehr and Vassiliev, *Spies*, pp. 64–5.
29 For this and much of the remainder of this paragraph, see *ibid.*, p. 67. Vassiliev's source was KGB file 82702, vol. 1.
30 Brown, 'Viennese Connection', p. 181. This is indeed what happened.
31 Source 'Kaspar' report, 'Dr E. Broda', 10 November 1945, TNA, KV2/2352/302a.
32 Source 'Kaspar' report, 'Edith Tudor Hart and E. Broda', 18 March 1946, TNA, KV2/2353/325d.
33 Source 'Kaspar' report, 'Dr Broda', 15 September 1946, TNA, KV2/2354/372b.
34 Brown, 'Viennese Connection', p. 185.
35 Against this, see, for example, MI5 report 'Broda', dated 23 April 1947, in which Tudor-Hart is cited as the source of a report on Broda's journey to Rome, which included details of a Yugoslav contact there, Ada Drakovitch: 'From what Tudor-Hart said it would seem that Ada Drakovich is employed by Russian Intelligence.' Just before this, Tudor-Hart had reportedly 'at last' admitted to MI5 that she herself had worked for Russian Intelligence in Austria and Italy in 1932–33 (see TNA, KV2/2354/400a; TNA, KV2/1014/112a).
36 See 'May's Contacts', 23 March 1946, TNA, KV2/2353/327b.
37 Source 'Kaspar' report, 'Edith Tudor-Hart and E. Broda', 18 March 1946, TNA, KV2/2353/325d.
38 Ministry of Supply, Directorate of Atomic Energy to MI5, 22 May 1946, TNA, KV2/2353/344a.
39 'Engelbert Egon Ernst August Broda', 14 October 1953, TNA, KV2/2354/495a.
40 Internal MI5 minute, 14 October 1953, TNA, KV2/2354/495b.
41 G.R. Mitchell (MI5) to J. Philip O'Brien, American Embassy in London, 31 March 1955, TNA, KV2/2354/547a.
42 R.T. Reed note, 17 October 1953, TNA, KV2/2354/497a.
43 Haynes, Klehr and Vassiliev, *Spies*, p. 67.
44 *Ibid.*, p. 143.
45 *The Times*, 10 June 2009.
46 Broda, *Scientist Spies*, p. xv.
47 Haynes, Klehr and Vassiliev, *Spies*, p. 67.

21

Parting company

MI5's surveillance of the political exiles did not cease with the end of the war but often continued well into the next decade, no matter whether the 'suspects' remained in Britain or returned to their country of origin. Perhaps surprisingly, one of the last post-war attempts that British officialdom made to control the movements of those political refugees who were anxious to return home was its efforts to postpone their departure from Britain. The British aim was to prevent Communists, in particular, from playing any active role in early political life back home. A Free German activist in British exile, Bruno Retzlaff-Kresse, frustrated at being unable to leave Manchester, later recalled the bitter irony of the situation 'that the same British authorities who had once tried to prevent us from entering England, now wanted to keep us in England at all costs'.[1] The majority of the political exiles were not finally permitted to return home until late 1946 or early 1947.

Some of the refugees managed by one subterfuge or another to return home ahead of time, however, among them the Austrian Centre functionaries Willi Scholz and Franz West. In October 1945, they seized the opportunity to leave Britain with a Yugoslav delegation, and without the permission of the British authorities, landing precariously on a small Russian military air base near Vienna. For Scholz, in particular, an early return to Austria was imperative since he had been selected as Communist Party candidate for Styria for the Austrian parliamentary elections scheduled for November 1945 (though in the event he was not elected). Scholz's and West's MI5 files contain various reports on their departure from Britain including several minutes on how the two men had managed to breach the security control regulations.[2] Reports continued to reach both files from Vienna: some arrived via the indefatigable 'Kaspar' who, while remaining in England for the time being, evidently had sources of information in Austria; some came from SIS or from undisclosed sources. Sporadic information on the movements of Scholz and West, including Scholz's break with the Communist Party following the Hungarian uprising,[3] was filed well into the 1950s.

Most of the political refugees whom MI5 had watched over the years of exile sooner or later left Britain to resume their political activities at home. Germany was now a divided country, the eastern Soviet zone or later German Democratic Republic proving generally more attractive to the Communist returnees such as Wilhelm Koenen or Jürgen Kuczynski. Austria, on the other hand, proved a disappointment: the eagerly awaited parliamentary elections of November 1945 in which the Communists won just four seats confounded the hopes of returning activists. For different reasons, one personal the other professional, both Eva Kolmer, who later made a substantial contribution in the field of public health, and the Austrian Centre's cultural organiser Georg Knepler, later a leading Mozart scholar, ended up in the GDR rather than in their native Austria.

Eva Kolmer, who first succeeded in paying a short visit to Austria at the start of 1946, also managed to circumvent the British travel restrictions. Kolmer, who had been given leave to participate in the inaugural meeting of the International Democratic Women's Federation in Paris, simply took the Arlberg Express from Paris to Austria. In Kolmer's case, MI5 was evidently less displeased that she had succeeded in returning to Vienna than at the news, just a few weeks later, that she was back in London again.[4] The reason for her reappearance was her relationship with the German Communist leader Heinz Schmidt and her desire to accompany him back to the Soviet zone of Germany.[5] The final MI5 file on Kolmer even contains a notification of Schmidt's and Kolmer's wedding on 27 September 1947, intercepted while on its way to William Rust of the *Daily Worker*.[6] Kolmer's name was still included on the Home Office Suspect Index as late as 1955.[7]

Yet another who succeeded in outwitting the British authorities was Jürgen Kuczynski who, despite strong objections to his being allowed to return to Germany from Lord Vansittart and others,[8] was recruited to work as a statistician under American auspices and then to serve in the German administration of Bavaria under the US Military Government. When in August 1945 Kuczynski finally managed to pay a short visit to the Soviet sector of Berlin and the Central Committee of the KPD, he was wearing American military uniform, which was initially the cause of some consternation. 'Come back as soon as you can without your uniform', he was instructed by the East German Communist leader Walter Ulbricht.[9]

However, life in the Soviet Zone/German Democratic Republic could be difficult for returnees from Western exile. Heinz Schmidt and Eva Kolmer, despite their loyalty to the Party in exile, had fallen from grace by 1949, having been dismissed from the positions of influence they had occupied since returning to Berlin and 'exiled' again to rural Mecklenburg. Here Schmidt, previously Director of Berlin Radio, had to spend five years managing a collective farm complex as an early victim of the Stalinist purges that had reached the GDR.

In 1947, Jürgen Kuczynski was appointed to the presidency of the Society for the Study of the Culture of the Soviet Union, the precursor to the influential Society for German–Soviet Friendship. He was dismissed from this post in 1950, however, in another instance of the purges that threatened all returnees from Western exile and particularly Jews. Reports of this setback also found their way into Kuzcynski's MI5 file where rumours were noted in July 1950 that he had been attacked in the GDR press[10] and in September 1950 that he had had to resign from the directorship of the German Institute of Economics. He still retained his professorship at Berlin University, the September 1950 report continued, and he remained a member of the Executive Committee of the Cultural League for the Democratic Regeneration of Germany as well as of the SED (the East German Communist Party). Kuczynski had, so it was concluded, not been expelled but he had certainly been discredited.[11] A further report from 1953, marked secret, noted rumours of impending arrests in East Germany, particularly of Jews. Kuczynski was amongst those endangered, his 'offence' being compounded by the fact that he had spent the war in London[12] (although in fact managing to avoid arrest in the GDR). Thereafter, Kuczynski continued to have occasional brushes with the SED leadership but appears to have been granted rather more licence than others, possibly because his international academic reputation offered him a certain protection.

Returning home was not an easy option, therefore, and was by no means a matter of course for everyone, not even for those political refugees professing themselves most anxious to participate in political, social and cultural reconstruction. The composer Ernst Hermann Meyer had developed many personal and professional links during his years in England, not least an English wife, which must have magnified the mistrust in which *Westemigranten* were held in East Germany. A number of his close family members had decided to remain in Britain. Moreover Meyer, as a specialist in early English chamber music, had made many friends and acquaintances in British musical circles. He himself admitted that his decision to return was hard;[13] nevertheless, acting from political conviction, he returned to the Soviet Zone in the autumn of 1948, rather later than the majority of returnees (he excused his delay on grounds of illness). In the GDR, Meyer took pains to toe the Party line on the musical principles of Socialist realism both in his own compositions and even in condemning the 'formalist' music of fellow musicians Paul Dessau and Hanns Eisler, the latter formerly his teacher. Rewarded for his orthodoxy, Meyer became a member of the SED Central Committee in 1963 and went on to play a significant role in the music of the GDR. It is perhaps surprising, given not only Meyer's prominence in East Germany but also his family contacts in Britain, that MI5 ceased to take note of his activities as early as September 1949 (when Meyer made a brief visit back to Britain).[14]

The pacifist Otto Lehmann-Russbueldt, who was neither a Jew nor a Communist, returned to (West) Berlin only in 1951, after eighteen years in British exile during which he was both watched by MI5 and used as a source of information. His advanced age – he was in his late seventies by then – and the reluctance of his third wife, a Viennese Jew, to settle in Germany, were factors in his delayed return. In Berlin, he was received warmly, granted a pension and awarded the prestigious Federal Order of Merit. He continued to write, work and campaign for peace for the rest of his life. In 1952, MI5 noted that Lehmann-Russbueldt had returned to Britain on a visit[15] but appears to have lost interest in him thereafter.

Some political refugees who might have been expected to return home ultimately chose to remain in Britain. One of these was the actor and FGLC activist Gerhard Hinze. Hinze, for many years a committed Communist, had become disenchanted with the Party, and by the end of the war had also established a foothold on the British stage. An MI5 report from August 1945 noted that Hinze was experiencing doubts about returning to Germany: 'The Party view his vacillation with grave disquiet, and his action may cast some shadow upon his standing in the Party.'[16] By 1948, Hinze had applied for and been granted British nationality. Nevertheless, MI5 still retained an interest in him for a while longer, recording in March 1950, for example, that Hinze 'is now telling everyone that he has changed his political views and is anti-Communist'.[17]

And what of those refugees who devoted so much of their time in exile to informing on their fellow refugees? 'Kaspar', Josef Otto (von) Laemmel, actually managed to turn his assistance to the Security Service to his own advantage in later life, exaggerating his importance and his standing with the British authorities – using the figure of his *Doppelgänger* Andreas – in his semi-autobiographical novel of 1981.[18] Laemmel remained in Britain for some years after the war, running a specialist Austrian travel agency. However, he returned to Graz in 1962 where he became known as a writer and public speaker. During the remaining eighteen years of his life, Laemmel presented himself as having played a pivotal role in Austrian exile politics whereby he had served Austria and the Austrians in England (while omitting to mention his work with MI5).[19] He was decorated by the Austrian state for his good offices. The myth that Laemmel created around himself was reflected in the glowing obituary that appeared in the *Tagespost*: 'Having emigrated to England in wartime, he rendered unforgettable service to countless comrades in misfortune at the time, service that has received official recognition but also a much finer recognition in his comrades' thankful hearts.'[20]

Kurt Hiller, though equally assiduous as an informer, did not attempt to make personal or political capital out of his own activities upon his return to Germany in 1955. Nevertheless, he remained as bitter about Communist 'perfidy' as ever, publishing his condemnation of the Communists in his *Rote Ritter* in 1951. He died in 1972, having spent the last years of his life as a writer, journalist and political activist. Hiller, who back in 1928 had issued a powerful defence of homosexuality, 'Appeal on Behalf of an Oppressed Human Variety', has since become something of an icon of the German Gay Rights movement.

Laemmel and Hiller both continued with their intelligence gathering well beyond the end of hostilities. Karl Otten, on the other hand, played no further part in British intelligence after becoming blind in 1944. He and his wife Ellen became British citizens in 1947, his wartime work entitling him to make a priority application. He resumed his writing career, and by the time he and Ellen finally left England in 1958, he had successfully re-entered the German literary market. However, he did not return to Germany, fearing that his wartime work for the BBC German Service (and for SOE, should it ever become known) would provoke hostility. Instead he moved to Switzerland, settling in Locarno, near the German colony in Ascona, a location which offered good access to German readers and publishers. In a series of interviews in the 1990s,[21] Ellen Otten responded fully and frankly to inquiries about Karl's personal life and literary work, but deflected questions on his intelligence activities by pleading ignorance or loss of memory, a notable intelligence example of silence by proxy. She died in 1999, the same year that MI5 began to release security files including, in 2002, the file on Karl Otten.

For the most part, the refugee informers can be said to have occupied their time in filling up MI5's files with little more than the trivia of the lives of others; the vast majority of German-speaking refugees under MI5 surveillance posed no threat to British security whatsoever. As for those few refugees who actually were Soviet agents, MI5's evident reluctance to proceed against Klaus Fuchs and Engelbert Broda has already been noted. In the end, Fuchs was only arrested after prompting from the United States; he was fortunate indeed not to have been charged in the United States where he would probably have been executed, like Ethel and Julius Rosenberg. As it was, he was released from Wakefield Prison in 1959 and left immediately for the GDR where he resumed his scientific career, rose to a position of some prominence and was repeatedly honoured for his services by the East German state.

Broda, for his part, succeeded in escaping from Britain scot-free. Back in Vienna, he continued to work as a scientist and to engage in national and international political activity, including participating in the Pugwash movement in support of nuclear disarmament. In keeping with his political views, he was made a foreign member of the GDR's Academy of Sciences; had his politics been different, so his son surmises, he would also have been elected to the Austrian Academy of Sciences.[22] He was nevertheless decorated by the Austrian government in 1980 and, on his death three years later, was buried in a Grave of Honour in the Central Cemetery in Vienna. Unsurprisingly, the British security services retained an interest in Broda for years after his departure from Britain. Only in 2009, however, were the suspicions MI5 had long harboured confirmed, when Broda's espionage activities were formally revealed.[23]

Similarly, the super-spy Ursula Beurton-Kuczynski, alias Ruth Werner, code name 'Sonya', managed to get the better of British intelligence. In her autobiography *Sonya's Report* she describes how in February 1950 she had left Britain in the nick of time, just as the Fuchs story was breaking. Fearing that she was about to be arrested, she took off with two of her three children for the GDR where she was initially helped to find her feet by her brother Jürgen Kuczynski.[24] In East Berlin, she was decorated for her services and granted the rare honorary title of Colonel in the Red Army.

Why the British Security Service failed to move against 'Sonya' more quickly remains a mystery. She herself later speculated on how she had managed to escape arrest and indeed why she had not been prevented from leaving Britain:

> Either it was complete stupidity on the part of MI5 never to have connected me with Klaus [Fuchs], or they may have let me get away with it since every further discovery would have increased their disgrace [with the Americans] [...] Or was it possible that there was someone at MI5 who was, at the same time, working for the Soviet Union and had protected us?[25]

There is a postscript to this story: in 1991, at the age of 84, Sonya returned to Britain in order to promote her recently published book. Several MPs called for her arrest, a call that the attorney-general, having consulted both MI5 and the Director of Public Prosecutions, resisted on account of her advanced age and because she was no longer considered a threat.[26] This episode recalls the case of the British agent Melita Norwood who, like Fuchs, had supplied 'Sonya' with information on the atomic bomb project, and who in 1999, when her espionage activities were finally revealed, was considered too old to prosecute (she was 87).[27]

'Sonya's' fellow Soviet agents, Edith Tudor-Hart and Margaret Mynatt, both remained in Britain. An MI5 narrative report on Edith Tudor-Hart in 1951 characterised her – in a notable instance of casual anti-semitism – as 'a rather typical, emotional, introspective and somewhat intellectual

Viennese Jewess', adding: 'She has for a long time had what possibly amounts to a morbid interest in psychology and psychiatry [...] constantly taking her small son to clinics and specialists.'[28] Tudor-Hart had indeed become an increasingly troubled spirit in the post-war years. Her personal life was darkened by the mental illness of her son, Tommy, who was eventually diagnosed as schizophrenic and placed in an institution. Meanwhile, the pressures of her double life as a Soviet agent had also begun to take their toll. For well over a decade, she was subject to sporadic surveillance by the security services; at different times she was shadowed, her post intercepted, her phone tapped and she was interrogated more than once, not least by the zealous MI5 officer Peter Wright.[29] The fragmentary evidence of her MI5 file suggests that this process yielded little apart from updates on her relationship with her lover Engelbert Broda.

As her health declined, her conduct became more incalculable; she became careless or even rash in her behaviour. A report from early 1947 stated that 'Mrs Tudor-Hart has at last admitted that she used to work for the Russian Intelligence in Austria and Italy 1932–33'.[30] By then she may already have begun to disengage from Soviet espionage; in any case MI5 seems to have lost interest in her. However, when MI5 began to interrogate the Soviet spy Kim Philby in 1951, attention was redirected to Tudor-Hart in view of her long-standing friendship with Philby's first wife Litzi, who had by then left Britain for the GDR. In a 'source report' dated 3 October 1951, focusing largely on Litzi Honigmann (as she had become), an informant [name redacted] described Tudor-Hart as 'a sick woman, highly neurotic and suffering from persecution mania'.[31] In the early 1950s, Tudor-Hart finally suffered a complete breakdown, spending some months in a sanatorium.[32] By then she had ceased to be a Soviet spy. She died in 1973.

Margaret Mynatt made a career in Britain in Party journalism and publishing, founding the Soviet Monitor (a round-the-clock radio service supplying news from the Soviet Union to the world press) and becoming a director of Central Books and Lawrence and Wishart. There are also references in Mynatt's file to an acquaintance with Litzi Philby who had left for Prague in September 1946 bearing a certificate from Mynatt testifying to her political reliability.[33] MI5 continued to monitor Mynatt's largely Party-related activities until 1960. When she died in 1977, she was engaged in what was arguably the culmination of her life's work, as editor-in-chief of the English edition of the *Collected Works of Marx and Engels*.

As for Roger Hollis, he rose to become Director General of MI5 between 1956 and 1965. We have noted more than once that the publications of Peter Wright, Chapman Pincher and others have left a sizeable question mark over Hollis's loyalties (though it should be reiterated that the allegation that he was a Soviet agent remains unproven). However, his apparent reluctance to investigate the cases of suspected spies such as Jürgen Kuczynski is not easily explained, his inertia even being reflected in the official statement accompanying the release of Kuczynski's MI5 files in 2005: 'It is clear that even at this early stage [1939] the possibility of Kuczynski being involved in espionage was acknowledged. Yet, except for a postal warrant, little effort seems to have been expended on this case.'[34] However Kuczynski's sister 'Sonya', despite wondering whether she was being protected by someone within MI5, has dismissed the suggestion that her protector might have been Hollis: 'I must [...] spoil the speculation or, as some writers state, "the fact", that I ever had anything to do with the one-time director of MI5, Roger Hollis.'[35] (It is of course far from certain that one can be confident of Sonya's reliability here.)

Hollis retired from the Security Service in late 1965, well aware that questions regarding his competence, not to say his allegiances, were being raised in both Britain and the United States. Within three years, he had divorced his wife in order to marry his long-term secretary at MI5, Edith Valentine Hammond. He died in 1973, but the debate about his action – and inaction – within MI5 has continued to the present day.

There remain those MI5 officers with special responsibility for the surveillance of the German-speaking refugees, of whom two in particular stand out: W.D. Robson-Scott and Claud Sykes. Each of them had spent periods abroad prior to working for MI5; each may well have already been engaged in intelligence work whilst abroad. Each was clearly familiar with the often tangled and fraught relations between the different groupings within the German-speaking exile community and – most importantly – each was an excellent linguist with a fluent command of German.

William Robson-Scott, who had returned to London from Vienna in 1939, was recruited to MI5 from his newly obtained post at Birkbeck College London. Upon leaving MI5, he returned to Birkbeck where towards the end of his career he was appointed to a Chair in German. Retiring from Birkbeck in 1968, he spent the next five years as Honorary Director of the University of London's Institute of Germanic Studies. His name lives on at the Institute in the form of a Travelling Scholarship for postgraduate students wishing to carry out research in Germanic Languages and Literatures.

In 1968, as Robson-Scott moved on from one stage of his academic career to the next, his colleagues paid him fulsome tributes as a man as well as a scholar, singling out his 'resources of urbanity and good sense' for special mention.[36] How Robson-Scott viewed his work for MI5 is not known: he evidently never spoke of it. However an occasional aside, such as his remark that the much-watched Otto Lehmann-Russbueldt was 'of no interest whatever from the security point of view despite his large number of files', betrays a certain impatience with the process.[37]

Claud Sykes had left the Security Service by December 1944 and had resumed life in Letchworth, where he became once more a pillar of local society, an active Rotarian who was entrusted with writing the foreword to the official guide for Letchworth, published in 1951.[38] But he had lost neither his penchant for assumed identity, nor his taste for detective mystery. In 1947, he published the book *Alias William Shakespeare*,[39] in which he set out to prove that the real author of Shakespeare's works was Roger Manning, Earl of Rutland. His book did not close the argument about the authorship of Shakespeare's works, but it may well have caught the attention of Richard Ellmann, the biographer of James Joyce. While researching his biography, Ellmann interviewed Sykes in 1954 about his collaboration with Joyce in Zurich during the First World War. In fact, the passages in Ellmann's book concerning this collaboration rest purely on Sykes's own testimony, in which he may have been as economical with the truth as he had been with the 'Primrose League'. Ellmann evidently had no inkling that Sykes had ever been a spy. If he did ask Sykes how he came to be in Zurich in 1917, the reply is not recorded.

By the end of the war, both Sykes's and Robson-Scott's work was done, MI5 feeling able to dispense with their services. Most of the others mentioned in this chapter, however, continued to be watched by MI5 for some time to come, whether they knew it or not. Ten years or more would elapse before the personal files of certain German and Austrian refugees were finally closed.

Notes

1 Bruno Retzlaff-Kresse, *Illegalität – Kerker – Exil: Erinnerungen aus dem antifaschistischen Kampf*, Berlin: Dietz 1980, p. 318.

2 See 'Extract for Foreign Office File', The National Archives [TNA], KV2/3069/138b.

3 'Extract from D4/FCD source report re Austrian Communist Party: ment. Scholz', 17 June 1957, TNA, KV2/3070/170a.

4 See MI5 memorandum, marked 'Secret', 25 March 1946, and MI5 comment to Home Office, 8 April 1946, TNA, KV2/2523/352a and 355a.

5 'Extract from Source Kaspar (Lamb) report dated 9.3.46 re the activities of the Austrian C.P.', TNA, KV2/2522/342c.

6 TNA, KV2/2523/384a.

7 TNA, KV2/2523, minute at front of file 426.

8 See Selby minute, 11 September 1945, TNA, FO371/46804/C5420.

9 Jürgen Kuczynski, *Memoiren: Die Erziehung des J.K. zum Kommunisten und Wissenschaftler*, Berlin/Weimar: Aufbau, 2nd edition 1975, p. 416.

10 MI5 to SIS, 20 July 1950, TNA, KV2/1879/534a.

11 21 September 1950, TNA, KV2/1879/543a.

12 'Extract from B.4.D. Source Report on Purges in Eastern Germany', 24 January 1953, TNA, KV2/1880/608b.

13 Ernst Hermann Meyer, *Kontraste, Konflikte: Erinnerungen, Gespräche, Kommentare*, Berlin: Verlag Neue Musik 1979, p. 189f.
14 See TNA, KV2/3503.
15 'Otto Lehmann-Russbueldt', 11 April 1952, TNA, KV2/2006/326a.
16 Internal MI5 note, 25 August 1945, TNA, KV2/2364/72b.
17 Extract MI5 report, 4 March 1950, TNA, KV2/2365/82a.
18 Josef Otto Laemmel, *Das Unzerstörbare: Eine Art biographischer Roman*, Vienna: Heimatland-Verlag 1981.
19 Josef Otto Laemmel, 'Ergänzungen zur Kurzbiographie', http://geneal.lemmel.at/JosefOttoLaemmel.html (accessed 8 August 2011).
20 'Josef Otto Lämmel', *Tagespost*, 3 July 1980.
21 With Richard Dove.
22 Paul Broda, *Scientist Spies: A Memoir of My Three Parents and the Atom Bomb*, Kibworth Beauchamp: Matador 2011, p. 299.
23 See John Earl Haynes, Harvey Klehr and Alexander Vassiliev, *Spies: The Rise and Fall of the KGB in America*, New Haven/London: Yale University Press 2009 (based on material from KGB records).
24 Ruth Werner, *Sonya's Report*, London: Chatto and Windus 1991, pp. 288–90.
25 Werner, *Sonya's Report*, pp. 288–9.
26 Chapman Pincher, *Treachery: Betrayals, Blunders and Cover-ups: Six Decades of Espionage*, Edinburgh: Mainstream 2011, p. 595.
27 David Burke, *The Spy Who Came in from the Co-op: Melita Norwood and the Ending of Cold War Espionage*, Woodbridge: Boydell Press 2008.
28 MI5 Narrative Report on Edith Tudor-Hart, 1 December 1951, TNA, KV2/1604/227. Strangely, this report is not on her file, but on her ex-husband's.
29 Wright describes an interrogation of Tudor-Hart in *Spycatcher: The Candid Autobiography of a Senior Intelligence Officer*, New York: Viking 1987, p. 248.
30 'Mrs Tudor-Hart', Report B4c/FCD, 24 February 1947, TNA/KV2/1014/112a.
31 TNA, KV2/1014/143. This is the final item in Tudor-Hart's file.
32 See Wolf Suschitzky, ed., *Edith Tudor-Hart: The Eye of Conscience*, London: Nishen 1987.
33 'Extract source Kaspar/173', 7 September 1946, TNA, KV2/3364/114b.
34 See www.nationalarchives.gov.uk/releases/2005/highlights_march/march1/jewish.htm (accessed 16 September 2012).
35 Werner, *Sonya's Report*, p. 289.
36 Paul Salmon and Ralph Timms, 'William Robson-Scott: A Tribute on the Occasion of his Retirement', *German Life and Letters*, 22, 1 (1968), 1.
37 Robson-Scott note, 4 March 1944, TNA, KV2/2006/285b.
38 Thanks are due to Peter Lowe for drawing attention to this item and for confirming the date of Sykes's death.
39 Claud W. Sykes, *Alias William Shakespeare*, with a preface by Arthur Bryant, London: Aldor, 1947.

Conclusion

The late Marxist historian Eric Hobsbawm famously wrote that it is 'the business of historians to remember what others forget'.[1] Following his advice, we have tried in our study to 'remember' a lengthy episode of counter-intelligence, which, after being hidden from history for seventy years, is now in the public domain but has remained unacknowledged and unrecorded: MI5's surveillance of German and Austrian refugees from Hitler between 1933 and 1950. Hobsbawm might well have approved of our project. Himself a refugee, he was also the subject of an MI5 file which he was refused permission to read in 2009 on the grounds that the Security Service did not hold any personal data to which he was entitled to have access.[2]

In the course of this study, three major questions regarding MI5's surveillance of German-speaking refugees have repeatedly emerged. The first is: why, in a period leading up to a war against Fascism and during the war itself, did MI5 remain so intensely concerned with the surveillance of Communists and why did this surveillance continue and even intensify after the Soviet Union had entered the war in June 1941? MI5 had a long tradition of anti-Communism which provided its major operational focus in the 1930s and which it found confirmed in the apparent perfidy of the Nazi–Soviet Pact in 1939. However, it was unable to suspend this judgement, let alone its surveillance, during the years when the Soviet Union was a war ally.

The second question, related to the first, is a matter of political judgement (on which, of course, the agenda of any Security Service depends). The vast majority of the political refugees on whom MI5 doggedly kept watch were categorised as 'Communists and Suspected Communists, including Russian and Communist Sympathisers', whether they were or not (the pacifist Otto Lehmann-Russbueldt is a good case in point, as is the unaligned Socialist Karl Otten). The Security Service also kept watch on the refugees' main cultural organisations, the FGLC, the Austrian Centre and the CRTF, declaring the first two to be no more than a Communist front, and the CRTF to be, in Dick White's phrase, 'about the most dangerous of all these organisations'. The truth was more complex. These examples prompt the question: Was MI5 watching, in some cases, the wrong Germans for the wrong reasons? Our research suggests that MI5's political reasoning was often highly reductive. Comment after comment in these files suggests a binary view of the world: friend or foe, good or bad, British or foreign, sink or swim, black or white.

If the first two questions are historical, the third brings us right up to the present: why has this particular surveillance operation, undoubtedly a costly one in terms of manpower and effort, not become part of the official history of MI5, failing to find a mention, for example, in Christopher Andrew's centenary study, *The Defence of the Realm*? Any answer to this question can only be conjectural. It may be because, even though the Soviet Union was a war ally for some years, this whole period of surveillance of Communists, and supposed Communists, is now viewed simply as a prologue to the Cold War and has thus been written out as the discrete security enterprise as which it began.

There is another possible reason. Both the official and unofficial histories of MI5 agree that the Service had a 'good war', citing among its triumphs the arrest of virtually every German spy infiltrated into Britain, 'the spectacularly successful British double-cross system'[3] and the equally successful 'Fortitude', the elaborate deception plan to deflect German attention from the intended site of the Allied invasion of occupied France. By contrast, MI5's operations against German and Austrian refugees, including the fiasco of internment and the evident failure to curb the activities of atomic spies Fuchs and Broda, do not fit into this triumphal narrative.

It may also be that this operation was eclipsed by the revelations concerning the 'Cambridge Five' – Maclean and Burgess in the Diplomatic Service, Philby and John Cairncross at MI6, and Anthony Blunt at MI5 itself. These very British spies were men from 'good families' and 'good schools' who, by passing secrets to the Soviet Union, did great damage to British security and even greater damage to the reputation of the Security Service. They have appeared only fleetingly in our narrative, and yet they too are linked, ideologically and personally, to the German-speaking refugees. MI5 says as much: the descriptor for Tudor-Hart's MI5 file states that it was 'almost certainly she who first talent-spotted [Kim] Philby to the RIS [Russian Intelligence Service]' and who briefly acted as a courier for Guy Burgess. However, this is not what MI5 knew, or even guessed, at the time; being wise after the event is the prerogative of the historian, not of the Security Service.

The question of whether the surveillance of German-speaking refugees was a success or failure – or in some cases, was really necessary – must of course be answered with reference to MI5's raison d'être: the defence of the realm. As we have seen, both before and during the war, the British Security

Service spent much time and energy keeping watch on individuals and organisations within the German-speaking refugee community, most of whom posed a negligible security threat. One obvious criticism is therefore that MI5 failed to distinguish between those who posed a genuine danger to British security and those who did not. There were some cases where, even by their own criteria, there seemed no reason for continuing surveillance. In the case of Otto Lehmann-Russbueldt, as already noted, nothing incriminating, indeed nothing of substance was ever discovered. A contrasting, though strangely comparable, case was that of Wilhelm Koenen, who led the German Communist group in British exile from 1942, and who was therefore viewed as a security threat – yet his preoccupation was almost entirely with events and prospects in his native Germany, and he therefore posed no direct, let alone immediate threat to domestic security.

On the other hand, MI5 largely failed to prioritise or even to identify those few cases which constituted a genuine security threat. In the case of Margaret Mynatt, it succeeded in having her removed from her post at the CRTF; whether this managed to reduce Communist influence within the organisation is open to question. In the case of the atom spy Klaus Fuchs, MI5 was slow to act, missing several chances to forestall his activities. While the case did eventually culminate in a successful prosecution under the Official Secrets Act, MI5 finally acted only after strong pressure from the Americans. In the case of his fellow atomic spy Engelbert Broda, it failed to take any action at all: as we have noted, he was simply allowed to return to his native Austria. His real role emerged only with the brief opening of KGB records in the 1990s; at the time, MI5 knew little and could prove even less.

In the case of Edith Tudor-Hart, MI5 was never able to muster enough evidence to charge her. It had her followed, intercepted her mail, tapped her phone and even broke into her flat, but despite surveillance over two decades, it failed even to realise that she was a member of the CPGB, under the alias 'Betty Gray', let alone suspect her true significance as a Communist agent – until she had already begun to withdraw from espionage activity.

The answer to the question of success or failure is however rarely black or white. Any assessment of the operations of the Security Service has to acknowledge the constraints under which it operated. Above all, MI5 was frequently hindered or deflected by the intervention of other government departments or agencies. We have referred to various cases which illustrate the extent and limits of MI5's power and influence, most strikingly in its relations with the Home Office. In the mid-1930s, for example, MI5's rather belated efforts to investigate Nazi spies in London, or even the British Union of Fascists, were hindered by Home Office refusal to sanction the required mail intercepts.

Moreover, the Home Office frequently ignored or overruled MI5 advice in individual cases. In 1938, for example, it overruled the Service's recommendation that the leading Communist Wilhelm Koenen should be refused entry into Britain; in 1941, the Interned Enemy Aliens Tribunal reviewing Koenen's case rejected MI5's recommendation for his continued internment. During the internment episode itself, the Home Office consistently rejected MI5's demand to re-intern Jürgen Kuczynski, declaring that he could not be interned simply because he was a Communist. In the case of the Austrian Communist Eva Kolmer, it simply ignored MI5's demands for her internment. Kolmer was probably too bound up in the affairs of her own country to constitute any real threat to British security (although it is known that she passed information from inside the internment camps to François Lafitte for inclusion in his critique of British internment policy, *The Internment of Aliens*).[4]

Even more crucially, the Department of Industrial and Scientific Research overruled MI5's advice against the employment of foreign Communists like Fuchs and Broda in secret scientific work, arguing that the urgency of scientific research outweighed any security risk involved, a widely held view among the British scientific establishment in wartime. Moreover, so secret was the work on which the Tube Alloys scientists were engaged that MI5 was not even apprised of its precise nature, a considerable handicap.

The case of Fuchs raises, once again, the spectre of Roger Hollis. As MI5's 'Communist expert' and head of F Division from 1941 to 1945, Hollis failed at several crucial points to recommend action against suspected spies like Fuchs and, to a lesser extent, Broda. He was asked to review Fuchs's case on several occasions, each time either choosing to ignore evidence or recommending that no action be taken. Hollis was indeed known within MI5 as a master of inaction. In the case of Broda, he undoubtedly prevaricated, showing a marked unwillingness to proceed against him. However, we have chosen not to re-open the question of whether Hollis was simply negligent or, as claimed by Chapman Pincher, was in fact a Soviet agent, largely because the case remains unproven and there is no new evidence. MI5 has never released details of its internal inquiry into Hollis and the question of whether or not he was a Soviet spy is one that perhaps only the organisation – or he – could have answered.

It is striking that some of the few successful spies within the German-speaking refugee community, like 'Sonya', Edith Tudor-Hart and Margaret Mynatt, were able to establish themselves in Britain more smoothly than most, thanks to a significant technicality – British nationality. In the first two cases, this was acquired through marriage, in the third it was the gift of an otherwise absent British father, but all three were thereby spared the threat of alien internment – although the prospect of internment under Defence Regulation 18B, the procedure for the internment of suspect Britons, was raised at least once in Mynatt's case, but not implemented.

It is also noteworthy that all three were women – and seem to have benefited from MI5's indulgent treatment of 'the fair sex'. Throughout the internment process, women were treated more leniently than men (category 'C' women were almost never interned, unlike their male counterparts), suggesting that women were perceived by British officialdom, a bastion of male chauvinism at the time, as posing a lesser threat than men and as generally less worthy of serious attention. Even the formidable Eva Kolmer was referred to ironically, if not patronisingly, by MI5 officer William Robson-Scott as 'the great Eva', a remark suggesting that the capabilities of women – and their potential role in espionage – were greatly underestimated. MI5, for example, opened a joint file for Len Beurton and his wife 'Sonya', and initially seems to have regarded him with greater suspicion than her. 'Sonya' herself appears to have exploited this situation, using her children to project an image of normal family life in order to deflect suspicion.

MI5's most valuable investigative resource at the time was its Central Registry, holding many thousands of 'personal' files. What do these 'personal' files tell us about the suspects they concern? And what do they tell us about MI5? Any modern reader consulting them will be struck by the often sparse and fragmentary nature of the information they contain. In several cases, little of substance was discovered; in others information was misconstrued or was simply incorrect. The reader may also be struck by the inadequacy of the weapons of surveillance available to the Security Service – the phone tap, the postal intercept, personal observation – particularly in comparison to the resources of the modern surveillance state. The use of a postal intercept on suspects like Kuczynski or Fuchs yielded nothing of note. Kuczynski's correspondence, for example, simply served to confirm his wide circle of friends and his academic reputation. Fuchs, on the other hand, received virtually no post at all. Both carefully avoided sending incriminating information by post.

Especially during the war years, MI5 used informants as an important source of information on refugee suspects. Our study puts a rather uncomfortable gloss on relationships within the refugee community, confirming that MI5 built up an extensive network of informers – who informed not only on fellow-refugees but also on each other. In the security files, the names of informers are usually redacted or concealed by a code name, but despite MI5's determined, if fitful discretion, they can, in most cases, be confidently identified. We know not only who they were but what they disclosed. In fact, the information they divulged on fellow-refugees constitutes the major part of some personal and organisational files. The question 'why did they inform?' has no simple answer, though our research shows that most were motivated by the wish to settle old personal and political scores (e.g. between Socialists and Communists). Few of the informers expected any remuneration, nor was any given.

It remains to be asked: how useful was their information to MI5? All the regular informers, such as 'Kaspar' or Kurt Hiller, were considered 'a reliable source'; not all of them deserved such confidence. Certainly, they often provided information which MI5 might not have obtained in any other way, correcting some of the shortcomings previously noted, but their information was not always accurate. Some informers, such as Hiller, already had a personal file of their own, and it is noteworthy that such watchers also continued to be watched. Interestingly, none of the many reports submitted by Hiller were posted on his 'personal file', being distributed among the files of those he informed against, presumably to help preserve his anonymity.

Surveillance is *per se* intrusive. Some of MI5's 'personal' files are indeed highly intrusive, revealing the mundane details of the private lives of their subjects. Reports on Edith Tudor-Hart make frequent reference to her mentally handicapped son and her consequent visits to psychiatric clinics. In the case of Klaus Fuchs, 'observation' revealed his intimate relations with the wife of a Harwell colleague, while Gerhard Hinze's file contains a short post-war report on the suicide of his first wife.

The internment crisis of 1940 provides the best yardstick of MI5's attitude towards refugees. The release of various files which had hitherto been withheld has enabled us to document for the first time MI5's attitudes to alien internment, and the policy advice they gave on the subject. They strongly advocated general internment in the lead-up to war, heartily endorsed it in May/June 1940 and voiced strong opposition to the scale and speed of releases authorised by the Home Office from September 1940. In the meantime, they attempted to establish a network of informers in different camps on the Isle of Man in order to extend their control over the refugee population. All in all, MI5's record in the internment crisis of 1940 represents one of its greatest failures and is among the less creditable aspects of its wartime record.

Most of the political refugees were Jewish, prompting the question as to whether anti-Semitism played any part in this surveillance exercise. MI5 files reveal occasional instances of routine anti-Semitism, but such prejudices reflected attitudes which were widespread within British society in the 1930s and 1940s, not least among the social classes from which MI5 almost exclusively recruited. Such 'low-level' anti-Semitism was not only widespread but socially acceptable and – perhaps most offensive to modern liberal sensibility – often had no bearing on the case in question. However, there is no evidence that such prejudice influenced the course of any MI5 operation, still less of what would now be called 'institutional anti-Semitism'. The government's introduction of general internment in 1940, eagerly supported by MI5, can be criticised on many grounds but hardly for being anti-Semitic. The refugees were interned not because they were Jews but because they were Germans.

Anglo-German relations remain an unspoken point of reference throughout our study. While Britain and Germany broke off diplomatic relations on the declaration of war, Anglo-German relations continued within Britain itself. The attitude of the British government (and more specifically its stepchild MI5) towards German refugees provides an interesting gloss on the subject. Even before the outbreak of war, MI5 had called for mass internment of refugees on the dubious grounds that, as Germans, they had divided loyalties and as refugees they had probably been infiltrated by Nazi agents and spies. This had certainly been the case with Hans Wesemann back in 1934–35 but subsequent investigations, as our research shows, discovered few if any suspected spies among the refugees; even the hapless Ludwig Max Warschauer, who was sent to Britain as a spy, evidently refrained from doing any actual spying.

But a more heartening aspect of Anglo-German relations also emerges from the internment crisis of 1940. The policy of mass internment was first suspended and then reversed, partly because public and parliamentary opinion shifted strongly against it – a remarkable development in wartime. We have noted at several points in our narrative the 'friends in need' who assisted the refugees as supporters, advisers and donors. They constitute an interesting commentary on Anglo-German relations at a personal level. Some of these associations rested on shared political convictions, some on personal friendship or shared cultural values, some on pure philanthropy. Almost all were maintained throughout the war, transcending the prevailing atmosphere of mistrust and hostility. On the other hand, MI5 kept 'personal' files on many of those who befriended the refugees, sometimes precisely *because* they did.

While the overwhelming majority of the refugees from Hitler chose to remain in Britain after the war, most political refugees did not. However, even those who went back had continuing links of family and friendship to Britain, often through intermarriage. While Jürgen Kuczynski returned to Berlin, no fewer than four of his sisters, Brigitte, Renate, Sabine and Barbara, remained in Britain, having married British husbands. Equally, the composer E. H. Meyer married an English wife, as did his Austrian counterpart Georg Knepler. While Meyer returned to Berlin, his sister, his younger brother and his daughter by his first wife all remained in Britain, taking British nationality.

Our study emphasises that many of the German-speaking refugees on whom MI5 spied were figures of some cultural or intellectual stature. During the same period, MI5 also held security files on various British cultural figures, ranging from writers such as W.H. Auden, George Orwell, Storm Jameson and Olivia Manning to composers Alan Bush and Ralph Vaughan Williams and the theatre director Joan Littlewood – quite apart from the files it kept on political figures such as D.N. Pritt and Fenner Brockway, and Communist activists like Bob Stewart and Harry Pollitt. In fact, MI5 seems to have kept files on many of the leading cultural and political figures in Britain in the 1930s and 1940s, although the full total may never be known. The time is certainly ripe for a parallel study to our own, investigating the relationship between British culture and politics – and the relation of both of these to the security services.[5] It might well add new and hitherto missing dimensions to aspects of British cultural history.

Notes

1 Eric Hobsbawm, *Age of Extremes: The Short Twentieth Century 1914–1991*, London: Michael Joseph 1994.

2 *The Guardian*, 2 March 2009.

3 Christopher Andrew, *The Defence of the Realm: The Authorized History of MI5*, London: Allen Lane 2009, p. 248.

4 François Lafitte, 'Afterthoughts Four Decades Later', Introduction to 1988 edition of *The Internment of Aliens*, London: Libris 1988, pp. xxi–xxii.

5 James Smith, *British Writers and MI5 Surveillance 1930–1960*, Cambridge/New York: Cambridge University Press 2013, which concentrates on a few key literary figures, takes a welcome first step in this direction.

A note on sources

The raw material from which this study is fashioned has been drawn largely from the security files which MI5 kept on political refugees from the Third Reich during the 1930s and 1940s. Since 1999, a stream of files containing information gathered by MI5 on various individuals and organisations suspected of subversive activity, including those on German and Austrian refugees, have been released to the National Archives. At the time of writing, the Security Service has made available some 5,000 files; further files are being released at regular intervals. While these files represent a unique documentary source for the historian or the biographer, furnishing a hitherto missing dimension of social and political history, they also have some inherent limitations and pose certain pitfalls for the unwary.

For the academic researcher, these sources are sometimes less than satisfactory since they are manifestly incomplete and in some cases unreliable. Firstly, MI5 has released only a small proportion of the files it once held. Many others still remain closed, while far more have actually been destroyed. According to MI5's own statement, between 1909 and the early 1970s more than 175,000 files were destroyed as 'obsolete or because of major contractions in the service' (although some were microfilmed prior to destruction) while since the fall of Soviet Communism, a further 180,000 files have been destroyed.[1] As to those which remain closed, MI5 does not always reveal which files have been 'retained', nor why. Requests for information about specific files may elicit the information that the file in question has been destroyed or that it 'does not meet our current release criteria'. In other cases, requests for information are met with the standard response: 'The Security Service is not a public authority subject to the Freedom of Information Act and we do not process requests for information of this nature.' Nor does MI5 reveal the criteria used to decide which files may be released and which retained or – more seriously for the researcher – destroyed.

Moreover, there is no guarantee that even those files which *have* been released represent the whole truth and nothing but the truth. Most of the files have been 'redacted', in order to conceal certain names or events, and to foreground others. (The names which have been blacked out are usually those of MI5 officers and agents, or those of their informants.) In places, there are obvious gaps in the records, where items have been removed, so that the content of certain files is incomplete and possibly misleading. This is so, for example, in the case of both Ernst Hermann Meyer and Engelbert Broda.

It is, of course, possible to fill some of the gaps through cross-posting; sometimes a copy of a document removed from one file comes to light in a different one, presumably having escaped the eye of the redactor there. A perhaps more reliable method has been to compare the records of MI5 to those of other sources, such as the Home Office or other official bodies. However, there are obvious difficulties inherent in cross-referencing, for example, between MI5 and Home Office files, since Home Office files on the same individuals are not always open to scrutiny and they too have been redacted, though not always in the same way.

Secondary sources

This lack of accessible information is partly the result of official policy, which binds former officers of the Security Service to lifelong silence – and in return guarantees their anonymity. The official policy of *omertà* has of course been breached in the past, most famously with the publication of *Spycatcher* by the disaffected MI5 officer Peter Wright.[2] More recently, Stella Rimington published her autobiography, which included major sections on her work for MI5, particularly her period as (the first female) Director General between 1992 and 1996.[3]

Official secrecy has not prevented the publication of various unauthorised histories, including two volumes by the intelligence expert Nigel West, covering respectively the years 1909–45 and 1945–72, the first of which, if only for the period it covers, is of obvious relevance to the present study.[4] West – a prolific writer on intelligence matters – gives a splendidly cloak-and-dagger account of the 'exploits' of MI5, adopting the organisation's own ethos to comment on its history. However, he has nothing to say about MI5 surveillance of German émigrés.

Winding forward to the present, it must be said that some of the characteristic features of MI5 in the 1930s and 1940s have now been modified. The 1989 Security Service Act marked an end to the days when, although MI5 officially existed, its operations did not. It is now a more open organisation, reflecting the prevailing expectation that institutions which are publicly funded should also be publicly accountable. While MI5 has inevitably protected the secrecy of current operations and continued to conceal the identity of officers and agents, a new spirit of (partial) openness is abroad. In 1992, Stella Rimington was named publicly as the new Director General of MI5, the first time such an appointment had been officially acknowledged. Beginning in 1997, MI5 began to recruit through public advertising rather than through personal contacts and recommendations. It has also established a public website, which offers a well-manicured version of the organisation and its history.

As part of this new openness, from 1999 onwards the Service began to release some of its historical files to the National Archives, including policy and organisational files as well as some of the 'personal files' it held on suspects, a move which has made possible the present study. Consistent with this release of its early records, MI5 also released an official account of its early years, published in 1999.[5] And most recently it has commissioned an official history of MI5, which appeared in 2009 to mark the centenary of the Service. The author of this work is the Cambridge historian and doyen of Intelligence Studies, Professor Christopher Andrew, handpicked as an academic expert who had already written extensively on the security services.[6] Andrew and his team of researchers were given exclusive access to MI5's entire archive, amounting to some 400,000 files. Unfortunately, when he cites the MI5 archive, which he does frequently and often copiously, his endnotes in every case refer only to 'Security Service Archives', so that the reader has no idea what kind of document he has drawn on. Moreover, as he alone has had this opportunity, nobody else can check the scope or accuracy of his references. In any case, Andrew's account, comprising over 1,000 pages, makes no reference to the large-scale surveillance operations MI5 conducted against German and Austrian refugees.

The appearance of Andrew's official history was preceded by 'the unofficial history' *Spooks*,[7] the authors of which did not enjoy access to the MI5 archive, although they made extensive use of the documents already released to the National Archives. However, like the official history, *Spooks* makes no mention of the surveillance of German-speaking refugees, except for the atom spy Klaus Fuchs.

Professor Andrew's 'authorised history' of MI5 was followed in 2010 by an equivalent volume commissioned by MI6 and written by Professor Keith Jeffery.[8] This 'independent and authoritative' history of the Secret Intelligence Service covers the first forty years of the organisation (1909–49) and naturally contains many cross-references to MI5, though it too fails to mention the surveillance of German-speaking refugees. The possible reasons for these omissions have been discussed in our conclusion.

Notes

1 See The National Archives, Records of the Security Service, www.nationalarchives.gov.uk.

2 Peter Wright, *Spycatcher. The Candid Autobiography of a Senior Intelligence Officer*, New York: Viking 1987.

3 Stella Rimington, *Open Secret: The Autobiography of the Former Director-General of MI5*, London: Hutchinson 2001.
4 Nigel West, *MI5: British Security Service Operations 1909–1945*, London: Bodley Head 1981 and West, *A Matter of Trust. MI5 1945–1972*, London: Weidenfeld and Nicolson 1982. See also West, *Mask: MI5's Penetration of the Communist Party of Great Britain*, London: Routledge 2005.
5 John Court Curry, *The Security Service 1908–1945: The Official History*, London: Public Record Office 1999.
6 Christopher Andrew, *The Defence of the Realm: The Authorized History of MI5*, London: Allen Lane 2009; Cf. also Christopher Andrew, *Secret Service: The Making of the British Intelligence Community*, London: Heinemann 1985.
7 Thomas Hennessey and Claire Thomas, *Spooks: The Unofficial History of MI5*, Stroud: Amberley 2009.
8 Keith Jeffery, *MI6: The History of the Secret Intelligence Service 1909–1949*, London: Bloomsbury 2010.

Select bibliography

Archival material held at

Arbeider bevegelsens Arkiv og Bibliotek, Oslo (ARBARK)
Archiv der Sozialen Demokratie der Friedrich-Ebert-Stiftung, Bonn (AsdD)
Archiv für die Geschichte der Soziologie in Österreich, Graz (AGSÖ)
BBC Written Archives Centre, Caversham (BBCWAC)
Bibliotheek van het Vredespaleis, The Hague (VP)
Bodleian Library, Oxford (BLO)
Columbia University Rare Books and Manuscript Library, New York
Deutsche Nationalbibliothek, Frankfurt am Main (DNB)
Deutsches Literaturarchiv, Marbach (DLA)
Geheimes Staatsarchiv Preußischer Kulturbesitz, Berlin (PK)
Home Office, London (HO)
Institut für Zeitgeschichte, Munich (IfZ)
Lambeth Palace Library, London
Politisches Archiv des Auswärtigen Amtes, Berlin (AA)
Schweizerisches Bundesarchiv, Berne (SBB)
Staatsarchiv des Kantons Basel-Stadt (StAB)
Stiftung Archiv der Parteien und Massenorganisationen der DDR im Bundesarchiv, Berlin-Lichterfelde (SAPMO-BArch)
The National Archives, Kew (TNA)
And papers in the private possession of Ernest Rodker and Edna Sovin.

Publications

Andrew, Christopher, *Secret Service: The Making of the British Intelligence Community*, London: Heinemann 1985.

Andrew, Christopher, *The Defence of the Realm: The Authorized History of MI5*, London: Allen Lane 2009.

Barnes, James J. and Patience P. Barnes, *Nazi Refugee Turned Gestapo Spy: The Life of Hans Wesemann, 1895–1971*, Westport/London: Praeger 2001.

Barnes, James J. and Patience P. Barnes, *Nazis in Pre-War London 1930–1939: The Fate and Role of German Party Members and British Sympathisers*, Brighton/Portland: Sussex Academic Press 2005.

Bearman, Marietta, Charmian Brinson, Richard Dove, Anthony Grenville and Jennifer Taylor, *Out of Austria: The Austrian Centre in London in World War II*, London: Tauris Academic Studies 2008.

Berthold, Werner and Brita Eckert, eds, *Der deutsche PEN-Club im Exil 1933–1938: Eine Ausstellung der Deutschen Bibliothek Frankfurt am Main*, Frankfurt a. M.: Buchhändler-Vereinigung 1980.

Bower, Tom, *The Perfect English Spy: Sir Dick White and the Secret War 1935–90*, London: Heinemann 1995.

Brinson, Charmian, *The Strange Case of Dora Fabian and Mathilde Wurm: A Study of German Political Exiles in London during the 1930s*, Berne: Peter Lang 1997.

Brinson, Charmian, 'The Gestapo and the German Political Exiles in Britain during the 1930s: The Case of Hans Wesemann – and Others', *German Life and Letters*, 51, 1 (January 1998), 43–64.

Brinson, Charmian and Richard Dove, *Politics by Other Means: The Free German League of Culture in London 1939–1945*, London: Vallentine Mitchell 2010.

Brinson, Charmian and Richard Dove, 'Friends and Enemies: The Freier Deutscher Kulturbund and the British, 1938–1946', *ANGERMION*, 5 (2012), 135–45.

Broda, Paul, *Scientist Spies: A Memoir of My Three Parents and the Atom Bomb*, Kibworth Beauchamp: Matador 2011.

Brown, Andrew, 'The Viennese Connection: Engelbert Broda, Alan Nunn May and Atomic Espionage', *Intelligence and National Security*, 24, 2 (April 2009), 173–93.

Buresova, Jana, 'The Czech Refugee Trust Fund in Britain, 1939–1950', in Charmian Brinson and Marian Malet, eds, *Exile in and from Czechoslovakia during the 1930s and 1940s: Yearbook of the Research Centre for German and Austrian Exile Studies*, vol. 11, 2009, pp. 133–45.

Burke, David, *The Spy Who Came in from the Co-op: Melita Norwood and the Ending of Cold War Espionage*, Woodbridge: Boydell Press 2008.

Cesarani, David and Tony Kushner, eds, *The Internment of Aliens in Twentieth Century Britain*, London: Cass 1993.

Curry, John Court, *The Security Service 1908–1945: The Official History*, London: Public Record Office 1999.

Dove, Richard, *Journey of No Return: Five German -Speaking Literary Exiles in Britain, 1933–1945*, London: Libris 2000.

Dove, Richard, 'Gerhard Hinze or Gerard Heinz? A Life in Two Acts', in Charmian Brinson and Richard Dove, eds, *German-Speaking Exiles in the Performing Arts in Britain after 1933: Yearbook of the Research Centre for German and Austrian Exile Studies*, vol. 14, 2013, pp. 61–86.

Fox, John P., 'Nazi Germany and the German Emigration to Great Britain', in Gerhard Hirschfeld, ed., *Exile in Great Britain: Refugees from Hitler's Germany*, Leamington Spa: Berg 1984, pp. 29–62.

Haynes, John Earl, Harvey Klehr and Alexander Vassiliev, *Spies: The Rise and Fall of the KGB in America*, New Haven/London: Yale University Press 2009.

Hennessey, Thomas and Claire Thomas, *Spooks: The Unofficial History of MI5*, Stroud: Amberley 2009.

Heumos, Peter, *Die Emigration aus der Tschechoslowakei nach Westeuropa und dem Nahen Osten, 1938–1945*, Munich: R. Oldenbourg Verlag 1989.

Hiller, Kurt, *Rote Ritter: Erlebnisse mit deutschen Kommunisten*, Gelsenkirchen: Ruhr Verlag 1951.

Jeffery, Keith, *MI6: The History of the Secret Intelligence Service 1909–1949*, London: Bloomsbury 2010.

Kapp, Yvonne and Margaret Mynatt, *British Policy and the Refugees, 1933–1941*, London/Portland: Frank Cass 1997.

Kuczynski, Jürgen, *Memoiren: Die Erziehung des J.K. zum Kommunisten und Wissenschaftler*, Berlin/Weimar: Aufbau, 2nd edition 1975.

Laemmel, Josef Otto, *Das Unzerstörbare: Eine Art biographischer Roman*, Vienna: Heimatland-Verlag 1981.

Lafitte, François, *The Internment of Aliens*, Harmondsworth: Penguin 1940. Republished London: Libris 1988 with a new introduction by the author.

London, Louise, *Whitehall and the Jews 1933–1948: British Immigration Policy and the Holocaust*, Cambridge: Cambridge University Press 2000.

Lützenkirchen, Harald, ed., *Kurt Hiller: Die Rundbriefe des Freiheitsbundes deutscher Sozialisten, London 1939–1947*, Fürth: Klaussner 1991.

Meyer, Ernst H., *Kontraste, Konflikte: Erinnerungen, Gespräche, Kommentare*, Berlin: Verlag Neue Musik 1979.

Pincher, Chapman, *Treachery: Betrayals, Blunders and Cover-ups: Six Decades of Espionage*, Edinburgh: Mainstream 2011.

Putlitz, Wolfgang zu, *The Putlitz Dossier*, London: Allan Wingate 1957.

Rimington, Stella, *Open Secret: The Autobiography of the Former Director-General of MI5*, London: Hutchinson 2001.

Röder, Werner, *Die deutschen sozialistischen Exilgruppen in Großbritannien 1940–1945: Ein Beitrag zur Geschichte des Widerstandes gegen den Nationalsozialismus*, Hanover: Verlag für Literatur und Zeitgeschehen 1969.

Seyfert, Michael, *Im Niemandsland: Deutsche Exilliteratur in britischer Internierung*, Berlin: Das Arsenal 1984.

Sherman, A. J., *Island Refuge: Britain and Refugees from the Third Reich 1933–1939*, 2nd edition, London: Frank Cass 1994.

Smith, Michael, *Foley: The Spy Who Saved 10,000 Jews*, London: Hodder 1999.

Suschitzky, Wolf, ed., *Edith Tudor-Hart: The Eye of Conscience*, London: Nishen 1987.

Ustinov, Peter, *Dear Me*, London: Heinemann 1977.

Vansittart, Robert, *The Mist Procession: The Autobiography of Lord Vansittart*, London: Hutchinson 1958.

Wasserstein, Bernard, *Britain and the Jews of Europe 1939–1945*, Oxford: Clarendon 1979.

Weinstein, Allen and Alexander Vassiliev, *The Haunted Wood: Soviet Espionage in America – The Stalin Era*, New York: Modern Library, paperback edition 2000.

Werner, Ruth, *Sonya's Report*, London: Chatto and Windus 1991.

West, Nigel, *MI5: British Security Service Operations 1909–1945*, London: Bodley Head 1981.

West, Nigel and Oleg Tsarev, *The Crown Jewels: The British Secrets at the Heart of the KGB Archives*, London: Harper Collins 1998.

West, Nigel, ed., *The Guy Liddell Diaries*, vol. 1 *1939–1942*, vol. 2 *1942–1945*, London: Routledge 2005.

Williams, Robert Chadwell, *Klaus Fuchs, Atom Spy*, Cambridge, Mass./London: Harvard University Press 1987.

Wright, Peter, *Spycatcher: The Candid Autobiography of a Senior Intelligence Officer*, New York: Viking 1987.

Index

CPSIA information can be obtained
at www.ICGtesting.com
Printed in the USA
FFOW03n0218270116
20701FF